MUSLIM TEXTUALITIES

In the first decade of the twenty-first century, Muslim women writers located in Europe and American entered the cultural mainstream. Literary and visual productions negotiated static visual emblems of Islam, most prominently "the veil." They did so not by rejecting veiling practices, but by adapting Muslim resources, concepts, and visual tradition to empowerment narratives in popular media. Mainstream reception of their works has often overlooked or misread these negotiations. *Muslim Textualities* argues for more flexible and capacious interpretation, with particular attention to visibility as a metaphor for political agency and to knowledge of cultural contexts. This provocative volume aims to articulate Muslim female agency through clear and accessible analysis of the theory and concepts driving the interpretation of these works. Scholars interested in the working representations of Muslim women, feminist subjectivities, and the complexities of gender roles, patriarchy, and feminism will find this volume of particular interest.

Jean M. Kane received a Ph.D. in English from the University of Virginia, an M.A. in English from Stanford University, and a B.A. in Comparative Literature and Art History from Indiana University. She is currently Professor of English and Women's Studies at Vassar College.

MUSLIM TEXTUALITIES

A Literary Approach to Feminism

Jean M. Kane

NEW YORK AND LONDON

Cover credit: © Getty Images

First published 2022
by Routledge
605 Third Avenue, New York, NY 10158

and by Routledge
2 Park Square, Milton Park, Abingdon, Oxon, OX14 4RN

Routledge is an imprint of the Taylor & Francis Group, an informa business

© 2022 Jean M. Kane

The right of Jean M. Kane to be identified as author of this work has been asserted in accordance with sections 77 and 78 of the Copyright, Designs and Patents Act 1988.

All rights reserved. No part of this book may be reprinted or reproduced or utilised in any form or by any electronic, mechanical, or other means, now known or hereafter invented, including photocopying and recording, or in any information storage or retrieval system, without permission in writing from the publishers.

Trademark notice: Product or corporate names may be trademarks or registered trademarks, and are used only for identification and explanation without intent to infringe.

Library of Congress Cataloging-in-Publication Data
A catalog record for this title has been requested

ISBN: 978-1-032-03832-2 (hbk)
ISBN: 978-1-032-03831-5 (pbk)
ISBN: 978-1-003-18929-9 (ebk)

DOI: 10.4324/9781003189299

Typeset in Bembo
by SPi Technologies India Pvt Ltd (Straive)

CONTENTS

Acknowledgments   *vi*

   Introduction   1

1 Sex and Other Cities: Abjected Age, Abandoned Flesh   14

2 Female Masochism and Textual Masquerade in Monica Ali's *Brick Lane* and *Untold Story*   43

3 Muslimah Seeing America: Local Colors in Mohja Kahf's *The Girl in the Tangerine Scarf*   70

4 Surface Violation: Parastou Forouhar's Domestic Sublime   93

5 The Mother Mark and Other Tongues in *Nylon Road*   124

   Conclusion   154

Bibliography   *162*
Index   *182*

ACKNOWLEDGMENTS

This book was germinated in a rich, disordered residue of interests, observations, questions, and experiences, particularly in the women's studies classroom. The cluster of themes and ideas required dialogues and shaping over years of drafts. They resulted in a clear and, I hope, compelling argument only in the last stages. I am indebted to the mentoring of Karen Robertson, my co-teacher, friend, and scholarly guide. Our dialogues have nurtured and strengthened this project throughout. She is a model of intellectual generosity and feminist collaboration.

I skidded into my editor, Michelle Salyga, at the bottom of an escalator at an MLA convention in Chicago. With prudence and calm, as well as fortitude, she has guided the manuscript through revisions and improvements, delays and hesitations, and a pandemic. My heartfelt thanks for her confidence in the project. Kudos go to editorial assistants, Bryony Reece and Saritha Srivasan, and my copyeditor, Claire Bell.

I am grateful to Karla Mantilla of *Feminist Studies* and James E. Clung and Esra Mirza Santesso for the scholarly responses to the chapter that began the book. Esra, as it turned out, was also an anonymous reviewer of the manuscript. She gave it her informed attention in two evaluations. Her guidance has been invaluable. The expertise of Kirsten Wesselhoeft, Julia Watson, Feroze Jussawalla, Jan Susina, Helene Meyers, and Iman Sohrabi has helped me in various ways.

Thanks as well to the invisible hands of anonymous reviewers, editorial assistants, and production staff, whose labor brings the actual and virtual book into being.

The artists I have met because of this research have been the most affable and generous people I could have imagined. Thank you to Parastou Forouhar and Parsua Bashi for their help with the illustrations and to Muriel Pérez of Kein and Aber for tolerating my initial foray into acquiring images and permissions.

Many thanks go to my research assistant of some years ago, Dylan Manning, who not only did the arduous work of organizing and annotating the artwork of Parastou Forouhar, but also worked as my editorial assistant in proofreading and compiling the bibliography. Another research assistant I had at Vassar, Ezra Babski, contributed to the editorial grunt work. Judith Dollemayer gave her experience, skill, and editorial knowledge to the shaping of the project as a book, and Scott Smiley has compiled the index. Vassar College has generously supplied funding for research, travel, and editorial support. Tracey Sciortino has helped me to figure out the byzantine ways of collecting and distributing it.

This book is dedicated to the Christopher G. Kanes.

An earlier version of Chapter 1 appeared in *Islam and Postcolonial Discourse: Purity and Hybridity* (edited by Esra Mirze Santesso and James E. McClung, 2017), and appears courtesy of Taylor & Francis Books.

An earlier version of Chapter 4 appeared in *Feminist Studies* (44.2 [2018]: 303–32), as an art essay, "Parastou Forouhar's Domestic Sublime" and appears courtesy of the journal.

Illustrations in Chapter 4 appear courtesy of Parastou Forouhar, artist, and Professor of Art, Johannes Gutenberg-Universität Mainz, Germany.

Illustrations in Chapter 5 on *Nylon Road* appear courtesy of Parsua Bashi and KEIN & ABER AG, Zürich-Berlin 2006 (translated into German by Miriam Wiesel).

INTRODUCTION

A tweet from the 2018 Women's March in Washington, DC shows the constraints of visibility as a metaphor for empowerment. Featured in the online magazine *Muslim Girl*, the tweet suggests that an image needs a linguistic supplement. "It's time for America not only to see women but [to] hear women. I march so my voice will be united with the millions of women in this country determined to work toward our equity," writes Nasrat Qadir Chaudry. The text appears below a logo of a stylized young woman's face in a red, white, and blue headscarf. Logo and language accordingly join the "voice" associated with mid-twentieth-century feminisms and the "visibility" currently preferred as the figure for social agency. Yet as Peggy Phelan anticipated decades ago, "the binary opposition between the power of visibility and the impotency of invisibility" may be "falsifying." She elaborates: "There is real power in remaining unmarked; and there are serious limitations to visual representation as a political goal."[1] Some critics argue that visibility assumes the structure of a trade-off. In emerging Pakistani global fashion, for instance, Inna Arzumanova observes, "the veil not only gains visibility but is reinscribed as an object of art" rather than an emblem of oppression. Such unintended "hegemonic leaks" both betray the static tropes of Orientalist imagery and suggest a "cultural futurity" for Islamic identity.[2] In Europe and America, Muslim women writers and artists of the early twenty-first century have grappled with this trade-off through tactics that have not been fully registered by mainstream critics steeped in the conventional neoliberalism of postfeminism and its successors.

In this book, what Claire Chambers calls "sensory studies"[3] meet the politics of scopic and affect theory. Chambers and others call attention to the use of

DOI: 10.4324/9781003189299-1

touch, taste, smell, and to some extent sound as sources of bodily knowledge that challenge the empirical privilege of vision in Western thought. *Muslim Textualities: A Literary Approach to Feminism* examines seeing as the preferred metaphor of recognition for ethnoreligious minority women. I question visual representation as a liberatory mode touted by feminisms centered on individual choice and freedom, particularly in digital media. How does the image relate to the second-wave valorization of the "voice," that is, as spoken and written language? How does visual depiction evade, complicate, or challenge the conventional emblems of Islam in Christian-derived cultures, in particular "the veil"? To say "Christian derived" is not to erase the presence of other religious groups—my focus is after all minority representation—but rather to use the "postsecular" as a critical vantage point. This perspective interrogates the purported neutrality of the post-Enlightenment secular in the West. The Western mainstream easily recognizes differences between belief or practice and evocation of themes, concepts, idioms, and signs drawn from the repository of Christian art. To some degree, the distinction seems natural and self-evident, if not acceptable to all audiences. Mainstream audiences and critics have seemed unable to open such a space for Muslim representations. If religion is the repressed of critical practice, cultural identity is the lacuna of Muslims' representation in the Western contexts.

What do diasporan Muslim women see when they claim not just the right to look but the desire to represent? I focus on culturally identified Muslim women as producers of antipatriarchal aesthetics in Europe and America. As a minority that is not phenotypically "marked," Muslim women are routinely represented through "the veil," their insignia in nonMuslim majority locations. This master signifier, according to Sahar Ghumkhor, catches Muslim women in a Lacanian imaginary, whether or not they wear robes, face coverings, or head coverings associated with Islam. The dynamic of "veiled-veiling-unveiling-unveiled" functions as a scrim of violence that must constantly occupy the participial *being* removed. In Ghumkhor's reading, Muslim women enter into the Western symbolic only through reenactment. In disavowing the religious body as different, women secure the purported "secular" unified corpus as natural, self-evident, and universal, without the lack at the root of subject formation. Even the "hypervisibility" of contemporary young women in hijab in social and digital media participates in this imaginary, Ghumkhor contends.[4]

I do not focus on veiling practices or their histories. Furthermore, the question of the secular body as an identity distinct from a modern or liberal, capitalist, or Western institutional formulation of bodies remains very open.[5] But Ghumkhor does helpfully point to the imaginary of a secular body as unified and natural. The poles of religious and secular are illuminating rather than fully descriptive, especially of women who identify as Muslim but whose relation to belief and practice are various. I investigate how Muslim women in the West entered mainstream media productions in relation to the master signifier of the veil as an image, even as cloth, fabric, fashion, and covering are used in many of them. My examination extends to the insignia's constrictions, affects, and somatic presumptions. The productions I discuss preceded the contemporary moment but they also informed and shaped it.

In the EuroAmerican imaginary, the visual sign of the veil has operated as a flat, dark blot that eliminates corporeality, depth, movement, and particular detail. Attempting to pry Muslim women's self-representations from this blot constantly threatens to lapse back into the binaries that it signifies. This study focuses on Muslim women's negotiation of the blot in mainstream representations that may draw on fabric and textiles as material and on covering as a multivalent practice. *Muslim Textualities* assumes flexible maneuvering between culture, practice, and belief. My field is not captured by "the veil," or "religion," "secularity" or "freedom," "belief" or "blasphemy." The six producers that I analyze here show the vibrant antipatriarchal energies in the literary and visual productions of Muslim women in Europe and America in the early twenty-first century. At the same time, I articulate the tactics and strategies the authors use in negotiating the frozen signifiers of Islam for nonMuslim majority audiences. I investigate the representations of bodily habitus, disposition, and cultivation that do figure in many of the works' representations of relational dynamics.[6] The productions do not necessarily forward a particular religious doctrine or a political agenda, though some do; they do not necessarily challenge a neoliberal construction of the individual woman, and in this may be appropriately cast as reenactments of "white femininity." Yet they do all demonstrate the relations of neoliberal, "secular" Muslim female identities and their critiques of sex/gender by drawing on Muslim knowledge. The makers that I treat may render modes of agency and personhood that do not entirely coincide with the paradigm of individuality or the body imagined to secure it: they promote hermeneutic flexibility in the presentation of bodies. While not all explicitly aligned with a prescribed, official understanding of adherence or practice, they call upon experience as an aid to interpretation, reminiscent of the Qur'anic principle of *tafsir*. While echoing critiques of state practices grounded in Qur'anic social and gender-justice imperatives, they forward theological concepts such as *tawhid*—the unity of God's creation—and draw analogies to women's *da'wa*, or devotional movements as agential. At the same time they may promote romance and dramatize competitive beauty standards or professional accomplishments, in accordance with neoliberal, "white," or empowerment norms.

The exploration of chick-it and its televisual offshoots reveals the subterranean but integral relations of women who belong to minority groups abjected by their ethnoreligious identities and women who belong to dominant groups abjected by age, disability, or other factors that render them ineligible for luminous bodily display. Rajaa Alsanea's *The Girls of Riyadh* (2007), translated from the Arabic *Banat al-Riyadh* (2005), shows the antipatriarchal critique tied to Muslim texts and practices, more evident in the original, as well as brand homogenization. Setting this translation next to the American movie *Sex and the City 2* (2010) demonstrates how "the veil" acts as an alibi. The profound affect of veiling and sequestering resonate with the fatality of exposure in the novels of Monica Ali, who explores masochism as a mechanism of empowerment for women acting under constraint. The similarity of her female protagonists in *Brick Lane* (2003) and *Untold Story* (2011) were rendered invisible in mainstream criticism because of their different class, social, and racial locations: one is an abjected brown migrant, the other a luminous white royal and global celebrity. Comparing the masochistic tactics of both works reveals their biopolitical subtexts as well as their different interpretations of "submission" to authority.

The problem of the veil as sign and affect is addressed through evasion in *Brick Lane*, but brought to the fore through bodily performativity. The protagonist's knowledge of God comes about through the incorporation of one body into another. The process parallels the internalization of Muhammad in Islamic practice, even though the protagonist achieves this understanding through doctrinal and cultural transgression. Mohja Kahf's *The Girl in the Tangerine Scarf* (2006) features the performativity of veiling as feminist empowerment, deep spiritual commitment, and revolutionary activity. The narrative attempts to imagine an American Islam based in the Africa-descended female body. But selective unveiling cannot register as an enactment of self-determination given the binary of epidermal racism in the U.S. as well as the imperial plot that emerges from the Mecca-centered Muslim migrants. The scopic regimes that operate in the time and place heavily shape this outcome.

With Kahf's narrative and several of her poems, my argument turns more decisively toward the epistemologies of vision. The digital productions of the German-Iranian artist Parastou Forouhar and the graphic narrative *Nylon Road* (2006), written and drawn by the Swiss-Iranian Parsua Bashi, intervene in scopic regimes through reinterpretations of looking and its protocols. Scopic regimes, or conventions, explicitly or implicitly determine how recognition operates through their assumptions, mechanisms, and circuits. Martin Jay, drawing from the cinematic theory of Christian Metz,[7] argued in 1988 that three major scopic regimes have operated in modernity, each roughly associated with a characteristic in modern European art and philosophy. They constitute "three ideal typical visual cultures." Each one is predicated on particular relations of surface and depth; of embodiment to vision and scene; and conceptual or narrative content.[8] In discussions of visual culture and visuality as a discipline in the early twentieth century, the social life of seeing and representing have flourished in relation to politics and power. W. T. J. Mitchell defines visual culture as "the visual construction of the social, not just the social construction of vision."[9] He insists that all media are mixed, and does so without canceling their particularities or contexts. Jay agrees that visual culture includes "optical experience" in all its manifestations and visual practice in "all variants."[10] In print as well as visual media, the "politics" of recognition and the "principles of exchange" undergird their operation, Wendy Hesford elaborates.[11] She belongs to a thick history of feminist theory investigating the look and the gaze, the relation of voice and language to image, and the semiotics of sexual identity and gender performativity as well as the racial, national, class, and belief identities shaping these categories.[12] The social fields through which we perceive bodies and the invisibilities that mold historical understanding are central to feminist visual studies. These include what Nicholas Mirzoeff identifies as the "right to look": who looks, at what, and how.[13]

Muslim Girl suggests what Rosalind Gill calls a postfeminist "disposition"[14] through the use of "girl" in the magazine's title, its visual identity in the logo, and the Instagram and tweet interactions with readers. At the same time, the sentiments expressed by the publication sound decidedly second-wave. The site emphasizes coalition and alliance among different identity and perhaps even age groups. The Muslim artists that I discuss modify and reposition female empowerment by claiming feminism while using the media, imagery, and genres that have been associated with feminism's aftermath.[15] Positing even a postfeminist disposition discloses the mainstream presumption that Muslim women are at best *becoming* feminist, as they do when they throw off their robes to show their full faces and bodily substance. The action signals their Western liberation, "white femininity," fashion consumption, and luminous, if modest, display.

I concentrate on postfeminist ideologies that dominated the era in which these works were created. Angela McRobbie defines the European and American "postfeminism" of the 1990s and into the 2000s as a habit of displacement and "disarticulation" of women from patriarchal structures and political alliances. These structures are ignored or diminished by emphasizing the individual woman and her choices.[16] Through the right actions, a woman may enter into the Deleuzean "luminous space of attention"[17] that empowers her, McRobbie says. Shimmering light washes out old forms of gender regulation and the dreary ghosts of conventional femininity.[18] Significantly, the offer of empowerment discourages intergenerational, intersectional, and intercultural alliances through its primary appeal to young, affluent women, modeled on a white, heterosexual, cis paradigm. As more recent critiques of white femininity show, the offer of inclusion to the girl of color or the "global girl" rests on her acceptance and incorporation of these apolitical values. There are many terms in circulation that contain elements of this orientation—commodity feminism and choice feminism among them—but McRobbie offers a well-established structural analysis of their foundation in a (chosen) disciplinary management that mirrors Muslim women's (enforced, unexamined) discipline by a harsh and extravagant patriarchy.[19] In some contrast to McRobbie, Gill argues that "postfeminist media culture" specifically should be the object of analysis. She defines it as a "sensibility" animated by feminist and antifeminist impulses. Among its chief features are a conception of "femininity as a bodily property" and an "emphasis on self-surveillance, monitoring, and discipline," both of which relate to discourses of "individualism, choice, and empowerment" as the alibi for freedom. These characteristics accompany a reinvestment in biological sexual difference, through commodification, diffuse sexualization, objectification, and consumerism. Gill elaborates, "These themes coexist with and are structured by stark inequalities and exclusions that are related to 'race' and ethnicity, class, age, sexuality, and disability—as well as gender."[20] Postfeminism has more recently come to operate as a "gendered neoliberalism" that "tightened its hold on contemporary life and bec[a]me hegemonic" as an affective disposition.[21]

McRobbie and Gill supply frameworks for my analysis of Muslim women as producers of the dominant popular imagery of women's agency.[22] The rubric offers a complex theoretical genealogy[23] intimately entangled in questions of expression and audience expectation, agency, and coercion.[24] Subcultural and transnational frameworks situate these issues in the polysemy of pleasure and politics. Calling attention to these frameworks presses forth the question: what is recognized as agential, by whom?[25] Postfeminist genres such as chick-lit, for example, have provided avenues of publication for marginalized groups; different female audiences are hailed in various ways by empowerment imagery. I focus specifically on the transactions between Muslim-identified women in Europe and America and their audiences. In this arena the equation of "visibility" and "agency" is highly fraught, but also imaginatively productive, as scholars have examined in both high art and mass media, particularly in relation to African-American women.[26] As I show, the binaries that women of African descent navigate may become even more rigid in the case of American Muslim identities, where epidermal colorism as a mark may supplant recognition of religious identities, expected to be "read" from corporeality.[27]

The relations of Muslim theologians to a Western monolithic or so-called hegemonic "feminism" has also been a complicated one. Some antipatriarchal critics have contended that "feminism," whether or not it is modified by the adjective "Islam," appropriates to itself all gender-equality or gender-conscious traditions, such as Qur'anic egalitarianism and Islamic jurisprudence. Others, while recognizing such historical hierarchies and conceptual differences, claim "Islamic feminism" as an acknowledgment of a political alliance. They share "modes of critical thought that they employ as part of a collective analytical project ... to criticize male power and normativity."[28] *Tafsir*, translated as "explanation," "interpretation," or "exegesis," and *ijtihad*, or "independent reasoning" are crucially important to critics of patriarchy and androcentrism. They inform the novels I discuss through citation, analogy, adaptation, and subtext. "Official" or historical male authorities have drawn on these tools since at least the eighth century CE.[29] To these methods must be added *siyaq*, an examination of historical context, introduced by "Muslim modernists" as an important technique of *tafsir*. The male modernists welcomed innovation and often argued that the Qur'an was accessible to anyone because of its compatibility with reason. The ulama's exclusive claim to textual authority was challenged by this interpretive emphasis, such as the Qur'an's ultimate aim of universal and ahistorical justice.[30]

These and other intellectual trends gave grounding to feminist and gender-justice exegetes of Islam in the late 1970s and early 1980s. Among the first generation are Amina Wadud, Riffat Hassan, Azizah Y. al-Hibri, Asma Barlas, and Kecia Ali, all of whom work in a U.S. context, though many of them are diasporan; and Sa'ddiya Shaikh of South Africa.[31] Asma Barlas, for instance, contends that though "patriarchal *tafsir*" has dominated historical interpretations of Islam, it has "no Qur'anic basis."[32] Barlas argues for a holistic reading of the Qur'an, based on its "best meaning" and contextual translations of key terms. Her "egalitarian" *tafsir* leads her to assert that the Qur'an "enjoins equality and warns against oppression based on gender without denying biological differences."[33] Because God transcends sex-gender, God's people are not engendered through "fatherhood," which is surpassed by God's "sovereignty." Similarly, Barlas contends that because God forwards "justice," the Qur'an is "antipatriarchal."[34] Since its message surpasses the specific constraints of seventh-century Arabia, the Qur'an encodes recognition of future injustices as well.[35]

Using *tafsir*, *ijtihad*, and *siyaq*, Barlas calls on the Islamic history of exegesis and reasoning in a context of belief to argue against gender injustice. In this she contests the designation "Islamic feminist." Margot Badran and Sa'diyya Shaikh, among others, endorse the term, some with reservations. Badran contends that "Islamic feminism" derives from discourses grounded in Islam but also from other texts: as such it is not "Western" or "Eastern" but rather constitutes a "universal discourse." She regards it as a necessary "analytic construct" for critique of patriarchy, a "common language" that transcends "the terrain of any particular religion."[36] Other scholars recognize overlaps and divergences between gender-equality or gender-conscious Muslim and so-called "feminist" work, and may see them as difficult to disentangle.[37] In treating the divergent viewpoints, Fatima Saeed questions the "apparent need to find equivalence between the two." Saeed argues that a "critical space" usefully allows different histories, politics, and frameworks to inform antipatriarchal work. "What happens," she asks, "when feminism as a discourse forecloses the possibility of theorizing sex equality from alternative cultural and intellectual paradigms?"[38]

These approaches to gender justice bear upon contemporary visuality and female empowerment, shot through as the works may be with commercial imagery; ambivalent as the works may be about feminism, claims of collectivity, intersectional politics, binary sex, and gender performativity. The genres in which these writers and artists work themselves enforce a cis heteronorm, coupled with culture and belief systems that may "overinvest" in an essential woman rather a spectrum of gender-sexuality, as Juliane Hammer argues.[39] According to Kecia Ali, the practice and resonance of "Islam" in locations that do not enforce its legal structures produce new formations of Islam and of Muslim identity: we can speak of "Western Muslims."[40] The producers that I treat all live in Europe and America, though many are diasporan. They reject the status of Muslim women as a lack their registered by an inert or bodiless robe. They refuse to stand singularly for a static alibi of "tradition" while they challenge the anonymity and facelessness that accompany the depiction of group submission, victim status, or entrenched modes of disavowal reiterated in mainstream genres. These producers often celebrate competitive individualism but also interrogate it in subtle ways that shape or challenge the model of personhood as the "individual." Because Muslim-identified women serve a shorthand for the opposite of individual "freedom," they must address structural impasses created by neoliberal[41] feminism, its disregard of race, class, disability, ageing, and violence. They attempt to overcome ethnoreligious difference read solely through the lens of phenotypic race—even as they revel in the beauty practices, aspirations for personal development, media circulation, and class privilege that characterize mainstream pop, born in the province of white femininity.

Chapter 1 establishes the terrain on which "becoming unveiled" is enacted in Anglo-American chick-lit and chick-film. The comparison reveals the interlocking of the mature (secular, white) postfeminist and the ever-immured Muslimah in a conventional EuroAmerican semiotic. I focus on two works in the emergence of the literary genre as a marketing niche that became televisual and transnational. *Sex and the City 2* (2010), a television series long paradigmatic by the time the second film appeared, leaves the domestic space to visit Arabian "Islamland," a pastiche exotic locale named "Abu Dhabi." Under the guise of its cheeky U.S. satire and parody, the movie is radically xenophobic and regressive even for its moment. But it also reveals the yearning of woman ageing out of luminous display for a legacy and a future that is decidedly not their mother's feminism. The lack telegraphed by the coming abjection of age, particularly acute for the nonreproductive wife, is answered by the imagination of a Muslim woman who is fashionable and stylized, the same as the Anglo travelers underneath the "cloak" of the robe. While *Sex and the City 2* is obliged to update heterosexual marriage by featuring a gay and selectively nonmonogamous marriage, it turns to the Orient to reinvigorate female bodies that will soon dim. The literary transformation of an initially spikier chick-lit into the niche commodity parallels the transformation of the Arabic *Banat al-Riyadh* (2005) into the English-language *Girls of Riyadh* (2007), as its co-translator has extensively described. While *Banat* pays explicit homage to the *Sex and the City* television show, it also in its original Arabic uses heteroglossia through different linguistic levels and regional dialects, promotes a gender-justice critique of Arabia, distinguishes its status and politics from those of other Muslim-majority states in the region, and alludes to the Prophet as the model of conduct, including his tolerance for disagreements. While the specifics of the original language are inevitably lost or dampened in translation, Marilyn Booth enumerates the ways in which the English-language text was further homogenized for consumption in the Anglo-American market. Still the translation reveals the deft use of nonvisual technology and the conceit of the zenana, or women's space, to open the perspectives of four competitive and ambitious friends. Because the narrator does not reveal which of the four characters the narrator is, and even leaves open the possibility that she is a fifth omniscient narrator, *Girls of Riyadh* finally celebrates a transcendent perspective *and* an embodied voice that circulates without the limitations of female flesh and its representation.

Chapter 2 examines the possibilities for female rejuvenation in two novels written by Monica Ali. *Brick Lane* (2003) focuses on a rural Muslim woman who migrates to London; *Untold Story* (2011) imagines the epitome of white femininity, Princess Diana, in an anonymous and posthumous existence in America. The two novels were subjected to nationalized and racialized receptions, contexts that have prevented readers from seeing the related structures of abjection shaping both protagonists. The specific contours of the spiritual-corporeal transformation of Nazneen has been read as a celebration of Western economic autonomy as well as a rejection of Islam. In fact, *Brick Lane* employs a masochistic camouflage of the visible and explicit insignia of Islam to dramatize the protagonist's internalization of the prophetic body. Her transformation accelerates when she engages in a transgressive love affair. The *tafsir* of experience, applied in a particular way, diffusely animates the protagonist's experience of divine reciprocity. *Untold Story* continues the trajectory of *Sex and the City 2* by melodramatically imagining that the exposure of the former Diana will be fatal to her children. Lydia, the Diana surrogate, seeks self-discovery through a plot of liberation and escape from self-destruction. Yet the masochistic dynamic imagined to have fueled her historical life increases its ascetic hold. The novel immures Lydia in a homogeneous white enclave that is imagined to protect her from exposure, but is in fact charged with the energies of death, affective isolation, and loss of purpose. Together, Ali's novels show the exchange of the stereotypical roles of the abjected migrant Muslim and the luminous freedom of white womanhood.

Chapter 3 comes up against the limits of ethnoreligious representation as visual display. Set in America in the era of Islamic revival, the scopic determinates of white and black, native and foreign, flatten distinctions among race, ethnicity, and religion. Mohja Kahf's *The Girl in the Tangerine Scarf* (2006) attempts to place an African migrant, and through her African-American Muslims of long standing, at the center of a "native" U.S. Islam. The novel promotes an antiracist Islamic feminism that rejects consumerism and has no claim on affluence. But Kahf's central metaphor, which casts hijab as a "second skin," cannot extend to the Africa-descended Muslimah in America. In the epidermal racial binary of rural America in the late twentieth century, selective unveiling would become a scene of subjection. Though the novel attempts to counter the "conversion narrative" attached to American Muslims by Mecca-centered migrants, the black Muslim woman becomes a site of mourning, absence, and collective grief without an image. Kahf's treatment of black Muslim women is more successful in the vehicle of her poetry. Her most recent volume, *Hagar Poems* (2016), is trained on the exemplary African woman of scripture and her conflicts and alliances with Sarah, the first, older wife of Abraham.

Chapters 4 and 5 move into revisions of looking and seeing as epistemologies in visual media. Both feature artists who refigure the iconography of Muslim women as immured and oppressed to present particular versions of corporeal subjectivity in relation to neoliberal individualism. The digital and sculptural work of German-Iranian Parastou Forouhar displays the structures of violence that shape female identification. Forouhar makes a broad critique of domestic terror that draws upon Islamic concepts and pre-Islamic aesthetics at the same time that it pertains to a Western legacy of decoration as a secondary order of high art. Her reception, however, initially emphasized her critique of state-sponsored violence in Iran because of the assassination of her parents in their home in 1998. Forouhar contributes strongly to recent feminist theory that concerns the "scaffolding" of patriarchal violence in Europe and America, and the conceptualization of women as "derivatives" of such structures. Significantly, her work revises the theory of the gaze through entanglements and duplications of forms that may change according to the viewer's position and concentration.

Chapter 5 treats a graphic narrative that departs from the life narrative's affinity with trauma, particularly in multimodal works. In relating the life of a privileged Iranian migrant to Switzerland, Parsua Bashi uses an enlarged face that echoes Disney princesses and glamour comic strips such as "Brenda Starr" to hail a global audience while typifying and characterizing a Muslimah face. Bashi uses the idiom of fashion, beauty, and design in which she was trained while she levels political critique of it. Using a strategy of psychomachia, *Nylon Road* (2006) challenges the notion of a unified subject by embodying the author's different selves at different ages. The dialectical procedure illustrates the discontinuities of a Lacanian subject who never achieves wholeness. Instead, these past figures collaborate with her current persona. In spite of its visual mixed medium and graphic format, Bashi emphasizes loss and fragmentation through the absence of her native language in Switzerland, and indeed from the work, initially published in German.

In Conclusion I refer to the current explosion of Muslim women's productions in contemporary media. I relate the representational strategies of earlier work I've discussed to that of an emerging Muslim-American artist who enthusiastically represents queer and antiracist female identity in her work. "To humanize Muslims—to make Muslims appear to be more human—is a radical act," Saba Taj proclaimed in a TED talk given in 2017.[42] Taj accomplishes this task through playful facialization and individual portraiture, but also through posthuman imagery. She uses ethnological and cultural stereotypes to invert species rhetoric, drawing upon the grotesque to break open fetishized images of Islam while showing affinity with "Afrofuturist" fiction, cinema, and visual art.

Notes

1 Peggy Phelan, *Unmarked: The Politics of Performance* (London: Routledge, 1993), 6.
2 Inna Arzumanova, "Veiled Visibility: Racial Performances and Hegemonic Leaks in Pakistani Fashion Week," in *Racism Postrace*, ed. Roopali Mukherjee, Sarah Banet-Weiser, and Herman Gray (Durham: Duke University Press, 2019), 278.
3 Claire Chambers, *Making Sense of Contemporary British Muslim Novels* (London: Springer-Macmillan, 2019), xxxiii.
4 Sahar Ghumkhor, *The Political Psychology of the Veil: The Impossible Body* (Switzerland: Springer Nature and Palgrave-Macmillan, 2020).
5 See Charles Hirschkind, "Is There a Secular Body?" *Cultural Anthropology* 26.4 (2011): 633–47; Talal Asad, "Thinking about the Secular Body, Pain, and Liberal Politics," *Cultural Anthropology* 26.4 (2011): 657–75.
6 Hirschkind, "Secular Body," 641–43.
7 Christian Metz, *The Imaginary Signifier: Psychoanalysis and Cinema*, trans. Celia Britton et al. (Bloomington: Indiana University Press, 1982). Metz uses the term to distinguish theatrical and cinematic viewing.
8 Martin Jay, "Scopic Regimes of Modernity," in *Vision and Visuality*, ed. Hal Foster (Seattle: Bay-DIA, 1988), 3–23.
9 W. T. J. Mitchell. "Showing Seeing: A Critique of Visual Culture," *Journal of Visual Culture*, 11.2 (2002), 170.
10 Martin Jay, "That Visual Turn: The Advent of Visual Culture," *The Journal of Visual Culture*, 1.1 (2002), 87–92.
11 Wendy Hesford, *Spectacular Rhetorics: Human Rights, Visions, Recognition, Feminisms* (New York: New York University Press, 2011), 29. In describing the "human rights spectacle" Hesford distinguishes singular images from the "social and rhetorical processes of recognition mediated by visual representations and ocular epistemology," which assumes that "seeing is believing," 155.
12 See, for instance, Amelia Jones, ed. *The Feminism and Visual Culture Reader*, 2nd ed. (New York: Routledge, 2010).
13 Nicholas Mirzoeff, *The Right to Look: A Counterhistory of Visuality* (Durham: Duke University Press, 2011), 2.
14 Rosalind Gill, "The Affective, Cultural, and Psychic Life of Postfeminism: A Postfeminist Sensibility Ten Years On," *European Journal of Cultural Studies* 20.6 (2017), 606.
15 See, for instance, Pamela Butler and Jinga Desai, "Manolos, Marriage, and Mantras: Chick-Lit Criticism and Transnational Feminism," *Meridians: Feminism, Race, and Transnationalism*, 8.2 (2008): 1–31; Lucinda Newns, "Renegotiating Romantic Genres: Textual Resistance and Muslim Chick-Lit," *Journal of Commonwealth Literature*, 53.2 (2017): 1–17; Muhammad Abdullah and Safeer Awan, "Islamic Postfeminism and Muslim Chick-Lit: Coexistence of Conflicting Discourses," *Pakistan Journal of Women's Studies* 24.2 (2017): 93–105; Wenche Ommundsen, "Sex and the Global City: Chick Lit with a Difference," *Contemporary Women's Writing* 5.2 (2011): 107–24.
16 Angela McRobbie, *The Aftermath of Feminism: Gender, Culture and Social Change* (London: Sage, 2009), 60.
17 McRobbie, *Aftermath*, 60.
18 McRobbie, *Aftermath*, 54, 60.
19 Myra Macdonald, "Muslim Women and the Veil: Problems of Image and Voice in Media Representations," *Feminist Media Studies* 6.1 (2006): 13.
20 Rosalind Gill, "Postfeminist Media Culture: Elements of a Sensibility," *European Journal of Media Studies* 10.2 (2007): 147–48.

21 Rosalind Gill, "The Affective, Cultural, and Psychic Life of Postfeminism," 606. Also see "Post-postfeminism? New Feminist Visibilities in Postfeminist Times," *Feminist Media Studies* 16.4 (2016): 610–30.
22 Trish Salah notes the simultaneous rise of "representations of (white) girl power" and "representations of oppressed (Oriental/Muslim) women." She argues that the conjunction has been "crucial in constituting a postfeminist public sphere." "Of Activist Fandoms, Auteur Pedagogy, and Imperial Feminism: From *Buffy the Vampire Slayer* to *I am Du'a Khalil*," in *Muslim Women: Transnational Feminism and the Ethics of Pedagogy: Contested Imaginaries in Post-9/11 Cultural Practice*, 167.
23 For an earlier interpretation of postfeminism as an epistemological shift away from foundational philosophies, see, for instance, Ann Brooks, *Postfeminisms: Feminism, Cultural Theory, and Cultural Forms* (London and New York: Routledge, 1997, 2002), 4. Gill, "Post-postfeminism," p. 612, gives an extensive list of scholars engaged in definitions of the term before 2000. Exemplary of "third-wave" feminism are works such as Jennifer Baumgardner and Amy Richards, *ManifestA: Young Women, Feminism, and the Future* (New York: Farrar, Straus and Giroux, 2000); Jennifer Baumgardner and Amy Richards, "Feminism and Femininity: Or How We Learned to Stop Worrying and Love the Thong," in *All About the Girl*, ed. Anita Harris (London: Routledge, 2004), 59–69; and, in a different vein, Chela Sandoval, *Methodology of the Oppressed* (Minneapolis: University of Minnesota Press, 2000).
24 Sadie Wearing, for instance, sets the formulations of McRobbie and Gill against critics who argue that postfeminist media culture may present "a new way of doing femininity and doing culture." "Representing Agency and Coercion: Feminist Readings and Postfeminist Media Fictions," in *Gender, Agency, and Coercion*, ed. Sumi Madhok, Anne Phillips, and Kalpana Wilson (Houndmills, Basingstoke: Palgrave-Macmillan, 2013), 223–24.
25 Clare Hemmings and Amal Treacher Kabesh, "The Feminist Subject of Agency: Recognition and Affect in Encounters with the 'Other,'" in *Gender, Agency, and Coercion*, ed. Sumi Madhok, Anne Phillips, and Kalpana Wilson (Houndmills, Basingstoke: Palgrave-Macmillan, 2013), 32.
26 See for instance, Peggy Phelan, *Unmarked*; Lisa Gail Collins, *The Art of History: African American Women Artists Engage the Past* (New Brunswick, NJ: Rutgers University Press, 2002); Nicole R. Fleetwood, *Troubling Vision: Performance, Visuality, and Blackness* (Chicago: University of Chicago Press, 2011); Sharon Holland, *Raising the Dead: Readings of Death and (Black) Subjectivity* (Durham: Duke University Press, 2000). On visibility, also see Linda Alcoff, *Visible Identities: Race, Gender, and the Self* (Oxford: Oxford University Press, 2006).
27 Joanne Hollows, *Feminism, Femininity and Popular Culture* (Manchester and New York: Manchester University Press, 2000), 26–27.
28 Aysha A. Hidayatullah, *Feminist Edges of the Qur'an* (Oxford: Oxford University Press, 2014), 44. She further argues that categorizing exegetes merely as "women" or as "gender equality" proponents presents a host of intellectual problems. In addition, such terms fail to suggest that these Muslim theologians make a "radical critique of power." She elaborates: "The exegetes of the Qur'an boldly claim the right to interpret the Qur'an in opposition to the vanguard of Qur'anic interpreters who have repeatedly done violence to women by presenting their sexist biases as the mandate of God; the authors of [such] works radically challenge the treatment of human beings in Islam as normatively male."
29 Hidayatullah, *Feminist Edges*, 24. Hidayatullah summarizes the historical development of *tafsir* as a category distinct from *hadith* and its development as a written rather than an oral form, 28–30.
30 Hidayatullah, *Feminist Edges*, 68–70.

31 Hidayatullah, *Feminist Edges*, 68–70; also see Juliane Hammer, "Introduction to Women and Gender Justice," in *Muslim Women and Gender Justice: Concepts, Sources, and Histories*, ed. Dina El Omari, Juliane Hammer, and Mouhanad Khorchide (New York: Routledge, 2019), 1–14.
32 Amina Barlas and David Rayburn Finn, *Believing Women in Islam: A Brief Introduction* (Austin: University of Texas Press, 2019), 40.
33 Barlas and Finn, *Believing Women*, 25, 2.
34 Barlas and Finn, *Believing Women*, 34.
35 Barlas and Finn, *Believing Women*, 7.
36 Margot Badran, *Feminism in Islam: Secular and Religious Convergences* (Oxford: Oneworld, 2009), 2–3, 242.
37 Hidayatullah, *Feminist Edges*, 44. See Margot Badran, *Feminism in Islam* and Amina Wadud, *Inside the Gender Jihad: Women's Reform in Islam* (Oxford: Oneworld, 2006).
38 Fatima Seedat, "Islam, Feminism, and Islamic Feminism: Between Inadequacy and Inevitability," *Journal of Feminist Studies in Religion* 29.2 (2013): 27.
39 Hammer, "Introduction to Women and Gender Justice," 13.
40 Kecia Ali, *Sexual Ethics and Islam: Feminist Reflections on Qur'an, Hadith and Jurisprudence* (Oxford: Oneworld, 2006), xxiii, xxii, 57.
41 George Monbiot summarizes the current form of this ideology, born in the 1940s. "Neoliberalism sees competition as the defining characteristic of human relations. It redefines citizens as consumers, whose democratic choices are best exercised by buying and selling, a process that rewards merit and punishes inefficiency. It maintains that the market delivers benefits that could never be achieved by planning." "Neoliberalism—The Ideology at the Root of All Our Problems," *Guardian* 15 April 2016. www.theguardian.com/books/2016/apr/15/neoliberalism-ideology-problem-george-monbiot.
42 Saba Taj, "Art, Resistance, and the Dominant Narrative," TEDX Duke, 10 April 2017. www.youtube.com/watch?v=mnE0Qn2eJMw. Accessed November 9, 2019.

1
SEX AND OTHER CITIES
Abjected Age, Abandoned Flesh

Head covering (as well as robing) has a variegated history in ancient cultures located in the Mediterranean, the Middle East, North Africa, the Arabian Peninsula, and the subcontinent. The rich semiotic of covering relates to prestige, practicality, affinity, and fashion as well as to gender and belief norms. Homa Hoodfar observes that in Muslim cultures "the veil's functions and social significance have varied tremendously, particularly during times of rapid social change."[1] Muslim women are "social actors" in these developments. In the European imperium, Orientalist imagery of the eighteenth century used the head covering as a primary marker of the exotic, linked in representations of women to sensuality, passivity, and seclusion—a fantasy erotic domain to be penetrated visually. Even European women travelers of the eighteenth and nineteenth centuries seldom related these stereotypes to the superficially different but prevailing patriarchies that governed them at home.

In the twentieth century, modernizing and decolonizing leaders cast veiling as regressive. Dictating women's dress, even at the expense of the agency that covering provided them in public spheres, became a key sign of "secularizing" or liberal political movements in Turkey, Egypt, India, and other locations. Whether mandated, stigmatized, or offered, female dress signified national values visually. Uma Narayan calls attention to these "pictures of history"[2] that condense and idealize "political and discursive struggles."[3] The images of nation not only substitute for knowledge, but they also distract attention from women's function as totalized vessels of national-religious values, loyalty, and reproductive service.

In the later twentieth century, revival, revolution, and diaspora made veiling practices synonymous with Islam, as feminist scholars in various fields have shown. Veiling's renewed religious meaning for many Muslim women in Muslim-majority cultures encompassed anticapitalist and social equity impulses founded

DOI: 10.4324/9781003189299-2

on religious belief. In the West, however, "the veil" froze as a signifier of Islamic patriarchy and its despotic exercise of violence. On book covers and magazine pages, newspapers and televisual sites, the "veil" appeared most frequently as an encompassing black robe. Megan McDonald calls it a "blank(et) signifier" that "saturates and evacuates" meaning.[4] As an emblem it resembles a large ink blot, lacking substance and mobility. The woman's face is conventionally turned away from the frontal plane to display her back. Her head is frugally distinguished from her figure. No one needs to speak to convey this sign's meaning. As a sign, "the veil" serves up a shorthand that passes for knowledge: the Muslim woman is uniquely oppressed and immured, in precise opposition to the freedom of the EuroAmerican (Christian/secular) woman. If only she could show some skin, some plasticity of flesh, she could *move*. Sahar Ghumkhor reads the constant reenactment of veiling and unveiling as symptomatic of "a hypnotic belief in the revealed flesh as a signature of freedom."[5] The performance of veiling and unveiling secures the imagined "secular" body as natural and homogenous. In a related vein Haneen Shafeeq Ghabia argues that a cultural "Muslim femininity" acts as a site where white femininity "is secured, reproduced, and sustained."[6] I share with these and other critics an interest in linking the sign of the veil to a persistent need for a supplement to a Western imago of free, coherent, and mobile women.

The writers and artists I treat here take as a starting point not hijab per se—a rich body of feminist scholarship in a number of fields already exists—but rather the Muslimah figured as a blot with a tenuous hold on the "subjectification" registered by figural plasticity and the capacity for "faciality." Deleuze and Guattari define faciality as the representation of the head as distinct from the body and the face as distinct from the head as a site of individuation.[7] "The Face" is produced when the head "ceases to be a part of the body, ceases to be coded by the body, when it ceases to have a multidimensional, polyvocal corporeal code—when the body, head included, has been decoded and has to be *overcoded*."[8] This chapter introduces the hijab[9] as an imagined materialization of female identity undefined and inert, lacking facialization. The blot captures a woman. I contend that the blot serves in the Western Christian imaginary as a totalized essence and a disguise, which only need be removed to allow for a facialized form, one also capable of movement.

The material masquerade solidifies elements of the psychological masquerade first identified by Joan Riviere. She argues that women may cloak their intellect and strength in charm and girlishness (in her Freudian terms, their possession of phallic power). In this way they mitigate their threat to masculine authority. Angela McRobbie coins the term "postfeminist masquerade" to describe women's simultaneous rejection and seeming acceptance of agency,[10] one that encompasses physical and behavioral elements. Mary Ann Doane grounds the perceptual and spatial dynamics of the masquerade: she contends that film offers "the potential to manufacture a distance for the image, to generate a problematic within which the image is manipulable, producible, and readable by the woman,"[11] who is always too present in her own flesh. The veil "manufacture[s]" a spatial and, I am adding, a temporal gap[12] between the viewing and viewed women, through a heavy affect of materiality. In my argument, Deleuze and Guattari's analysis bears upon feminist theories of disguise that are psychic, somatic, affective,[13] gestural, and representational.

The little distance between the screen (or other reproduced) image and the female viewer parallels the little distance between the image of the covered woman and the woman visibly ageing out of postfeminist display. The two signifiers sustain and animate one another. *Sex and the City 2* (2007) translates the masquerade into an actual hijab as the field of emergence for the face as the sign of a subjectified agent. The movie telegraphs the possibility of her substance and movement. Here the proximity of a fashionable covered Muslim woman shows a route to rejuvenation for older Anglo-American women: "old flesh" and "veiled flesh" reveal affinities between "women not fit to be seen" and "women not able to be seen."[14] Ageing flesh becomes a kind of forthcoming skin-veil in the movie. It sends the four friends, three of them now married, to Abu Dhabi, where they wear flowing (though not necessarily modest) fashions, enjoy luxuries, flirt, and ride camels against the backdrop of voiceless women in dark robes. Yet in an early scene, a hijabi actually *models* innovation to the American protagonist. Dubbed "the real housewife of Abu Dhabi," a made-up woman in a decorated, fashionable hijab and abaya offers a mediating supplement to the movie's formulation of U.S. feminism. Her expressive face and gestures elicit a shiver of delight and recognition from Carrie, the protagonist, who spots her across a hotel patio. At the conclusion of the movie, the real housewife's greater significance is revealed: she offers a redesign of "tradition," which links women globally. As Rafia Zakaria notes in another context, the imagery of veiling can be understood as a "wish for reclamation."[15] In a very different affective position, the real housewife also offers Carrie a disguised and compensatory connection to a (default Christian, American, white feminist) mother who never appears in the *Sex* televisual narrative. Through such links, Carrie imagines a future for a nonreproductive heterosexual marriage as it ages out of glamor.

Arab women speak their empowerment and shape their own presentation in Rajaa Alsanea's *Banat al-Riyadh* (2005). Published in Beirut and London,[16] *Banat* has been called the Arabic *Sex in the City*; indeed, the TV show features in the novel. It was translated into English as *Girls of Riyadh* in 2007. *Banat* imitates the television series *Sex and the City* by presenting four female protagonists of the "velvet class" seeking companionate heterosexual union and a balance between marriage and career. In the novel, social strictures on marriage partnership generate a major obstacle to women's fulfillment. *Banat/Girls* takes up the very issues of legal and social equity that *Sex* assumes are essentially resolved in the U.S. Promoting a reformist Islam based on scripture, the Arabic and English texts adumbrate a politics of response to an authoritarian nation-state whose strictures fall most heavily on women. Here, older women appear, but usually as agents of patriarchal control. Gender justice advocacy takes the form of an appeal to *isnan*, or the Qur'anic principle of human equality. Such commentary on Saudi laws and social norms emerges among depictions of self-management as a product in an exclusive marketplace of romance. Advice for securing a marriage partner, assessment of other women's appearance (even among friends), and material consumption (particularly of fashion) figure significantly in the text. The marriage plot shapes but does not entirely limit careers. Nonetheless an actual encounter in the U.S. of an Arab migrant wife and the secret Asian-American lover of her Arab husband exposes the lie of mobility and inclusion imagined or desired by identification with postfeminism of the *Sex and the City* variety.

Sex and *Banat/Girls* reveal the essential attachment of disciplinary regimes to women's bodies, through private and public regulation. Like "choice," "religion" can serve as an alibi for this regulation. Only the anonymous narrator of *Banat/Girls* escapes the marriage plot. As a stand-in for any one of the characters or as the author function in relation to them, she finds her fulfillment in forthcoming celebrity. She enters into McRobbie's luminous postfeminist space, only as a voice. She is not characterized visually. Ultimately fame can potentially free young women from the dictates of the pictured flesh and even from the disembodied "voice" of writing. The conclusion of *Banat/Girls* offers a trade-off between a feminist or Islamic gender-equality politics and a postfeminist spectacle of individual power. Through this transaction, the narrator hopes to gain public speech from her throat *without* giving her body over to the signs of freedom and unfreedom, youth and age, home and abroad.

Chick-Lit and Lit-Crit: Legacies of Romance

As Amy Burge shows in her analysis of medieval and contemporary romances in English, the genre has been used transhistorically to "manipulate[e the] hybrid representations of religious and ethnic difference in order to create successful romance unions." Romance manages Christian hostility to Islam.[17] Since the Middle Ages in the West, Burge argues, "religious difference" has often been read as "somatic difference." Conversely, "race" in its contemporary meanings incorporates various elements associated with religion or belief, language, and culture. In short, Burge sees consistency in the categories of difference employed at disparate moments. At the same time she notes their distinct valences. Belief holds primary status as the mark of difference in medieval texts and race as biology in modern ones. In neither epoch can nature and culture be easily distinguished from one another: belief, language, custom, behaviors and cultures mix with somatic or phenotypical differences understood as racial or ethnic.[18] Such destabilizing of custom and bios, race and religion, ethnicity and language or habit features, however weakly, in the desert and sheik romances published in the U.K. by Mills & Boon into the twenty-first century.[19] The "romance East" of the desert and sheik subgenre is distanced from territorial, political, and social realities while using geographic and other cues to locate settings in the Middle East. In earlier decades, when Britain maintained an imperial presence, the books were most often set in actual locations, predominantly in North Africa.[20]

Girls of Riyadh and Sex and the City 2 bear a crucial relationship to a belated romance genre of chick-lit. The term's evolution roughly parallels the source material's journey to its later translation, whether linguistic or televisual. "Chick-lit" entered circulation as the title of the Cris Mazza and Jeffry DeShell anthology, *Chick-Lit: Post Feminist Fiction* (1995), published by Fiction Collective 2, a venue for avant-garde work at the Illinois State University Press.[21] The anthology's aims were progressive. According to Stephanie Harzewski, "Mazza and DeShell announced a feisty and unapologetically female literary category that distanced itself from the staid second-wave disposition: the *chick* of their chick-lit supplanted the serious *woman* and the gynocentric *womyn* of an earlier, more inviolate, feminist age."[22] The New York publishing industry took up the term after James Wolcott, in a May 1996 *New Yorker* article, used it to mock the style of editorialist Maureen Dowd and her ilk for their "sheer *girlishness*,"[23] suggesting that such writers revealed the problematic legacy of feminism.[24] In 2006, critics Suzanne Ferriss and Mallory Young praised chick-lit's mixture of romance with issues of everyday life while acknowledging that "ambiguity lies at the genre's core."[25] In the same collection, *Chick-Lit: The New Women's Fiction*, Cris Mazza descries the "perversion" of the subgenre by "the commercial book industry machine."[26] More recently, Heike Missler contends that "chick lit as it once was may … be a residual genre," but one that remains a significant site of online culture, female identification, and publishing opportunity for first time novelists.[27] In fact, the genre continues to produce work by women from nondominant groups, whether in "masquerade" as chick-lit or in fact centered around its salient characteristics.[28]

Neither *Sex and the City*, the newspaper column that Candace Bushnell wrote for the New York *Observer* beginning in 1996, nor *Banat al-Riyadh* exactly fits the genre of "chick lit" that emerged in the same year. As a niche publishing term, "chick lit" downplayed the progressive aims and the literary experimentation of the *Chick-Lit* anthology while reveling in the rejection of second-wave feminism's purportedly dour and dowdy style. The "girlishness" that Wolcott derided became a dominant characteristic of the books as a brand. Bushnell's *Sex and the City* columns, and the collection that immediately succeeded them, helped to ignite the popular genre. Both early and later chick-lit favors urban settings for white, middle-class protagonists who work in media. But the more unruly source material lacks the "girlishness" that became the brand hallmark. In the column, Bushnell and her compatriots are older, shrewder, more upwardly mobile, and more sexually competitive than the mother of chick-lit protagonists, Bridget Jones of Helen Fielding's newspaper column and later novel, *Bridget Jones's Diary* (1996).[29] Bushnell represents men more critically than is conventional in later chick-lit, and romantic partnership, when not in conflict with the acquisition of money and power, ultimately may take second place to it. In these ways Bushnell's texts "share more ... with glamour novels than with chick lit," according to Harzewski.[30] The HBO television show (1998–2004) counterbalanced the column's insider knowingness and will-to-power with softer romantic comedy. The protagonists sought heterosexual partnership as a dominant life goal and eschewed competition with one another in favor of friendship and humor.[31] Glamor remained a staple in the television series, and the display of cutting-edge fashion became more central because of the visual medium.

Banat imitates the television series *Sex and the City* by presenting four female protagonists of the "velvet class" encountered through the audience's entrance into the intimate space of the women's zenana. *Banat* issues this invitation specifically to young Saudi women. The narrator renders the young women's world through Arabic literary and cultural references as well as pop "global" ones, with an emphasis on youth culture. Marilyn Booth, who co-translated *Banat* into English, argues that the Arabic original demonstrates that "chick lit can be chick crit," as the Shell and DeMazza anthology envisioned. Booth continues:

> [O]ne can read the Arabic *Banat al-Riyadh* ... as a critique of patriarchal Saudi culture not simplistically as uniformly oppressive of females but rather as a system that exploits consumer culture to compensate or reward privileged youth (male or female) of the majority Sunni population for adhering to status-quo social arrangements.

Literary complexity forwards this reading "through the use of varying regional dialects and linguistic levels."[32] *Banat*'s deployment of "Arabenglish" interacts with gendered constructions and regional linguistic variations to deliver a carnivalesque dimension.[33] Booth describes the Arabic original as "bold in its use of not one but multiple vernaculars (in a situation of diglossia where spoken Arabic varies markedly from place to place as well as from the 'learned' or 'literary' language)." Though not alone in her use of the vernacular in fiction, author Rajaa Alsanea makes a "controversial" choice because of "the strong emotional and ideological associations that obtain between the ancient language of the Qur'an and today's 'literary' Arabic."[34]

The desire to diminish and homogenize difference governed many decisions about the translation of *Banat* into English,[35] just as it did the adaptation of Bushnell's *Sex and the City* columns into the TV show. While *Banat* and *Girls of Riyadh* share features, the English translation is a "version" of the original not only because of the inherent difference of language and framework, but also because of the editorial privileging of accessibility to Anglo-American markets and of adherence to the publishing industry's emergent "chick-lit" conventions. *Girls* dilutes the address to young women as its audience, generalizes the depiction of Saudi patriarchy, and carefully manages other issues of class and cultural difference. Effacing as much as possible the traces of translation, the English version further creates a certain kind of "individuality-in-celebrity" for the narrator and author that, as "it resists and challenges certain stereotypes (by, for example showing [such] authors as media-savvy and articulate transnational figures), may sustain others," according to Booth.[36] *Girls* weakens the threat of cultural and sexual difference. The process is best understood, Booth argues, through "the apparatus of publicity and public-image making along with the less visible process of actually producing the text of a translation."[37]

What do the translations of popular source texts reveal about representation of the elite female "person"? She sounds much like McRobbie's "global girl," whose disciplined femininity is styled for the widest possible exposure, and whose religious, racial or ethnic, national, or class identities must be subordinated to dominant paradigms of beauty and presentation.[38] The individual woman as celebrity brand stages a mise-en-abime of surfaces. Her highest form of accomplishment is diffuse circulation. As writers, Bushnell and Alsanea become the *fait accompli* of their stories. Both relate the achievement of a goal emplotted through the texts themselves. The ultimate postfeminist freedom is not self-disciplined embodiment, but transcendence of embodiment altogether in favor of the image or avatar.[39] Simulation might overtake the masquerade, without needing to bother with issues of surface and depth, immediacy and distance, as well as possibilities of intimacy and transformation.[40] At the same time, *Banat/Girls* encodes a longing for orality, through the recitation of the narrator's writing by herself and other women in concert.

White and Velvet Weddings

As a television series, *Sex and the City* chronicles the sexual lives of thirtysomething affluent, single, straight, white, cis women in Manhattan. The narrator presents herself as the sexual anthropologist of this tribe, focusing on the umbrella group of her kin, three close women friends. The opening montage assumes the ethnologic vantage point of the sidewalk, looking up to the Chrysler Building from below and allowing its heroine to be splashed by a bus that bears her image in an ad.[41] The introduction anticipates the show's aim to celebrate and to spoof the image of a glittering metropolis. Glossy and gritty, New York is a cosmopolitan center and a parochial town. In the early seasons, the show uses *vox-pop* direct address to the camera, usually voiced by Carrie, or occasionally by an acquaintance or stranger. In noting the series' formal and thematic debt to Woody Allen's "nervous male" romantic comedies, Tom Grochowski observes that the documentary style underscores Carrie's authorial position as ethnologist.[42] Media critics and, later, scholars heralded the show for its focus on women as agents of their own sexual and economic desires, and as builders of their own small community in an agonistic urban milieu. All four women work, three in the business of representation, but Carrie's job, as a columnist for the fictional

New York *Star*, most closely ties her private life to her work, and her reportage to memoir. In this world, labor rarely interferes with the pursuit of pleasure, except in the case of Miranda, an attorney. The show's fantasy content reaches its heights not in the realm of sex, but rather in the realm of economics. On the salary of a weekly columnist for an alternative newspaper, Carrie lives in an Upper East-Side brownstone, her apartment is a one bedroom, she never takes public transportation, and does not seem to benefit from family money. To signify her poverty (relative to her social set), the show casts her as a renter, one who spends too freely on designer clothes and shoes. By the end of the series, Carrie herself has become a celebrity author, but her economic status improves only when she is helped by others: one of the women sells her engagement ring to help Carrie buy her apartment, and boyfriends are responsible for other improvements in her real estate.

During the adventure in Abu Dhabi that comprises most of *Sex and the City 2*, the cheeky satires of American regionalism become ethnographic. As a "type" in the American imagination, a Muslim woman is not available for parody in the way that a (white) Angelenos model or an affluent Connecticut mother is. Yet the film *Sex and the City 2* suggests that imperial history is ripe for similar satire, as if the inequities it produced have already been ameliorated. The movie begins with images of clouds and then zooms down, first to an aerial map of Manhattan and then to its landmarks. Rather than lampoon and celebrate urban glamor, the opening just illustrates it. "Once upon a long time ago," Carrie Bradshaw (Sarah Jessica Parker) begins her cosmopolitan ethnography, "there was an island, some Dutch, some Indians and some beads." These "beads," echoed by the diamond-encrusted letters of the title, "led to steamboats and skyscrapers, Wall Street, electric lights, newspapers, Ellis Island, the Yankees, Central Park, the Chrysler Building and Studio 54, and the first World's Fair."[43] The voiceover parallels the arrival of Carrie Bradshaw in Manhattan in 1986 to this genealogy, which ends the "B.C." or "before Carrie" era of Manhattan's commerce, media, and cultural life. "Beads" as flashy jewels, money, and imperial or settler loot allude to the female group that formed a decade before. Three of the four are now married. Two have children. The fourth, the oldest, a committed single woman, is experiencing a waning libido that she attributes to menopause. Pictured then and now, the four meet at Bergdorf's to purchase a wedding gift for friends, but they are gay male friends, whose lavish wedding supplies an occasion for examining "traditional" marriage with a contemporary urban twist.

The "gay sensibility" of the TV series has been established in the popular and academic press,[44] and the show's strong preference for male queers is well documented. While the series makes forays into lesbian sex, anything resembling a lesbian perspective is virtually absent from it. Mandy Merck argues that the show "makes its women not fantasy partners [as in *Will and Grace*] but the fantasy equivalents of metropolitan gay men. ... If the content is straight, the form is gay."[45] The representation of gay male sexuality acquires new force in the movie as an alternative model for companionate marriage, as well as a containment of queerness. The union affords a luminous staging of the white wedding as politically progressive *and* normative, hip and traditional, queer and straight, ironic and clichéd. The event takes place in the "country," a Connecticut bed and breakfast at which a Broadway-level production is staged. Out of the closet, the tuxedoed "brooms" relish the visibility of gay marriage as a spectacle and as a legal right. Many jokes turn on the gayness of the wedding, with its swans, gay men's chorus crooning show tunes, and Liza Minnelli-officiated vows. "Queering" marriage and straightening queerness also point to the advantages of the male-male bond. Much is made of the possibility of an agreed upon "cheating" in the men's marriage, and attention is called to the fact that both men will keep their surnames "because [they're] men."[46]

Carrie's role in the ceremony drives the point home. She acts as her friend Stanford Blatch's "best man," wearing a tuxedo and a strip of black lace across her forehead. In a production obsessively attentive to dress, this slightly pointed strip of lace carries great semiotic weight, at once suggesting lingerie, a tiara, and a quasi veil. Carrie's "drag" must still mark her as a heterosexual cis woman. The frisson of sexy gender-bending increases when her husband is turned on by the outfit—just like his own, absent the headband—and they have sex before proceeding to the ceremony. Like the three-way (with two women) that appears in an episode of the series, this faux gay male coupling aims to excite heteronormative cis desire. But it also underscores a gay male relationship, with a more flexible commitment and a nonreproductive teleology, as a fantasy paradigm for straight marriage. As Merck observes:

> As both straight and gay commentators have argued for years, gay men can be seen as the pioneers of post-Fordist lifestyling, in which the ethos has shifted from production (of goods and services, as well as future workers in procreative sex) to consumption (of goods and services as well as recreational sex).[47]

Whatever the realities of gay male lives that interfere with this portrayal, the representation of gay male sexuality acquires new force as an alternative model for companionate marriage.

The *Sex and the City* version of Friedan's "problem with no name" suggests a desire for domestic partnership and intimacy without its dullness and routine, even as the film enters the dangerous terrain of the nonreproductive married woman. The marriage of men, notably not of women, models this utopian possibility; so does the symbolic return to virginity. The thematic of virginity first appears through snippets of Frank Capra's *It Happened One Night* (1934). The movie is famous for "the walls of Jericho"[48]—the blanket of chastity hung between Claudette Colbert and Clark Gable as they sleep, unmarried, in the same space—that come tumbling down on the couple's wedding night.[49] In bed together after the men's wedding, Carrie and her husband watch the movie while the sounds of sex and children filter through the walls. The environment resonates with the passionate past of young single life and the future of parenthood, the replacement satisfaction of mature partnership. Virginity preserved until marriage would also have enlivened the romance of Carrie's marriage, which is young, though the couple's sex life is not. Here *Sex* expresses yearning for the old-fashioned values it normally repudiates. Soon this nostalgia[50] produces the possibility of return, through travel to a land that spatializes the past. Samantha Jones, the publicist whose client funds the four women's international trip, later claims that because they have not previously visited the Middle East, the women will all be "virgins" there. The wordplay serves to figure the American women as newly, if comically, chaste. Trading cultural for sexual innocence, they can borrow the "clothes," that is the signification, of the "traditional" unmarried Muslim woman in Abu Dhabi. If the male pair figures the possible future of the metrosexual couple, the Middle Eastern woman comes to figure the lost pleasure of female history,[51] revived to dramatize innocence and mystery. Inhabiting the fantasy of "traditional" virginity eventually allows Carrie to refashion a heterosexual marriage that is not reproductive in a space of personal choice and luminosity.

Banat/Girls also presents the writer-narrator as a guide to a particular ethnographic group. After introducing it, the narration opens onto a wedding. Using a Yahoo mail group, the narrator hides from view and invites the audience into intimate proximity with elite women on the marriage market. The anonymous, Scheherazade-like narrator depends on a trope of invisibility articulated but never illuminated in the interlaced stories of four women friends. The relationship of the first-person narrator to the four protagonists is never disclosed. She is potentially "inside" or "outside" each one. She may even be all of them, the collective "author function" of each character. If the knowing, satirical voice of the author belongs to the downtrodden Gamrah, for instance, the novel adds dimension and surprise to her portrayal. Isolated and depressed, she of all the characters would have the time to write, and she tries on a different identity in her instant messaging.[52] What power might Gamrah gain through writing? Such possibilities suggest that practice can fabricate selves, or dimensions of the self, particularly in relation to a community. Practice may alter the sovereign contours of the neoliberal individual.

The omniscient third-person perspective animates the "I" who opens with an address to the reader: "Ladies and Gentlemen," she begins her frame,

> You are invited to join me in one of the most explosive scandals and noisiest, wildest all-night parties around. Your personal tour guide—and that's *moi*—will reveal to you a new world, a world closer to you than you might imagine. We all live in this world but do not really experience it, seeing what we can tolerate and ignoring the rest.

She appeals to the audience's courage "to read the naked truth laid out on the World Wide Web" and its patience to remain with her "through this insane adventure."[53] Booth notes that the English translation "ungenders" *Banat*, here by omitting "girls" or "young misses" (*anisati*)[54] from the introduction. This category appears between "ladies" and "gentlemen" in the Arabic original and so highlights the primary audience that the narrator is addressing: her peers. In many similar ways, Booth argues, the published translation "neutraliz[es] the narrator's voice into a bland translatese" of homogenized diction that reduces the use of figure and idiom. The changes dilute "the text's thoroughgoing emphasis on female experience and feminine perspectives."[55]

In *Girls*, the narrator's breezy tone changes when she quotes Syrian poet Nizar Qabbani (1923–98). His verse establishes a common identity between the unnamed storyteller and the women she represents: "I shall write of my girlfriends/for in each one's tale/I see my story and my self prevail." These women are "jailed" and "martyred" by the lives imposed on them (3). Though the gossipy language of "scandal" at first sits uneasily with the spiritual and political metaphors, Alsanea uses the juxtaposition to relocate scandal from personal reputation to social system. The use of Qabbani also inflects the link, as the widely read poet portrays the sensual and political as inseparable. According to Mohja Kahf, "Political oppression from outside the bedroom as well as the traditional social strictures that render women hunks of meat—or *mensafs*, as Kabbani likes to put it——make real love and sexual delight impossible."[56] But Booth insists that the English translation downplays such coding. *Girls* fails to mark the thick allusiveness of the "sirah" communicated in the narrator's web address, "seerehwenfadha7et." Moreover, Booth notes that *sirah* is commonly used to signify "auto/biography," in contrast to "memoir." It also means "conduct" or "way of life," and as such "connotes the ultimate model of good conduct, the life of the Prophet Muhammad."[57] In changing *infadahat* to *fadaha*, the address also emphasizes exposure of a story, with possible connotations of disgrace. The translation of Qabbani's verse additionally shifts the audience who is hailed: "I will write of my friends who are female" becomes "girlfriends." The translator argues that this choice "los[es] metrical and line patterns ... while de-emphasizing the poem's political emphasis on kinds of oppression visited solely on females and highlighting instead the personal and limited."[58]

Like *Banat*, *Girls* takes political rather than stylistic advantage of the technological conceit that it employs. As Moneera al-Ghadeer notes, "it is not a cyberfiction or cyberpunk novel since there is no exploration of the futuristic effects of technology on individual lives."[59] Nor, it should be added, does Alsanea employ visual effects other than the orthographic to indicate the conceit of the online text: each entry of the epistolary novel begins with an email slug, in a typeface that differs from that of the body text.[60] *Girls* does capitalize on the emerging prominence of social media in forming new Muslim networks, without using these media to present actual visual representations of the women.

Alsanea makes the "cloth" of robes a cloak of invisibility that also "exposes" the figurative *zenana* of the women's private lives. In their partial refusal of the chick-lit alliance with visual culture, both versions exploit internet technology to assert contemporary women's identities in more culturally particular ways. Alsanea "signals Muslim women's interstitial insider-outsider status" as she uses new media to "produce radical connectivity" that "fosters a new kind of cosmopolitanism marked by religion," in accord with miriam cooke's "Muslimwoman," her alternative reading of the stereotype.[61] The narrator's email postings and the comments that they elicit from readers also call to mind the *da'wa* or piety and outreach sites associated in part with women's blogs. While devotional, these sites are not sanctioned by the *ulama*, or official, learned authorities.[62] In positioning herself inside and outside the *ummah* without directly invoking it, Alsanea suggests a conflictual field that is "mobile and malleable" rather than "unified and homogeneous," in keeping with populist practices.[63] Olivier Roy says, "The virtual *ummah* of the Internet is the perfect place for individuals to express themselves while claiming to belong to a community" as active members rather than as mere audience.[64] Bunt describes this revision of the concept of the classical, unified *ummah* in similar dynamic terms.[65] While in no way presenting her fictional listserv as an Islamic or Muslim devotional site, Alsanea gives observant women a public voice that responds to authoritative male discourses. In the original Arabic, she also gives expression to the female interlocutors, as most of the comments posted online are men's.[66]

In the years since *Banat*'s publication, such sites have gained prominence, challenging the topos of the "romantic Middle East" described by Burge.[67] Social media sites have become important to the project of Muslim visibility and identity formation as well as to entrepreneurship. British author Shelina Janmohamed claims,

> It's almost as though being fashionable is a duty for Generation M [that is, young Muslim women] in order to dispel stereotypes that may be held about Muslims being oppressed, backward, or simply out of touch with the modern world.[68]

Banat al-Riyadh anticipates the fashion and beauty blogs that disseminate such issues of presentation and "lifestyle" as compatible with belief. Reina Lewis observes,

> Unusual for fashion blogging, the modest blogosphere directly situates fashion practices within and as contributory to wider forms of social and political discourse ... Modest fashion discourse also extends into online domains concerned with home-sewing, thrifting, and parenting, incorporating fashion considerations into the quotidian practices of "everyday religion"

that lend themselves to more porous boundaries.[69] Lewis mentions in particular the Muslim American Winnie Detwa of winniedetwaland, and the Jewish-American Nina Cohen of alltumbledown.[70] These bloggers, who often use Instagram and YouTube as platforms, may be linked to actual fashion companies, such as *Haute Hijab*, or featured in digital versions of publications such as *Teen Vogue*.[71] Though many of them feature hijabi, the same models and bloggers may feature photos of themselves without a head covering, a trend that Lewis calls "situational veiling." The practice has attracted mainstream attention that dovetails with the interlocking stereotypes of veiling.[72] Nonetheless Lewis contends that "the fundamental reflexivity of digital cultures … provid[es] a spatial pluralization of authority" without seeking to supplant "existing forms."[73]

Girls' internet conceit, in omitting photographs, offers the perfect *hortus conclusus* for the stories of observant unmarried women revealed. The lavish wedding they attend is a festival of scrutiny. All the guests are preoccupied with the young women's conduct and appearance, whose every aspect is coded with their identities within family, class, tribe, region, and language. The young women themselves—though her friends—cruelly criticize the bride. "Hey! Check her out. The pharaohs are back!" one says. Her dress is a "mess," her make-up "painful" as "her skin is too dark for such a chalky foundation." The contrast between her face and neck elicits the remark, "Eww … so vulgar."[74] (Or, as Booth renders it in her Arabenglish, phonetically spelled, "*Eww—so falguu'r.*"[75]) For her part the bride sees the "envy half hidden in their eyes" (8) when her friends later hypocritically praise her appearance. While they pose for pictures and begin to dance—before the men arrive in the women's reception room—"the eyes of all those older women who devote themselves to arranging marriages [are] glued to all of [the young women's] bodies" (8). The single women in turn exhibit themselves, conscious of their virtues and deficiencies in relation to one another. Gamrah's wedding introduces the plight of elite young women, three of whom will be dramatically duped by men. They suffer for violating as well as for adhering to the rigid codes of Saudi patriarchy. Well-traveled, educated, and encouraged by their families to develop careers, the women enjoy little power on the marriage market. They encounter danger, trickery, and censure at every turn. Gamrah's immediate experience after her wedding portends ill for the successfully married woman as well.

Both *Sex and the City 2* and *Girls of Riyadh* represent the home as an arena of spectacle and surveillance. No one can completely escape the domestic sphere while inhabiting a female body. Everyone negotiates this reality through dress as a tool of assertion or compliance. *Girls'* opening wedding scene is followed by a flashback to the wedding preparations, in which the four friends, a *shillah* or clique, zoom around Riyadh in "disguises." Michelle drives. She has an international drivers' license and rents, through subterfuge, a BMW X5 SUV with tinted windows. The women adapt both male and traditional female garb to enable their adventure. The narrator reports of the driver, for instance:

> [Michelle] greeted [her friends] wearing baggy trousers with lots of pockets and an oversized jacket—gear that artfully concealed any sign of femininity—plus a bandanna that hid her hair. To top it all off, she had on a pair of colored sunglasses that gave her the appearance of an adolescent boy who has escaped parental surveillance.
>
> (14)

Men on the road nonetheless recognize the tinted windows as a sign of eligible women within, and a persistent fellow at the mall evades security guards to accompany the women as a family escort (16). The narrator remarks resentfully,

> That's the way things are here in the shops and malls: guys stare at women for their own reasons, while women stare at each other just because they are *nosy*! ... A girl can't stroll about in the malls under the protection of God without being checked out thoroughly by everyone, especially her own kind, from her *abaya* to the covering over her hair to the way she walks and the bags she carries and in which direction she looks and in front of what merchandise she stops.
>
> (17)

To negotiate codes of respectability, a young woman must conceal her identity while appearing as an attractive commodity herself. Of course she is free to consume other commodities.

Location, Location, Location

Sex and the City 2 matches the homogeneity of Manhattan with that of a pastiche Orientalist Muslim world. The film recognizes no distinction between Arab and Muslim, much less among Gulf states. The protagonists vacation in Abu Dhabi, which resembles Dubai, another U.A.E. country. Burge associates Dubai with the pastiche of the desert and sheik romance because so many have been set there—but also because "Dubai can itself be understood as a construction."[76] Yet it is here that *Girls'* Michelle can balance the demands of family and independence, as she cannot in Riyadh or even in San Francisco. Nonetheless *Sex and the City 2* portrays Abu Dhabi as Arabland, complete with camels and sheiks. The director acknowledges this typification: "We had to take Morocco and make it the Middle East," says Michael Patrick King. "[I]t's an exotic country and it's exoticized, but the Middle East is just different [from Morocco]."[77] More specifically, "Abu Dhabi is a coastal metropolis" while the hotel in Marrakech, where much of the film was shot, is near "an expanse of barren desert scrub with the Atlas Mountains rising in the distance." The skyline of Abu Dhabi, a digital creation inserted post-production,[78] is the one distinction from this old Orientalist imagery: the newer one of OPEC wealth. Samantha claims that the emirate has superseded the "old" Dubai. Yet she is detained by forbidding-looking, silent airport screeners in hijab, who are convinced that her homeopathic menopause medicine is an illegal drug. Ironic and comic, the scene associates drugs and the Orient. At the same time it suggests that women must be deprived of innocent comforts in this land, deprivations enforced by other women.

The adventure into "traditional" femininity is marked by the exchange of fabrications, which here can be soft and loose, with much excess cloth, though still revealing and fashionable. The American women change masquerades without giving up their agency because they do not "become" what they wear. Brandi Thompson Summers notes an analogous concept in American high fashion in which unmarked, neutral white bodies can "occupy" blackness "through the performance of race as an aestheticized category."[79] In the exotic locale the boredom of privilege and the ennui of ordinary life can be revitalized and cured: Charlotte worries that her husband is attracted to the nanny and feels overwhelmed by motherhood; Miranda is tired of fighting the sexism of her workplace; Samantha is overwrought by the waning of her libido in menopause; and Carrie is concerned about the tedium of monogamy, the loss of excitement in a partnership of just two forever. The specters of ageing into unattractiveness, dispensability, and nonproductivity, whether biological or material, haunt the trip.

The Arab/Muslim man cannot supply this reinvigoration, as he does in the desert romance. In *Sex and the City 2*, the men of Abu Dhabi appear as genial hosts and attractive, sometimes sexualized servants devoted to cosseting the memsahibs, but none of them appears as an object of true desire for the American women. Here the male hero of the Eastern romance is a citation of a fantasy of difference, not a dramatization of the fantasy. White, Western (presumably Christian) men, supplied with the accoutrements and swaddled in the garb of the adventurer and the sheik, instead occupy the romance roles. Out in the desert during their caravan picnic (a break from the camel expedition), the women meet a Danish architect, a parodic Lawrence of Arabia who careens over the dunes in a jeep. He reawakens Samantha's dormant libido. And Carrie encounters her old boyfriend Aidan, the "rescuer"[80] of the TV series, at the marketplace. She later meets him, decked out in keffiyeh or shemagh (a scarf held around the skull by a rope or other binder) and robes, in a moonlit arcade. Though both are seemingly happily married, the former lovers find their desire for one another rekindled. Aidan comes to figure the seduction of the personal and the social past retailored. Their kiss creates a crisis in Carrie's marriage when she later confesses, on the phone, to her husband.[81]

The secondary female figures who appear in the film are in a sense worn by their robes. They function largely as props. Like the locations and digital recreations, robed women "fabricate" the scriptwriter's "Middle East" through the stock Muslim woman. She is both flattened and essentialized. She wears dark, traditional garb, does not speak aloud, and rarely moves. She fits absolutely with the argument of many gender justice advocates that the stress in postfeminism and its related formulations have moved from critique of patriarchy to distinguishing *"majority woman"* from the oppressed "other woman," often Muslim.[82] If the skyline is "a piece of the real" created digitally and dropped into the background of Marrakech, the Middle Eastern, that is Muslim, woman must appear to signify backwardness but also the mystery and seductiveness of withholding. At her hotel, Carrie watches in fascination while a woman in niqab eats French fries by inserting them under the cloth. Like the colonial photographers of the harem in the early twentieth century such as those Malek Alloula examines, the movie's gaze is fascinated by the hijab or niqab that denies the (here female) Western eye access to Muslim women's bodies. Now the lure of the harem signifies less as a communal female space than as a single female body. It is here, too, as I mention above, that Carrie encounters the woman she dubs "the real housewife of Abu Dhabi."

Arab women of the cosmopolitan elite who populate Abu Dhabi's discos and hotel restaurants, such as the Riyadh women would, don't register visually in the movie as such. Thus the equation of the niqab with the silenced woman finds its dramatic parallel in the virtual absence of other women's voices from the film. The robed women are only image, not character; they withhold, as the virgin does, as a tactic of seduction. The climax of this projection, a staging of almost every conceivable parody of the privileged white, imperialist "feminist" takes place in a club, where the American women perform a drunken, triumphalist "I Am Woman" karaoke. Appearing as cut-aways during the song are a woman in Indian dress, signified by her forehead jewel, a matronly Asian woman, and an Africa-descended woman. Women coded as Arab or Middle Eastern appear only as belly dancers on a level above the Americans. Director Michael Patrick King states that the song is performed "from a campy point of view," yet it is "still relevant to different women in different parts of the world."[83] The Muslim woman would appear to be one of them precisely because she is erased. At the same time she is *not* a woman, because she does not wear fashion, and because she does not wear fashion, she does not have a voice, or even a substantial body.

The privileged young women of Riyadh claim agency in their manipulation of their clothes, their consumption of luxuries, their travel, education, and in some cases careers. *Girls* portrays these privileges as entrapping as well as liberating. In a sense the Arab women resemble the American travelers in that their degree of freedom seems to inhere in their "blood." At home, their status places additional limits on the women's choice of marriage partner. Abroad, it exercises constraints through family and community. Michelle, who falls in love with a man she meets at the mall, relocates to San Francisco after his family disapproves of the match; in San Francisco, she falls in love with her cousin; her family insists that she leave school there and move with them to Dubai. Sadeem, formerly an excellent student, flunks out of King Faisal University after her fiancé convinces her to have sex with him before they are fully married, and then dumps her for being a loose woman. Sadeem "pack[s] away her wound along with her clothes and carrie[s] it all from the Dust Capital of the World to the Fog Capital of the World." Though she removes her abaya and head covering in the plane's bathroom before landing at Heathrow, she experiences London only as "a huge sanatorium" (61). Gamrah, the bride of the opening scenes, fares the worst abroad: she winds up in Chicago in a loveless, sexless, and eventually abusive marriage. With no English and few skills, she *is* a virtual prisoner in her Chicago high rise, the wife of a man who married her to satisfy his family.

Global Girls

What happens when the *Girls of Riyadh* meet the girls of Manhattan? In its portrayal of the young women as highly engaged with consumption, bodily management, and female competition, *Girls* assumes that this meeting has already taken place. The feminist elements of social critique and community with other women mix with the individualism of the postfeminist elite woman. But *Girls* also portrays a fight between the postfeminist global-American girl and the more conventional though international Saudi wife. In Chicago with her husband Rashid, Gamrah loves to watch the television series *Sex and the City*, even though she can't understand much of the dialogue (77). When a *Sex and the City*-like postfeminist actually materializes, however, she trounces Gamrah. Kari is Rashid's long-time girlfriend. After discovering the relationship, Gamrah gets dressed up to go confront Kari, but the Asian-American completely overpowers Gamrah with her "firmness and confidence, without any sign of confusion, and without stumbling over her English even a little." Kari renders Gamrah silent as she advises her to "work to improve [her]self, from the inside and out, so that [she] can move up to the standard [Rashid] wants and needs. So that she can come up to [Kari's] level." When Gamrah finally explodes, Kari "burst[s] into shameless laughter at the furious sentences that ma[k]e absolutely no sense, and Gamrah fe[els] herself getting smaller and weaker in front of her" (83). Heaping abuse on her because of his family's insistence on the arranged marriage, Rashid strikes his wife when she calls Kari an "Asian housemaid" and a "whore" (84, 85). He sends her back to Riyadh, divorced, even though she is now pregnant with his child.

The narrator opens the chapter that relates these confrontations with a hadith that prohibits men from striking servants and women with their hands. She claims that her internet provider is trying to block her site (87). In the following chapter, the narrator acknowledges the many and varied comments that she received in response to Gamrah's story, claiming to "enjoy" reading even the ones with which she disagrees because she "want[s] to be sure we are a people who agree to disagree" (87). Though it withholds any comment on Kari, the narrative clearly shows that Gamrah suffers the graver consequences from the social arrangement of her marriage, while the "global" American woman colludes with patriarchal arrangements through her superior articulation of the codes of postfemininity.

In this scene, as elsewhere, Alsanea deploys Islam to render it distinct from Saudi patriarchy and from Arab nationality. The narrator uses scripture as well as popular religious figures such as televangelists to make her case for women's agency and for her culture's capacity for historical revision. Her egalitarian interpretations invoke *isnan*, the Qur'anic principle of the equality of human beings.[84] Furthermore, the narrator claims a pedagogical aim for her exposure of the marriage market. Like Muhammad, she does not claim perfection; she "works hard" to "correct" her errors and "cultivate" herself. She cites the Prophet's assertion that "deeds are measured by the intentions behind them" and asks God to consider her "writings as good deeds" (57). Muhammad is the model of conduct and perfection. His compassion for human flaws demonstrates this trait. Michelle's narrative draws the distinction between the Islamic state and a Muslim-majority one, often through Michelle's plot. She explains:

> Saudi Arabia [is] the only country ruled solely and completely by the law derived from the Qur'an and the way of the Prophet, peace be upon him, applying that law—the Shari'ah—to all spheres of life. Other Muslim nations might draw upon the Islamic Shari'ah for their basic principles and outlook, but as society changed and new needs arose, they left specific rulings to human-made law.
>
> (221)

Her claims accord with the views of Muslim feminists and gender justice advocates such as Amina Wadud and Asma Barlas, who stress the significance of historical change within Muslim practice and belief. Because its message surpasses the specific constraints of seventh-century Arabia, Barlas argues, the Qur'an encodes recognition of future injustices as well.[85] Wadud regards the Qur'an as "neutral" toward gender equity and argues for figurative reading of certain sura that are problematic when interpreted literally.[86] The "intellectual heritage" of Islam figures importantly in the work of scholars such as Kecia Ali and Aysha Hidayatullah, who do not see the Qur'an as entirely antipatriarchal. Ali contends that tension between "hierarchy" and "egalitarianism" has always been present in the Qur'an, the sunnah, and the hadith. Legal methods offer a "flexible approach" that mitigates the binary of halal and haram with intermediate categories of "recommended, reprehensible, and indifferent."[87] The sunnah and the hadith, non-Qur'anic but sacred texts, constitute "significant sources of knowledge of wisdom." Ali points out that "official Islam" is at times more protective of women than gender-equality interpreters acknowledge: "much is lost when Muslims—Qur'an only feminists or pro-hadith salafi—choose to bypass [the sunnah and jurisprudence] for a literalist approach to source texts," she states.[88] The legal tradition derived from these other sacred sources actually describes an ethic that is adaptive over time, in accordance with God's forwarding of justice. Ziba Mir-Hosseini also points to the important distinction between "Shari'a (the path, found in the Qur'an and the Prophet's practice) and fiqh ('understanding', the jurists efforts to deduce laws from these textual sources)." She observes that "the distinction enables us to see patriarchal laws as divine Shari'a,' but as outdated human fiqh."[89] Alsanea, as I have noted, does not engage with the complexities of theological interpretations (which vary widely among antipatriarchal theorists)[90] but does call upon the tradition of women's *tafsir* and *da'wa* discussions to articulate the distinction between the nation-state and its dominant religion. Avoiding claims of hermeneutic authority or intent, as I have said, the novel calls upon "everyday religion," marked by syncretism, mixing, and paradox.[91]

Girls of Riyadh, like Gamrah before her encounter with Kari, loves *Sex and the City*. But the novel cannot entirely assimilate the postfeminism of *Sex*—in part, perhaps, because postfeminism meets its limit, or even its crutch, in the stock image of the Muslim woman. Yet within the Riyadh scene, Michelle launches the same kind of competitive attack on a rival that Kari makes against Gamrah. The wedding of Faisal bookends the narrative through another bout of female competition, based on appearance as empowerment. Michelle gains satisfaction from displaying herself as free and desirable, not just by exhibiting herself to the groom, but also by asserting her beauty in comparison with the frumpiness of his betrothed. The bride's "large body [is] stuffed into the wedding gown, which [is] stretched tightly around her ... unappealingly, creating unsightly folds of skin at her armpits" (265). Just as Kari does with Gamrah, Michelle makes another woman the target of her anger over oppression, in order to enjoy some measure of power. Other less attractive, often more constrained women become scapegoats for patriarchal injuries.

Less explicitly, *Sex and the City 2* also bears larger political intentions by using Muslim women as a confirmation of American might. Mitu Sengupta sees the film as a deflation of the American economic power of the 1990s everywhere evident in the TV show. Michael Patrick King supports this reading when he notes of this sequel:

> This time I was more than aware of the downturn in the economic climate. There were reminders everywhere of how people were being forced to cut back and tighten their belts, and I thought—perhaps like the filmmakers during the Great Depression of the '30s did—that what might be in order in the sequel was a big, fun decadent vacation for the girls on-screen as well as for the girls in the audience.[92]

Sengupta rereads King:

> If anything, the film reflects the self-serving auto-Orientalism of the new Arab capitalism, which markets cities such as Dubai and Abu Dhabi as

enviable hybrids of mystical traditionalism and cutting-edge cosmopolitanism; where one can enjoy a romantic Arabian Nights lifestyle while achieving mega business success.

She notes that "Abu Dhabi may be a paradise filled with peacocks and Lamborghinis, but it's a 'backward' land of sexually silenced women."[93] It's a small leap from Sengupta's reading to see America as a nonproductive middle-aged woman trying to hold on in the midst of crisis, as her youth, or glimmer in the spectacle of bodies, begins to wane.

The Muslimah can be recuperated if she can enter into the optic of contemporary postfemininity, the detachable masquerade of womanliness, and in Ghumkhor's reading the "hypervisibility" that reenacts the "natural," secular body.[94] The film's conclusion allows the American (Christian) woman to style herself as both invented and conventional through her contact with the Arab (Muslim) woman as a potential postfeminist. Spectacular fashion affords the new bond between the American and Arab woman, as well as covert access to a feminist legacy, displaced and separated from the image of the mature "mother." The hook for this transformation appears in the early scene on the hotel patio, which I mention above. Carrie spots "the real housewife of Abu Dhabi," whose bejeweled scarf, bared (though partly covered through sunglasses) made-up face, and cell phone signify her embrace of "old traditions" in new and personal ways. The woman's beaded headscarf in particular aligns her with the "glimmer" of the Manhattan Anglo-elite, and it is not necessary for her to speak in order to register her entrance into the visual regime of the woman as spectacle. "What if the veil, which has been portrayed as a site of activity and agency [by Muslim feminists], is nothing more than an empty signifier, a means to insert the body into the world of consumer capitalism?" Minoo Moallem asks.[95] *Sex and the City 2* does not present veiling practices in this way, as they still signify silence and oppression, but the beaded hijab and abaya sleeves of the "real housewife of Abu Dhabi" suggest that Muslim women can be acknowledged by the American women once they enter the realm of visible consumption and expressive gesture. (The beaded veil, singular in the film's iconography, also marks the absence of production and consumption of fashion as an Arab or Muslim industry, much less as a female one.)

Here the American postfeminist can access the *jouissance* of a rejected tradition while still holding on to Western scorn. At the same time what Deleuze and Guattari call "facialization" portends the "subjectification," or individualization, that the American women possess. Deleuze and Guattari describe facialization as a process of distinguishing the face from the mass of the head, as I have noted. The process also endows the face with particular significance: the face emerges from the "white wall/black hole system,"[96] an interesting parallel to the black sunglasses and otherwise bared face of the "real housewife." Here, however, the face emerges not from the head as a distinct feature but rather from the mass of the black, encompassing robe as it appears in most of the film. The conventional black abaya, niqab, and hijab little distinguish the head from the body of the wearer. The Muslimah's face in a sense acts as the harbinger of a female *form* or anatomy emerging into visibility. Notably, the "real housewife" figure speaks into her phone, gestures and smiles broadly. Her gestural language portends her movement and animation. The film does not record her voice or include that of the interlocutor in niqab shown, in wider shots, to be sitting at the same table. Carrie's shiver of recognition across the patio "answers" the "real housewife" bodily.

The Arab-Muslim despot, largely absent (though everywhere evident) until this point in the movie, must appear to spur the encounter between the two groups of women. The shopping trip that concludes the overseas adventure takes place after the Americans have been expelled from their hotel as a result of Samantha's arrest. The night before, she was caught having sex on the beach with the Danish architect. Samantha's disciplining is repeated in the souk. The women enter an illegal trade room, and thinking she has stolen it, one of the vendors chases Samantha and grabs her "Birkin," an expensive purse. When condoms fall out, she is surrounded by angry men, at whom she screams, curses, and makes obscene gestures. A chase ensues.

The American women's escape is facilitated by women in niqab who witnessed the scene. They follow the Americans and call them into another back room. Though they look stern and silent, and though the American women cower before them, the robed group turns out to be a book club. They are pleased by the men's outrage at Samantha. The climactic moment of recognition, fulfillment, and sisterhood occurs when they open their robes and remove their niqab to reveal the high Western fashion underneath: under "hundreds of layers of tradition," they reveal "the spring collection." At once, they too become women of the Helen Reddy variety, celebrated in an earlier scene. The movie allows them to speak as it achieves penetration of the scopically virginal harem of the veiled woman's body, in a hidden female space, a dried flower shop. The women of Abu Dhabi wear the burqa as a masquerade. Patriarchal fabric does not define them after all: they merely wear the cloth that appears to imprison them. Robes conceal their appetite for consumption and their individual tastes. Secretly, all they covet is Western fashion, and they beg for news from the fashion capital, New York. United in their opposition to Arab men and in their love of Western couture—hence affirming the productive preeminence of New York— the Arab women lend their robes to the Americans as a disguise so they can escape from the souk unrecognized. It is the match of robe and couture, never robe *as* couture, that allows the women to recognize their commonality, and permits the Muslim woman not only bodies that register on the EuroAmerican symbolic grid, but also actual speech heard in the film. In fact, subsequent years have seen the emergence of a "fractured geography" of fashion locations. Inna Arzumanova contends that ethnoracial and national differences are made visible in order to be neutralized and then used to display racial progress.[97]

Girls of Riyadh homogenizes many particularities evident in *Banat*, yet the intelligence, persistence, and strength of the narrator's voice remains evident in the translation. Criticism does not silence her. *Girls'* narrator claims a female community; she is speaking for the voiceless, though only a select group of them. (The Arabic title suggests that she speaks for all the young women of Riyadh.)[98] Of course, the narrator is the ultimate "winner" among the Riyadh women. Like Carrie, she achieves renown through her writing. Celebrities discuss her column in magazines (157); she playfully imagines herself as the anchor, like Barbara Walters or Oprah Winfrey, of a talk show (167); she is offered a book contract and even a TV show based on her writing (198). Dyer reads the celebrity realm as coveted because it represents freedom, autonomy, validation, and scope—the pinnacle of contemporary personhood.[99] If, as Kim Allen reminds us, we need to understand the aspiration to fame as a kind of "identity work" that reveals "how young women negotiate, rework, and resist the images and narratives of femininity, class, sexuality, morality, [labor], and success that celebrity appears to offer,"[100] what does the invisible celebrity of the narrator signify in *Banat/Girls*? It implies an escape from the relentless scrutiny and discipline exercised over young women, whether practiced by young women themselves or by media representation. Moreover, it offers the narrator a public voice more powerful and recognized than the one she already possesses online, in part because it is at one with her body, her own speech. The narrator may therefore imagine the acquisition of male privilege through an authoritative voice not thoroughly mediated by the discipline of female optics and at one with her own throat, what Stephens calls the "skin" of the voice. This fantasy is implicit in her delight in reading her posts to her family, as she merges not only with her own spoken voice but with the throats of her audience, who in her imagined scenario are also reading aloud: "I read [my email] out loud to everyone in the house," she announces. "Mind you, no one at home knows that I am the one behind these emails! In other words, I do what every other girl is doing at exactly the same time! In those moments I feel such intense pleasure!" (150). These voices raised in the fantasy of simultaneous reading echo communal recitation of a text.

The real housewife of *Sex and the City* externalizes visibly and conveniently the disciplinary regimes of Anglo-American postfemininity. Exemplified by the silent, robed woman, she never appears in New York, reinforcing her territorial congruence with the Middle East and assigning her racial and cultural difference to a distant land. Muslim women, in their imagined spatial and temporal distance from the postfeminist American, supply the gap necessary for critical interpretation of women by women, the assertion of agency over the always-too-close female image as essence. In her final voiceover, Carrie finds her model for a nontraditional marriage not in an American feminist legacy, but rather in the film's real housewife. The cloth of the Arab woman's bejeweled scarf and abaya sleeves model the self-fabrication of an American wife who does not reproduce. The fabric of "tradition" can be "decorated" to suit a unique woman such as Carrie and can pave the way for a Muslim Arab woman, whose voice we do not hear, but whose gestural and expressive body language portends luminosity.

The public presentation of Rajaa Alsanea herself grants another dimension to the novel's adaptation. Booth notes that Alsanea's image appeared on the British edition of *Girls*. Though it did not appear on the paperback American edition, her photo accompanied articles about her in the English and American press. Her photo also appeared on her website.[101] Like the character Lamees, who decides to veil in acknowledgment of her blessings—she is professionally very successful, happily married, and a mother—Alsanea reports that she decided to wear a head covering when she emigrated to the U.S. to attend dental school. Her photo portrays her as a beautiful young woman, tastefully made up, in a dark scarf that covers her hair and neck. One side of her head covering, near her eyes, is decorated with embroidered vines that match a similar pattern on the bib of her robe. A patch of lighter cloth echoes elements of the same design on the side opposite the headscarf pattern.[102] The effect is one of a pleasing and neat asymmetry. Though she lacks the sunglasses and cell phone of her *Sex and the City 2* counterpart, Alsanea's authorial image does bring to mind the real housewife of Abu Dhabi. Her picture has been featured on style blogs and fashion sites.[103] Such an image signifies achievement of the "mediagenic"[104] celebrity author status portended by the narrator's success, and reinforces the generic alliance with memoir that characterizes many chick-lit novels.[105] The iconography of Alsanea's brand of transnational Muslim postfeminism harmonizes elements of display and modesty, tradition and modernity. Punctuated by embroidery that evokes the lyrical and the organic, her dark clothing frames and highlights a smiling face. But it also marks her, in a way the other dress—the dress she wore before emigrating—would not. The celebrity author registers identity as visibility. Her narrative conceit exploits the literary advantages of anonymity and invisibility, allowing for the speaker's interchangeability with each of her characters.[106]

In spite of its final nod to difference, *Sex and the City 2* succeeds in thoroughly redefining the "cosmopolitan" New York woman as a (white) hometown girl.[107] Through its global travel, *Sex and the City 2* recasts the big city narrative as a return home, a home that affords freedom as well as organic connection, all without calling up a domestic feminist legacy. In particular Samantha underscores the dominant xenophobic thrust of the movie as she achieves orgasm with her Danish architect on a Hamptons beach on the Fourth of July. They copulate on the hood of a car as the fireworks of American independence render spectacular the orgiastic pleasure of her economic and sexual agency restored.

Notes

1 Homa Hoodfar, "The Veil in Their Minds and on Our Heads: Veiling Practices and Muslim Women," in *The Politics of Culture in the Shadow of Capital*, ed. Lisa Lowe and David Lloyd (Durham: Duke University Press, 1997), 251.

2 Uma Narayan, *Dislocating Cultures: Identities, Traditions, and Third World Cultures* (New York: Routledge, 1998), 402.
3 Narayan, "Dislocating Cultures," 402.
4 Megan McDonald, "Sur/Veil: The Veil as a Blank(et) Signifier," in *Muslim Women: Transnational Feminism and the Ethics of Pedagogy: Contested Imaginaries in Post-9/11 Cultural Practice*, ed. Lisa K. Taylor and Jasmin Zine (New York: Routledge, 2014), 25–58. Her discussion of the role of visuality in the contemporary French debate about hijab is illuminating.
5 Sahar Ghumkhor, *The Political Psychology of the Veil: The Impossible Body* (Switzerland: Springer Nature and Palgrave-Macmillan, 2020), ix.
6 Haneen Shafeeq Ghabia, *Muslim Women and White Femininity: Reenactment and Resistance* (New York: Peter Lang, 2018), 32.
7 Gilles Deleuze and Felix Guattari, *A Thousand Plateaus: Capitalism and Schizophrenia*, trans. Brian Massumi (Minneapolis: University of Minnesota Press, 1987), 170.
8 Deleuze and Guattari, *A Thousand Plateaus*, 170.
9 I use the term in accordance with vernacular practice in Europe and America, to designate modest dress. The term is not Arabic for "veil" but means "curtain." Fadwa El Guindi, *Veil: Modesty, Privacy, and Resistance* (Oxford: Berg, 2003), 7. Daphne Grace explains that Arabic contains no single term for the head and body coverings and garments used in various locations. *The Woman in the Muslim Mask: Veiling and Identity in Postcolonial Literature* (London and Sterling, VA.: Pluto Press, 2004), 16–17.
10 Joan Riviere, "Womanliness as a Masquerade" (1929), 35–44. McRobbie, *Aftermath*, 67. Luce Irigaray asserts that femininity itself is a masquerade that women have to assume to become "normal." *This Sex Which Is Not One*, trans. Catherine Porter and Carolyn Burke (Ithaca: Cornell University Press, 1985), 131. Peggy Phelan provides an interesting analysis of feminist scholars' attachment to Riviere's essay. It includes discussion of Riviere's white analysand's fantasy of sexual attack by a "negro" she would make love to and then prosecute. Phelan interprets this drama as a sadistic "racial masquerade" that accompanies the analysand's gender masochism. *Mourning Sex: Performing Public Memories* (London: Routledge, 1997), 139–40.
11 Mary Ann Doane, *Femmes Fatales: Feminism, Film Theory, Psychoanalysis* (London and New York: Routledge, 1991), 32.
12 Mary Ann Doane, *Femmes Fatales*, 26.
13 Sara Ahmed contends that affect "does not reside in an object or sign, but is an effect of the circulation between objects and signs … [T]he more signs are circulated, the more affective they become." *The Cultural Politics of Emotion* (New York, Routledge, 2004), 45.
14 Sharron Hinchliff, "Sexing Up the Midlife Woman: Cultural Representations of Ageing, Femininity and the Sexy Body," in Imelda Whelan and Joel Gwynne, *Ageing, Popular Culture, and Contemporary Feminism* (Houndmills, Baskingstoke: Palgrave-Macmillan, 2014), 63–77.
15 Rafia Zakaria, *Veil* (New York: Bloomsbury, 2017), 86.
16 The novel was first published in Saudi Arabia in 2005 but was withdrawn. It circulated on the black market until a court judgement overturned the ban. See Vron Ware, "The New Literary Front: Public Diplomacy and the Cultural Politics of Reading Arabic Fiction in Translation," *New Formations*, 73.85 (2010): 59. For an account of the Arabic text's influence, see Madawi Al-Rasheed, "Deconstructing Nation and Religion: Young Saudi Women Novelists," in *Novel and Nation in Muslim Women's Literary Contributions and National Identities*, ed. Daniella Kuzmanovic and Elisabeth Özdalga (Oxon: Palgrave Macmillan, 2015), 133–51. Marilyn Booth notes that the two versions made *Banat/Girls* a rare text, popular among both Arabophone and Anglophone audiences. "Three's a Crowd: The Translator-Author-Publisher and the Engineering of *Girls of Riyadh* for an Anglophone Readership," in *Translating Women: Different Voices and New Horizons*, ed. Luise von Flotow and Farzaneh Farahzad (Oxon: Routledge, 2016), 119.

17 Amy Burge, *Representing Difference in the Medieval and Modern Orientalist Romance* (Houndmills, Basingstoke: Palgrave, 2016), 9.
18 Burge, *Representing Difference*, 4.
19 The company is united with American Harlequin Romance lines.
20 Burge, *Representing Difference*, 56–57.
21 Stephanie Harzewski, *Chick Lit and Postfeminism* (Charlottesville: University of Virginia Press, 2011), 44.
22 Harzewski, *Chick Lit*, 44.
23 James Wolcott, "Hear Me Purr: Maureen Dowd and the Rise of Postfeminist Chick Lit," *New Yorker* 20 May 1996, 54–57. Cris Mazza contends that Wolcott got the term from the collection. Cris Mazza, "Who's Laughing Now? A Short History of Chick Lit and the Perversion of a Genre," in *Chick Lit: The New Woman's Fiction*, ed. Suzanne Ferriss and Mallory Young (New York: Routledge, 2006), 22–23.
24 Harzewski, *ChickLit*, 45–46.
25 Ferriss, Suzanne, and Mallory Young, eds. *Chick Lit: The New Woman's Fiction* (New York: Routledge 2006), 1–13, 9. The anthology calls attention to subgenres in locations outside Europe and America, as well as to African-American "sistah" lit, Latina and Asian-American authors, and lesbian authors. See, for example, Lisa Guerrero, "Sistah's Are Doin' It for Themselves: Chick Lit in Black and White," 89–101; Jess Butler, "For White Girls Only? Postfeminism and the Politics of Inclusion," *Feminist Formations* 25.1 (2013): 35–58; Kimberly Springer, "Divas, Evil Black Bitches, and Bitter Black Women: African American Women in Postfeminist and Post-Civil-Rights Popular Culture," in *Interrogating Postfeminism: Gender and the Politics of Popular Culture*, ed. Yvonne Tasker and Diane Negra (Durham: Duke University Press, 2007), 249–76; and Sarah Banet-Weiser, "What's Your Flava? Race and Postfeminism in Media Culture, in *Interrogating Postfeminism*, ed. Yvonne Tasker and Diane Negra (Durham: Duke University Press, 2007), 201–27.
26 Cris Mazza, "Who's Laughing Now?" 17, 18.
27 Heike Missler, *The Cultural Politics of Chick Lit: Popular Fiction, Postfeminism and Representation* (New York and Oxon: Routledge, 2017), 2. For some discussion of minority authors, see 33–35.
28 Ommundsen refers to Annie Wang's *The People's Republic of Desire* (2006) as "social commentary masquerading as chick-lit" through its structural allusion to *Sex and the City*. "Sex and the Global City," 112.
29 Harzewski, *Chick Lit*, 94–95.
30 Harzewski, *Chick Lit*, 94–95.
31 Rocío Montoro lists comedy as a topos of the "original genre" of chick lit. *Chick Lit: The Stylistics of Cappuccino Fiction* (London: Continuum, 2012), 3.
32 Marilyn Booth, "'The Muslim Woman' as Celebrity Author and the Politics of Translating Arabic: *Girls of Riyadh* Go on the Road." *Journal of Middle East Women's Studies* 6.3 (2010): 167.
33 Marilyn Booth, "Translator v. Author (2007): *Girls of Riyadh* Go to New York," *Translation Studies* 1.2 (2008): 199–209.
34 Booth, "Translator v. Author," 198.
35 Booth, "Translator v. Author," 199–209.
36 Booth, "The Muslim Woman," 151.
37 Booth, "Three's a Crowd," 119.
38 McRobbie, *Aftermath*, 75–77.
39 Gwynne, "The Lighter," 50–51.
40 Hoda Elsadda writes of blogging in Egypt, "Cyberspace also provides a measure of anonymity ... Moreover presence in virtual space ... allows for masquerading, a choice of identity or identities, all factors that alleviate some of the constraints that limit free expression and interaction." "Arab Women Bloggers: The Emergence of Literary Counterpublics," *Middle East Journal of Culture and Communication* 3.3 (2010): 318.

41 *Sex and the City*, Darren Star and HBO Productions, 1998–2004.
42 Tom Grochowski, "Neurotic in New York: The Woody Allen Touches in *Sex and the City*," in *Reading* Sex and the City, ed. Kim Akass and Janet McCabe (London: I.B. Taurus, 2008), 150, 156.
43 *Sex and the City 2*, dir. Michael Patrick King, Warner Home Video, 2010.
44 See, for instance, Jane Gerhard, "*Sex and the City*: Carrie Bradshaw's Queer Postfeminism," *Feminist Media Studies* 5.1 (2005): 37–48.
45 Mandy Merck, "Sexuality in the City," in *Reading* Sex and the City, ed. Kim Akass and Janet McCabe (London: Tauris, 2004), 61–62.
46 *Sex and the City 2*.
47 Merck, "Sexuality," 60.
48 *It Happened One Night*, dir. Frank Capra, Columbia Pictures, 1934.
49 Another allusion to the movie appears when the four women are fully robed and niqabed in Abu Dhabi and unable to hail a cab to the airport. Carrie bares her leg and immediately cars stop for her, as a driver does for a hitchhiking Claudette Colbert in the earlier film.
50 Missler, 174–75, notes that such nostalgia recalls Bushnell's *Sex and the City* collection in 1997, when the speaker welcomed readers to the age of "un-innocence," in contrast to Edith Wharton's New York.
51 History also carries with it connotations of age and intergenerational bonds. Cf. Sadie Wearing, "Subjects of Rejuvenation: Ageing in Postfeminist Culture," in *Interrogating Postfeminism: Gender and the Politics of Popular Culture*," ed. Yvonne Tasker and Diane Negra (Durham: Duke University Press, 2007), 277–310.
52 Gwynne, "The Lighter," 50.
53 Rajaa Alsanea, *Girls of Riyadh* [*Banat al-Riyadh*], trans. Rajaa Alsanea and Marilyn Booth (New York: Penguin, 2008). Page references to this edition will subsequently appear in parentheses within the discussion.
54 Booth, "Three's a Crowd," 121.
55 Booth, "Translator v. Author," 202–203.
56 Mohja Kahf, "Politics and Erotics in Nizar Kabbani's Poetry: From the Sultan's Wife to Lady Friend," *World Literature Today* 74.1 (2000): 44. The English version also entirely deletes a passage that alludes to the well-known suicide of Qabbani's elder sister when she was prevented from marrying her beloved. The tragedy provoked the poet's challenge to "the prevailing norms of gender relations," according to Booth, "Three's a Crowd," 125.
57 Booth, "Translator v. Author," 204.
58 Booth, "Translator v. Author," 203.
59 Moneera al-Ghadeer, "*Girls of Riyadh*: A New Technology of Writing or Chick Lit Defiance," rev. of Banat al-Riyadh [Girls of Riyadh] by Rajā'al-Sāni', *Journal of Arabic Literature* 37.2 (2006): 297.
60 The listserv address alludes to a talk show whose name means "speaking of which" or "since it came up, let's talk about it," in Lebanese dialect. The English transliteration of the show's title differs, according to al-Ghadeer, "*Girls*," 297.
61 miriam cooke, "The Muslimwoman," *Contemporary Islam* 1.2 (2007): 140.
62 Gary Bunt, "Defining Islamic Interconnectivity," in *Muslim Networks from Hajj to Hip Hop*, ed. miriam cooke and Bruce Lawrence (Chapel Hill: University of North Carolina Press, 2005), 247; Jon W. Anderson, "Wiring Up: The Internet Difference for Muslim Networks," in *Muslim Networks from Hajj to Hip Hop*, 257–58.
63 Taieb Belghazi, Afterword, in *Muslim Networks from Hajj to Hip Hop*, ed. miriam cooke and Bruce Lawrence (Chapel Hill: University of North Carolina Press, 2005), 277.
64 Olivier Roy, *Globalised Islam: The Search for a New Ummah*, London: Hurst, 2004, 183.
65 Gary Bunt, *iMuslims: Rewiring the House of Islam* (Chapel Hill: University of North Carolina Press, 2009), 30–32.
66 Booth, "Three's a Crowd," 121.

67 Phillipa, "*Girls of Riyadh* and *Desperate in Dubai*: Reading and Writing Romance in the Middle East." Review of Amy Burge presentation. *Synaesthezia: An Arts Blog*, August 4, 2018 www.synaesthezia.com/girls-of-riyadh-and-desperate-in-dubai-reading-and-writing-romance-in-the-middle-east/. Burge contends that these novels are developing their own "local forms of romance" for a global audience.
68 Shelina Janmohamed, *Generation M: Young Muslims Changing the World* (London: IB Tauris, 2016), 155.
69 Lewis, "Uncovering Modesty," 244.
70 Lewis, "Uncovering Modesty," 245.
71 Haute Hijab Staff, "The 28 Most Influential Hijabi Bloggers You Should Be Following in 2017," January 10, 2017, www.hautehijab.com/blogs/hijab-fashion/28-most-influential-hijabi-bloggers; Maha Syeda, "Make Up: Muslim Beauty Bloggers You Need to Follow," *Teen Vogue*, www.teenvogue.com/gallery/muslim-beauty-bloggers-to-follow. Accessed April 3, 2018.
72 Lewis, "Uncovering Modesty," 245.
73 Lewis, "Uncovering Modesty," 249.9.
74 Alsanea, *Girls of Riyadh*, 6–7.
75 Booth, "Translator v. Author," 204.
76 As models of a fantasy East, Dubai and the Mills & Boon romance are analogous fabrications of homogeneity, Burge says. *Representing Difference*, 57. Also see a similar argument about the mixture of Western commodity and local identity in Lava Asaad. "'A Girl Is Like a Bottle of Coke': Emptied and Recycled Identities in *Always Coca-Cola*," in *Memory, Voice and Identity: Muslim Women's Writing across the Middle East*, Feroza Jussawalla and Doaá Omran, eds. (New York: Routledge, 2021), 131–38.
77 Eric Cyphers, *Sex and the City 2: The Stories. The Fashion. The Adventure* (Philadelphia: Running Press, 2010), 163.
78 Cyphers, *Sex and the City 2*, 165.
79 Brandi Thompson Summers, "'Haute [Ghetto] Mess': Postracial Aesthetics and the Seduction of Blackness in High Fashion," in *Racism Postrace*, ed. Roopali Mukherjee, Sarah Banet-Weiser, and Herman Gray (Durham: Duke University Press, 2019), 248.
80 Joanna di Mattia, "'What's the Harm in Believing?' Mr Big, Mr Perfect, and the Romantic Quest for *Sex and the City*'s Mr Right," in *Reading Sex and the City*, ed. Akass and McCabe, 19–22.
81 Notably, Carrie wears a black shift-like dress when she first encounters her husband after the trip, again recalling Muslim women's "tradition," but in the final scene she wears green, and lies beside him on a couch as they watch Jean Arthur and Cary Grant in *Talk of the Town* (1942).
82 Birgit Rommelspacher, "Emanzipation als Konversion: Das Bild von der Muslima in christlich-säkularen Diskurs," *Ethik und Gesellschaft: Ökumenische Zeitschrift für Sozialethik* 4.2 (2010): 23. Qtd. in Riem Spielhaus, "Islam and Feminism: German and European Variations on a Global Theme," in *Muslim Women and Gender Justice: Concepts, Sources, and Histories*, ed. Dina El Omari et al. (New York: Routledge, 2020), 46.
83 Cyphers, *Sex and the City 2*, 169.
84 Gender justice Muslim theologians who claim a primary framework arising from authoritative texts express considerable differences about what constitutes the core texts and hence how this framework should be understood. For more comprehensive treatment of these differences, see Fatima Seedat, "Islam, Feminism, and Islamic Feminism," 25–45, Hidayatullah, *Feminist Edges of the Qur'an*, Juliane Hammer, "Introduction to Women and Gender Justice," 1–14, and Jerusha Tanner Rhodes, "Feminist Exegesis and beyond: Trajectories," in *Muslima* Theology, 17–32, both in in *Muslim Women and Gender Justice: Concepts, Sources, and Histories*, ed. Dina El Omari et al. (New York: Routledge, 2020).

85 Barlas and Finn, *Believing Women*, 7.
86 Wadud, *Inside the Gender Jihad: Women's Reform in Islam* (Oxford: Oneworld, 2006), 187–216.
87 Kecia Ali, *Sexual Ethics and Islam*, xxi.
88 Kecia Ali, *Sexual Ethics and Islam*, xx.
89 "Ziba Mir-Hosseini, Legal Anthropologist and Activist." www.zibamirhosseini.com/. Accessed August 20, 2020.
90 Hidayatullah, *Feminist Edges*, 123–95.
91 Reina Lewis, "Uncovering Modesty: Dejabis and Dewigies Expanding the Parameters of the Modest Fashion Blogosphere," *Fashion Theory* 19.2 (2015): 244.
92 Cyphers, *Sex and the City 2*, 7.
93 Mitu Sengupta, "Sex, the City and American Patriotism," *Counterpunch*, June 18, 2010, www.counterpunch.org/2010/06/18/sex-the-city-and-american-patriotism/. Accessed April 3, 2014.
94 Ghumkhor, *The Political Psychology of the Veil*, 22.
95 Minoo Moallem, *Between Warrior Brother and Veiled Sister: Islamic Fundamentalism and the Politics of Patriarchy in Iran* (Berkeley: University of California Press, 2005), 54.
96 Deleuze and Guattari. *A Thousand Plateaus*, 167. I am also indebted to the application of this theory by Michelle Ann Stephens, *Skin Acts: Race, Psychoanalysis and the Black Male Performer* (Durham: Duke University Press, 2014), 32.
97 Inna Arzumanova, "Veiled Visibility: Racial Performances and Hegemonic Leaks in Pakistani Fashion Week," in *Racism Postrace*, ed. Roopali Mukherjee, Sarah Banet-Weiser, and Herman Gray (Durham: Duke University Press, 2019), 266.
98 Booth, "Translator v. Author," 201.
99 Richard Dyer, *Stars*, 2nd ed. (London: British Film Institute, 1998), 99.
100 Kim Allen, "Girls Imagining Careers in the Limelight: Social Class, Gender, and Fantasies of 'Success,'" in *In the Limelight and under the Microscope: Forms and Functions of Female Celebrity*, ed. Su Holmes and Diane Negra (London: Continuum, 2011), 152.
101 Booth, "Translator," 162.
102 The website has been removed, but the image can be found at Siraj Wahab, "Interview with Rajaa al-Sanea, Author The Girls of Riyadh (2006)," *Notes from Saudi Arabia*, February 17, 2007, http://notesfromsaudiarabia.blogspot.com/2007/02/interview-with-rajaa-al-sanea-author-of.html. Accessed July 26, 2014.
103 See, for instance, the images embedded in "Review: Girls of Riyadh by Rajaa Alsanea," *The Picky Girl*, July 27, 2010, www.thepickygirl.com/?p=598; "Rajaa's Life Shots," under "January's Female of the Month, Rajaa Alsanea," 2010 http://beautyalkhaloud.blogspot.com/2010_01_01_archive.html; Pixie, "Beautiful Muslimati," under "Style Steal: Rajaa Alsanea's paisley print orange-and-pink Shayla," March 11, 2009, http://ilovehishmatheblog.blogspot.com/2009/03/i-love-this-paisleyprint-orange-and.html. In 2011, Alsanea, a practicing dentist, presented a more sober appearance. See Miriam Abdullah, "Rajaa al-Sanea: Beyond Girls of Riyadh," Al Akhbar English, October 20, 2011, http://english.al-akhbar.com/node/1110. All sites accessed June 22, 2014. Alsanea's reception and reaction to the English translation are treated in Ware, "The New Literary Front," 5, 22.
104 Joe Moran, *Star Authors: Literary Celebrity in America* (London: Pluto, 2000), 11.
105 Novels such as Asne Seierstad's *The Bookseller of Kabul* (2003) and Khalid Husseini's *The Kite Runner* (2003), which exemplify what Fatemeh Keshavarz calls "new Orientalist" fiction, filled out this niche. Åsne Seierstaad, *The Bookseller of Kabul* [Bokhandleren i Kabul, 2002], trans. Ingrid Christophersen (Back Bay Books 2003); Khaled Hosseini, *The Kite Runner* (New York: Riverhead-Penguin, 2003). Fatemeh Keshavarz, *Jasmine and Stars: Reading More than Lolita in Tehran* (Chapel Hill: University of North Carolina Press, 2007), 3.

106 Young Muslim women who claim the romance and chick-lit labels as well as a positive Muslim identity have appeared in English. Among them are *Sofia Khan Is Not Obliged* (2016) by the British Ayiesha Malik, *Courting Samira* (2012), by the Australian Amal Awad, *No Sex in the City* (2014) by the Australian Randa Abdel-Fattah, and *Ayesha at Last*, by the British Umza Jalaluddin.
107 Diane Negra, *What a Girl Wants? Fantasizing the Reclamation of the Self in Postfeminism* (London: Routledge, 2009), 21.

2
FEMALE MASOCHISM AND TEXTUAL MASQUERADE IN MONICA ALI'S *BRICK LANE* AND *UNTOLD STORY*

In *Sex and the City 2*, empowerment feminism rejuvenates ageing white bodies through proximate but still foreign Muslim-Arab women's bodies. The movie presents the little difference between the mature Anglo and the covered woman as an external one. Fashion underneath or on the hijab signals this revision of the essentialized image. Black-robed women hidden in the souk can converse privately with the American women in English. The real housewife speaks to her table companion (not necessarily in English) but cannot be heard by the American. *Banat/Girls* would like the Saudi and the American woman to speak in a shared public language. When they do, however, the hijabi returns to abjection. The Arab's wife poor English, unfashionable clothing, and lack of mastery of migrancy make her vulnerable to shaming, just as her dress and make-up did in Riyadh among friends. The Asian-American postfeminist Kari treats Gamrah with scorn, aligning herself completely with male privilege and global girl freedom. *Banat/Girls* extends the possibility of the marriage plot to deliver on its postfeminist promise of romance and career while promoting an Arab gender critique. Transcending the female flesh altogether to gain a public speaking voice remains the novel's final desire.

Monica Ali's novels *Brick Lane* (2003) and *Untold Story* (2011) incorporate the distance and disguise of masquerade performances into their own textual procedures. Literary decisions attempt to *overcome* the visual affect of the veil and the entrapment of luminous appearance. In *Brick Lane*, the abjected Muslim migrant wife finds her agency in spiritual and erotic rejuvenation. In *Untold Story* the ageing postfeminist celebrity princess flees her abjection to the image, and with it her public agency and affective connection. Not dying becomes the measure of the former princess's accomplishment, and melodrama her mode. Through

DOI: 10.4324/9781003189299-3

mere survival, she secures the preservation of sovereign succession and reveals the absence of a "choice" of a way of life.

As a British writer of Muslim and Bangladeshi descent, Monica Ali discovered her own entanglement in affect, visuality, and nationalism through the quite different reception of the two novels. In a 2019 interview, Ali relates:

> Nazneen, the protagonist of *Brick Lane*, is a virgin bride, uneducated, unworldly, has an arranged marriage to a much older man, suffers the scrutiny of the wider community, has an affair, but decides that a man is not the way to salvation, and reinvents a new life for herself.

The writer continues:

> Lydia, the protagonist of *Untold Story*, on the other hand, is a virgin bride, uneducated, unworldly, has an arranged marriage to a much older man, suffers the scrutiny of the outside world, has an affair, but decides that a man is not the way to salvation and reinvents herself and her life. But one story has brown people in saris in it, and the other doesn't.[1]

In the course of the interview Ali describes the expectation that "minority and queer" novelists will write about "identity-based things and the struggles of that identity." If they do not, critics become "confused."[2]

I argue that Ali's narratives anticipate the affect of ethnoreligious difference and visual cues, even though they were not able to surmount the racial, national, and religious frameworks that governed their reception. To show Nazneen as a rounded character, *Brick Lane* disavows the master signifiers of Islam. It makes no explicit reference to the Prophet and refers to "God," not Allah. Perhaps most significantly, Nazneen wears a sari. Only a few times does the narrative refer to her use of it as a head covering. Ali represents a woman who achieves recognition and power through belief practices usually made synonymous with masochism and subjugation in the Western imaginary. Diminishment of "the veil" allows the protagonist to register as flesh. Nonetheless the novel's early reception demonstrates that countering the affect of the veil leads to the reading of a "choice" feminism[3] unimpeded by community, whether political or spiritual. *Untold Story* is the "what-if" version of Diana, Princess of Wales, had she survived her historical death. In contrast to *Sex and the City 2*'s celebratory conclusion, *Untold Story*'s Lydia Snarebrook must disappear to live, attempting to become a "body without image."[4] Ali's equation of recognition with death shows the impossibility of an afterlife for the luminous feminine spectacle. As a construction, Diana-Lydia fits the concept of "assemblage," that is, "'complex constellation of [the] objects, bodies, expressions, qualities, and territories' that arrange themselves and connect through desire," as in the *agencement* of Deleuze and Guattari.[5] Plastic surgery and other means of cosmetic rejuvenation in this instance enact a "cutting off" as a line of force, to disrupt or redirect a habitual movement. Surgical removal becomes a camouflage and an act of maternal sacrifice.

Masochism appears in additional guises in the two works. Its interpretation becomes pivotal in each one. Is Nazneen "masochistic" in submission to her "fate," as a traditional woman? She regards her disposition as sinful when she protests her son's death, and sinful when she gives herself over to her attraction to Karim. She attributes both events to fate. Lydia both resists her fate as Diana the assemblage and submits to an increased threat of fatality to herself and her children. The question of what registers as agential and what role recognition plays in agency are crucial to interpretation of these dynamics. The issue brings to the fore judgments about "what kinds of choices and actions count in identifying agency and which do not" in a feminist reading.[6]

Feminist thinkers have reassessed masochism, particularly as formulated by Gilles Deleuze, to argue that it can be employed as a strategy for managing power relations. Amber Jamilla Musser approaches masochism by developing Hortense Spillers' conception of the "flesh" as a liberated subject position distinct from that of the captive "body."[7] Musser reorients the analysis to "structures of sensation in … performances of acts of submission."[8] Masochism in such readings becomes a highly plastic analytic and a bodily practice not limited to overt sexual acts. This distinction bears upon the understanding of submission as a cultivation of potential in Islam. Nazneen does not capitulate to an indifferent "fate," or succumb to an "Asiatic fatalism" linked to a "quietist" Islam,[9] though she regards her behavior as masochistic and fatal. The text grounds Nazneen's renewal instead in everyday experiences that lead her to distinguish passivity and self-destruction from Muslim belief. The "*tafsir* of praxis" foregrounds women's experience as a mode of Qur'anic exegesis.[10]

Untold Story secures its premise by presenting as credible Lydia's conviction that her sons will be killed if her identity as the historical Diana is discovered. In this Lydia becomes the "cold mother"[11] of Sacher-Masoch that Deleuze describes. Deleuze revises Freud's formulation of sadomasochism by separating the two dynamics through return to the literary works of Sade and Sacher-Masoch.[12] Masochism employs the aesthetic techniques of suspense and disavowal, which produce qualitative delay instead of quantitative repetition. Postponing fulfillment, especially through elaboration of contractual conditions, only intensifies masochistic pleasure.[13] Female masochism stems from a desire for recognition by an objectified or subordinated subject, and a desire for relief from guilt by a dominant subject.

Lydia's masochism is based in Diana's actual practices, but also on the literary premises of her survival, which respond to the removal of Diana's status as a transcendent white global mother. Lydia is thrust into Giorgio Agamben's "naked life" narrative,[14] in which the keeping alive of the body surpasses all other values, aims, or qualities. Rakia Shome ponders the mediations that allowed Diana to become "a simultaneous signifier of a national popular and a global popular without rupture or contradiction."[15] *Untold Story* reveals the collapse of such mediations. When the Diana figure detaches from representation, she must be reinstalled in Anglo nationality, racial whiteness, heterosexuality, and a homogenous provincial life. Lydia stands in need of the biopolitical rescue and protection she once extended to abjected populations in Britain and the naked lives of the postimperium. At the same time she expects to find her "self" as a lost origin and potential site of rejuvenation.

The exchanges of biopolitical zones contribute to Ali's latent content, particularly when the novels are considered together. Agamben states that producing biopolitical power is the original activity of sovereign power, which arose from the contradictions in the Greek formulation of *zoë*, or mere life at home, and *bios*, a particular way of life afforded by political status. The *homo sacer*, or victim who may be killed but not sacrificed, obscures the foundational paradox of this binary. In modern democracies, Agamben contends, citizenship became the vehicle of *bios*, or rights discourse. But the "mobile state of exception" established by the *homo sacer* allows for the deprivation of human rights or even human status through denaturalization, dislocation, and other means of managing populations. Evelyn Alsultany associates this dynamic with the "ambivalent racism" used to justify curtailing Arab-American civil rights after 9/11. It interacts with the affect of remorse and sympathy.[16] The death camp, rather than in the Foucauldian prison, is the model of contemporary sovereign power. Biopolitics have completely absorbed the polis.

Literary Pop, Migrant Images

Though regarded as literary novels, *Brick Lane* and *Untold Story* both gained pop currency through media hooks and tie-ins. In its marketing, *Brick Lane* capitalized on Ali's "immigrant" status, though her family left Bangladesh when she was three. She was named as a Granta Top Twenty young British novelist. The novel was shortlisted for the Booker Prize. Like Salman Rushdie's *The Satanic Verses* (1989), *Brick Lane* represents subcontinental migrants in London as sites of generative Muslim practice. Like *The Satanic Verses*, too, *Brick Lane* incited protest upon its publication and again, more dramatically, when it was being filmed in the East End of London, the novel's primary setting. Protestors complained about colonization of the neighborhood as well as about the portrait of an unfaithful Muslim wife. Filming had to proceed in a different location.[17] In literary circles, in the popular press, and in subsequent scholarship, the novel also occasioned much complaint about authenticity and identity.[18] Mrinalini Chakravorty observes that "the controversy elucidates ... the intersection of culture and the biology of race as the formative basis on which stereotypes about South Asia and its migrants are extended in the transnational moment."[19] In her subsequent career Ali has resisted a profile intimately connected with her own racial or religious heritage. She depicts her work as centered on issues of "identity" and makes no distinction between *Brick Lane* and the later fiction.[20] Rather than emphasizing her status as a "migrant," "transnational," or "feminist" writer, Ali has presented herself as a British writer with an international or cosmopolitan (rather than a "global") reach.[21] Her fiction treats spaces of migration, all of which are located in Europe and America. One of the three novels features a male protagonist. *Alentejo Blue* (2006), a set of interconnected stories, takes place in a Portuguese village frequented by tourists from other European nations, and *In the Kitchen* (2009) focuses on an internal migrant from the north of England to London, whose restaurant jobs draw him into class and cultural conflict. Notably, however, the themes of sexual inequality, geographical mobility, and transnational identity have characterized the works in different ways.

Ali's web materials and press highlighted the link between her fourth novel, *Untold Story*, set to be released in Britain around what would have been Diana's fiftieth birthday, and the marriage of her older son, Prince William.[22] The author refused pre-publication interviews "to preserve some of the mystique about the book," according to a publicist, but Ali published her own articles about it in papers such as the *Telegraph*.[23] In them she counters charges of the triviality of her subject matter as well as her connection to it. In response to a *New York Times* review that portrayed the novel itself as "a curious marriage of author and subject matter," Ali emphasizes her Britishness: she points out the reviewer's assumption that Diana's fans are all Anglo-English. If in the *Brick Lane* controversy, Ali was seen to be insufficiently Bangladeshi, she was later imagined as insufficiently English. In response, the author wrote,

> Like everyone else in this country, I grew up with the royal family in the background and watched the Diana fairy tale/nightmare unfold, and ultimately explode. Diana had her detractors, but she was someone who fascinated people of all backgrounds.[24]

Into this characterization of broad social appeal Ali also inserts a long discussion of Diana's relationship with Dr. Hasnat Khan, supposedly foiled by his disapproving mother, and elsewhere presents her own pop reading of Diana as a "gorgeous bundle of trouble,"[25] language that might be taken from a tabloid. To offset such associations, she stressed the novel's similarity to serious literary works about historical figures and celebrities.[26] Though Ali made such gestures in the context of an established literary reputation, they suggest her continued cultivation of the profile of a literary writer, whose own marked identities do not define her subject or her audience.

Ali's stylistic choices have contributed to her careful designation and placement. The heightened playfulness, linguistic and generic mixture, and social comedy associated with novelists of mixed British heritage at the time are absent from her prose. The author, like many of her reviewers, highlighted in her debut press her affinities with nineteenth-century British novelists such as Dickens and

Thackeray[27] and her use of historical sources. Yet the fantasy elements of both novels have been treated only as failures of realism, not as techniques if melodrama and romance injected into the surface realism. As some critics have noted, Ali even takes up the task of representing conversation and writing that do not take place in English entirely in English, using relatively little Bengali. *Brick Lane*, like the later *Untold Story*, invites the conventional readings I have described through this style: domestic realism in third-person narratives with some shifts in perspective. The focus on Nazneen, beginning with her childhood in Bangladesh, is interspersed with epistolary passages, written in the first-person (yet translated) voice of her sister Hasina, who remains in Bangladesh. *Untold Story* shifts point of view more often, in pairing the third-person account of Lydia with the perspective of John Grabowski, the British photographer who discovers her and who brings the detective/persecutor role of mass media to a plot climax. The third-person accounts are interspersed with the first-person narration of the courtier Lawrence, who helped Diana escape, and of Diana-Lydia herself, delivered in correspondence with him.

In both novels "fate" serves pivotal functions that contend with realist conventions. Geoffrey Nash contends that Nazneen's "fate," like the later political agenda introduced by Karim, is also a form of Islam, one ultimately nullified by the couple's adultery.[28] I contend that the vernacular understanding of "fate" has little to do with representing Islam per se, though the family is Muslim. *Brick Lane* casts belief in fate primarily as *maternal* resignation before the abjection of poverty and powerlessness, the overweening dominance of contingency in bare life circumstances.[29] Second, I do not tie Nazneen's adultery as a narrative rejection of Islam. To read a Christian woman as implicitly rejecting her religion because she commits adultery would certainly seem curious, yet this equation is readymade in the shorthand of the Islamic imaginary of the West. Nazneen's somatic incorporation of the body of belief is neither morally nor "doctrinally" acceptable, but it does *not* dovetail with a rejection of her faith, as the narrative shows. The protagonist's change is affective, somatic, performative, and here coded female. Nazneen dramatizes a mode of Muslim practice produced by a contemporary migrant woman who enacts a somatic and affective drama, her ways of everyday "living and being"[30] related to the *tafsir* of practice.[31]

If *Brick Lane* withholds in order to revise the masochism of veiling, *Untold Story* shows the failure of female masochism as a strategy for managing power relations for the luminous assemblage of nationalized and globalized postfeminism. Diana's boundless power depended on the charge of her photographed image. It consisted of the haptic and ocular, of affect and pose, of white missionary beauty and curative labor. Her image illustrates Brian Massumi's contention that "affect is synesthetic, implying a participation of the senses in each other: a measure of a living thing's potential interactions is its ability to transform the effects of one sensory mode into another."[32] In *Untold Story*, the former princess cannot exterminate the means of her production and its affect, just as Lydia cannot discover an origin as a self prior to her assemblage of feminine mediations. Lydia's actual existence, like Diana's posthumous one, becomes "redundant," as Diana Taylor has noted.[33]

Assemblage in *Brick Lane*

Brick Lane opens with a flashback to Nazneen's birth, when her mother detached emotionally from her sick infant. Nazneen's move to Britain to marry improves her biopolitical position but does not eradicate her vulnerability or grant her much further economic, social, or emotional mobility. In her linguistic and social isolation upon her arrival in London, she fits the stereotype of a lower-class Muslim village women as sequestered, passive, and mentally curtained. She acts as a "blockage" in or a "betrayal" of the national ideal, in Sara Ahmed's reading of British multicultural dynamics.[34] Nazneen's exchanges with her sister Hasina, a poor, unmarried, itinerant laborer in Dhaka, keep in the foreground her proximity to death. The threat culminates early, but in London, where Nazneen's own child dies.

The protagonist acquires the capacity to "inhabit" the national body[35] through the text's reluctance to represent her through stock signifiers, as I have noted. Nazneen wears a sari. In a few instances, she uses it to cover her head.[36] Noemi Pereira-Ares observes that the novel illustrates a "conspicuous profusion of sartorial descriptions" that form a subtextual "language of clothes": other characters' "dressed bodies silently project a wide spectrum of attitudes toward *hijab*, attitudes which range from rejection to ardent celebration."[37] The focal point of Nazneen's identity is not her head covering, in part because the sari is a more ambivalent signifier than "the veil" or "hijab." When Nazneen covers, she does so by pulling her sari over her head or her "headscarf" over her face (53–54, 143, 232, 254).[38] Moreover, especially in part one, Nazneen spends much of the time in her apartment alone, or with her husband, where the need to cover does not arise. Her reaction to other characters suggests that she dresses modestly.[39] Yet the narrative primarily represents Nazneen's body through her activities, not through her garb. Finally, Nazneen is poised to move from a mere laborer to a designer of clothes as she and her friend Razia plan to open a shop. *Brick Lane* can thus be read, and has been read, as a story of containment and absorption of difference into the neoliberal feminist body-politic.

The "stickiness" or blockage of the migrant Muslim woman's affect is countered through particularity, including specific placement in the history of postimperial Britain and its former colony, the Bangladesh that once belonged to the Raj. Beginning in 1985, the story of Nazneen and her husband in London adheres closely to the demographic and labor history of the East End, according to Garret Ziegler. *Brick Lane*, set in the historically immigrant neighborhood of Tower Hamlets, portrays Bengalis from the Sylhet region. The group migrated to the area in greater numbers after World War II. Mostly male, the migrants worked primarily in the garment industry, "picking up work then being abandoned by previous waves of Eastern European immigrants."[40] Not until the 1970s did (the now) Bangladeshi women begin migrating in greater numbers: commonwealth legislative restrictions enacted in the beginning in the 1960s limited immigration largely to the family members of British nationals, who often dealt with these restrictions by traveling to Bangladesh to marry.[41] *Brick Lane* maps onto this history rather precisely, as Chanu, who migrated to London in the 1960s as a young man, has returned with a much younger Bangladeshi woman as his bride in 1985.

According to Ali, as well as critics, Nazneen's later labor as a home garment worker, as well as her sister Hasina's factory and domestic labor in Bangladesh, draw on historical and sociological research too. Ali has acknowledged as a significant source Naila Kabber's *The Power to Choose: Bangladeshi Women and Labor Market Decisions in London and Dhaka* (2000).[42] As Ziegler observes, Nazneen experiences London not just as a European capital, but also as a global marketplace. Her empowerment in London follows a trajectory of interpellation into a transnational city and its economic opportunities. He asserts: "The novel traces the transformation of Nazneen from a dependent, isolated wife to an independent, socialized Western actor." She becomes one less by claiming rights than by gaining "political membership in the neo-liberal capitalist metropolis." In the process she "discard[s] the laws of her religion, slough[s] off decades, or even centuries, of gender norms, and end[s] up in control of her own labor power" at the novel's conclusion. Ziegler contrasts her ascent with the poverty of her sister in Dhaka.[43] John Marx finds such a progressive reading problematic. He defends the rationality of Hasina's final decision to elope with a cook and argues that the narrative breaks decisively—and intriguingly—with realism by suggesting Nazneen may become an entrepreneur.[44] Other critics have complained of the implausibility and the didacticism of the novel's conclusion.[45]

My own reading of *Brick Lane* attempts to revise neoliberal readings through attention to their biopolitical, gendered, and religious premises. Some readers' judgment of the plot resolution as fantastical may stem in part from persistence of the affect that Ali's substitutions attempt to avoid, and from the latent content's quiet dramatization of feminist Muslim practice, not conceptualized as such by Nazneen. The network of stereotypes that confine Nazneen's representation[46] is not only evident but is clearly manipulated in the novel's formal practices. Nazneen's matrilineal heritage, her female bonds, and her understanding of their relation to her changing understanding of God crucially situate her. Long before the protagonist takes up work as a garment producer, *Brick Lane* shows her attempt to "pattern" her life through understanding of her own isolated and drab domestic world as part of God's creation.[47] Her fantasies of independence similarly evidence her realization of increased agency as relational rather than autonomous, and fleshly as well as psychic and material. Pattern exemplifies the eventual coincidence of sensual, aesthetic, spiritual, and economic labor.

Nazneen's "conversion" of awareness begins with a dramatization of the Qur'an's physical and emotional power. The scene takes place in the early years of her marriage, when she is marooned at home in her council flat, afraid to venture out without her husband because she speaks no English and knows nothing of the city. Though she cannot recall ever being alone before she came to London, she now is confined day after day in a "large box" with nothing to do but dust furniture and listen to "the muffled sounds of private lives sealed away above, below, and around her."[48] Dusting leads Nazneen to pick up the Qur'an and experience its somatic influence.[49] "The words calmed her stomach and she was pleased," the narrator reports. "How would it sound in Arabic? More lovely even than in Bengali, she supposed, for those were the actual Words of God" (8). After Nazneen touches the real, or Arabic, Qur'an, the narration highlights the connection between God's creation and her flat:

> Nazneen stared at the glass showcase stuffed with pottery animals, china figures and plastic fruit. Each one had to be dusted. She wondered where the dust came in and what it came from. All of it belonged to God. She wondered what He wanted with clay tigers, trinkets and dust.

She mentally recites a sura, or verse, that she memorized in school. Though she doesn't know the meaning of the Arabic, the rhythm "soothe[s]" her and becomes one with her breathing (8).

Nazneen soon begins to order her day through spiritual practice. The narrator relates: "She began to pray five times each day, rolling out her prayer mat in the sitting room to face east" (27). The discipline of her physical practice is often set against her propensity to lose herself in fantasy. Both point to Nazneen's attraction to pattern and physical discipline as ways of endowing her circumstances with meaning. And as critics such as Ziegler gloss over, Nazneen initiates her own practice. Her inclinations contrast with her husband's decided lack of religiosity as well as, eventually, with her mother's submission to "fate" as a masochistic coldness. (Nazneen's sister's culminating revelation is that their mother Rupban committed suicide.)

These contexts inform Nazneen's initial forays out of the neighborhood and into greater London. The first time the novel represents her venturing out, her husband takes her to buy a new sari. Nazneen experiences the Bethnal Green Road as "as a roaring metal army tearing up the town" (28): the taste, smell, and sight of machines dominate her body and her perceptions. The "white women" she sees on the street belong to the scene of indifference or aggression. In "clinging trousers," the mothers work their mouths "furiously" as they "screec[h back]" at their screeching children. When professional women, "their shoulders padded up and out" wide enough to bear buckets, catch her scrutinizing them, they snicker derisively at her (29). Ziegler juxtaposes this scene with Nazneen's first attempt to navigate London on her own. Lost, presumably in the city, she occupies the position of ethnographic observer, a transparent eyeball. Ziegler argues that her neutral posture is quickly cancelled. "She is spotted, the moment of empowerment she experienced becomes ephemeral, and Nazneen is punished for believing that she could merely observe and not participate" (153). A woman stares back at her, a man accidentally hits her with his briefcase, and the outsider Nazneen "learns … that the global city allows no outsiders, no extra-economic agents, no detached observers" (153–54).

Angela Poon counters that the novel shows "the everyday and seemingly mundane ways in which migrant bodies experience the city as sources of alternative forms of knowing."[50] Shao-ming Kung calls Nazneen a diasporan "flaneuse" employing a gendered and raced consciousness.[51] Both interpretations treat Nazneen as an engaged and interactive observer. The protagonist gains power and confidence through "acknowledgment" on the British street, as Ziegler notes. But I want to call attention to the portrayal of a migrant woman as an actual blockage in the flow and Ali's recourse to sensation and bodily habitus as specific conditions of response. Ziegler interprets the professional women's dress as "masculinized" in Nazneen's view because of their aggressive or defensive individuality. The women's heads are "puffed up" like snakes in bouffant hair styles, their demeanor is "angry," and one woman's coat is "armor" (39–40). Yet Nazneen is also "puffed up," not around her head but around her middle. Her roundness and bulk in fact make her a bigger, more vulnerable body as she moves slowly among the skyscrapers and pedestrian flow. Nazneen is disoriented amid the brisk professional figures engaged in commerce. The affect they produce in her is a flinch reaction to barrage. She revises the aggression suggested by these descriptions when she connects the angry color of a red suit to that of "a bride's sari" and interprets it as granting its wearer solidity (39–40). Nazneen understands the working women's armor as a necessary defense, a way of granting themselves status and protection, not merely a mimesis of their male counterparts.[52] The idiom of clothing as protection becomes particularly significant in relation to Nazneen's history. Her mother died from a sword driven into her chest (by herself, it is later revealed). Her sister is "lost" as an unattached, impoverished woman in Bangladesh (41). The wandering Nazneen, who has begun to understand herself as connected to the dust in her apartment and who soothes herself in the rhythms of recitation, arrives home banged up, cold, and exhausted but proud of herself for having asked, presumably in English, for directions and for use of a pub's bathroom.

Against the assumption of autonomy as independence and freedom as pure mobility, then, Ali represents Nazneen as belonging to a "pattern" and desiring connection. Figure skating signifies a disciplined capacity arising from practice. The first English word Nazneen attempts in direct dialogue is "skating." She vividly merges with a female skater, pictured in a magazine, right after she realizes that her husband Chanu will never achieve any of his own goals. She "falls" into another embodiment, which is female and open to the environment but also disciplined and supported in a challenging new movement:

> [The skater] stood on one leg. Her body was horizontal and the other leg perpendicular. Her arms reached out and held on to [her partner's] hand, but she looked up and smiled directly at Nazneen. Her body was spangled, silver and blue. Her legs were as long as the Padma. She was a fairy-tale creature, a Hindu goddess. Nazneen fell, somehow, into that picture and caught hold of the man's hand. She was shocked to find she was traveling across the ice, on one foot, at terrible speed. And the man smiled and said, "Hold on tight." Little green gems twinkled in his black suit. Nazneen squeezed his hand. She felt the rush of wind on her cheeks, and the muscles in her thighs flexing. The ice smelled of limes. Applause. She could not see the audience but she heard them. And the man let go of her hand but she was not afraid.
>
> (71)

The woman is a spectacle, a center of attention, as Nazneen imagines that she could become in the commercial district only by waving a gun, forcing herself into visibility as a dangerous or deranged person (31). She glosses the skating fantasy as "silly" as is the vision of herself as "an independent woman," like her sister. She chides herself for daydreaming rather than praying (63). Skating, however, formally parallels belief practice in its disciplinary reworking of corporeal reciprocity. Nazneen's merging with the skater anticipates her affair with the young Muslim activist Karim as a partnership and a corporeal awakening. The fantasy parallels her desire to be "spool[ed]" and "threaded" to Dhaka through the words in her letters, where she imagines working alongside her sister (64).

Brick Lane retains a surface of domestic realism to dramatize Nazneen's somatic transformation. It connects to her realization that God has acknowledged her. The novel presents this development discursively and characterologically rather than stylistically. But the concept of merging with another crucially informs Nazneen's development. In Islam adherents internalize and incorporate the Prophet through practice. Nazneen's change manifests through sensation, emotion, and corporeality, but does so only after the death of her own child. When her son Raqib becomes ill, she prays on the tasbee, or prayer beads as if "drugged" by the repetition. The narrator relates Nazneen's later memory of the period, long after her son's death:

> In prayer she had sought to stupefy herself like a drunk with a bottle, like a fly against a lantern. This was not the correct way to pray. It was not the correct way to read the suras. It was not the correct way to live.
>
> (103)

After Raqib's death, the narrative takes a long temporal hiatus and resumes in 2001. Nazneen and Chanu now have two daughters, and Nazneen is working at home sewing jeans. Chanu's professional status has declined. Karim, a young British-born Muslim who picks up her garments for delivery, first provokes an imagined corporeal conjunction reminiscent of the skating fantasy. When Karim performs namaz in her apartment, the novel reports: "It was he who moved, but she who felt dizzy" (190). Initially, Nazneen cannot experience the attraction as a function of her own emotions. She understands her erotic desire only as an oppressive external force:

> She had submitted to her father and married her husband; she had submitted to her husband. And now she gave herself up to a power greater than these two, and she felt herself helpless before it. When the thought crept into her mind that the power was inside her, that she was its creator, she dismissed it as conceited. How could a weak woman unleash a force so strong? She gave in to fate and not herself.
> (247)

Though neither her style nor her explicit markers call attention to the workings of a kind of Muslim habitus in her text, Ali represents the practice of Islam as physical and emotional capture. Belief practice is a disciplinary production of corporeal reciprocity, of submission or surrender to Allah and the Prophet. *Brick Lane*, like *The Satanic Verses*, represents a mode of spiritual belief that produces an epistemology from regulated bodily actions. In so doing, both novels challenge the "repressive" thesis usually applied to spiritual discipline in modernist and contemporary narrative. Yet *Brick Lane* carries none of the ideological baggage central to Rushdie's binary between literal and figurative meaning, between sacred truth and fiction. Rushdie constructs "submission" to spiritual belief as an absolute counter to free agency, calling upon the modernist religion of art so central to his skepticism. Ali illustrates the powerful constraints on applying such a model to women, for whom the question is often what to submit *to*, not whether to submit *at all*. Saba Mahmood illuminates this difference in agency when she asks:

> How do we conceive of individual freedom in a context where the distinction between the subject's own desires and socially prescribed performances cannot be easily presumed, and where submission to (external) authority is a condition for achieving the subject's potentiality?[53]

Brick Lane gives one answer to this question.

Ali in fact poses a body in practice that differs from the "secular" body that Asad and Hirschkind posit and question. Islam differs as a *mode* distinct from the doctrinally oriented premises of a religion such as Christianity. As I have discussed at length elsewhere,[54] Islam, like Judaism, bases belief on disciplinary practice, understood as integral to the disposition and episteme of moral formation. Conceived as "an act, not a thing," as a practice more than a doctrine, Islam in this modality strongly differs from the Christian formation of "religion." Frederick Denny explains that the term *orthopraxy* approximates "the reality of Muslim devotion and obedience to God." Christianity, in contrast, "stresses doctrinal clarity and understanding by means of creeds, dogmas, and theologies." Islam and Judaism conceive of belief "as a way of life and a ritual patterning of that life under God's lordship."[55] These instrumental, or orthopractic, modes of belief do not emphatically differentiate emotion and knowledge, thought and act, or particular skin from communal flesh. Rather practice produces knowledge as a moral, somatic, and affective totality, training the adherent in concert with the community. The "orthodox"—that is, doctrinally oriented—and affective formation of liberal Christianity assumes a corporeality, through which sentiment and belief are expressed in relation to an accepted theology. Disciplined practice in contrast aims to produce physicality as an "ability," a "potentiality," or a "power," Asad explains.[56] Mahmood chooses the example of musical practice to explain this concept:

> We might consider the example of a virtuoso pianist who submits herself to the often painful regime of disciplinary practice, as well as to the hierarchical structures of apprenticeship, in order to acquire the ability—the requisite agency—to play the instrument with mastery.[57]

After they become lovers, Nazneen incorporates Karim physically as a "missing sense" (248) and feels that she "inhabit[s] her body for the first time" (284). Unlike her husband Chanu, the "god-conscious" Karim invites her into his knowledge, as well as into his practice of Islam in the community. In him, Ali collapses Nazneen's desire for "a place in the world" as spiritual, social, physical, and civic incorporation. The relationship opens confined spaces in which she feels entrapped (61).

At the same time that Ali draws on the agential potential of regulated practice, she demonstrates Nazneen's own adaptation of it from the *tafsir* of experience. The sensational and affective charge of touching the Qur'an, reciting the suras, and praying are solitary experiences until she meets Karim. The narrative then describes these activities more explicitly in terms of "regulated prayer or its postures and actions."[58] Even as she violates principles, Nazneen gains a sense of community and develops a somatic disposition through her practice with Karim. Similarly, as in women's *tafsir* of experience, generative potential relies less on following prescribed rules than it does on everyday practices and history. Bodies themselves become instruments of ordinary modes of spiritual communication and of habit.

Against the narrative of "becoming terrorist" attached to Muslim men in Jasbir Puar's view,[59] the spiritual and political Karim promotes Nazneen's sensual enjoyment, agential growth, and sense of communal affect. Yet Ali sets the intellectual or political programs of both Karim and Chanu against Nazneen's ultimate rejection of their larger agendas. Her husband's relaxed attitude toward religious practice and his worship of European learning—ultimately a thwarted attempt to assimilate—send him back to a Bangladesh he has idealized. Similarly, Karim's desire for an "origin" reveals a benighted and romantic master narrative. Both men seek palliatives for their fractured and subordinated positions in Britain by returning to a native "mother" for which Nazneen realizes she has acted as a surrogate. Idealized through distance and absence, Bangladesh represents coherence, unity, and recognition for the men. While the novel is not dismissive of their vulnerability and desire, it shows Nazneen's knowledge as less neat and more experientially derived.

Nazneen's emotional figure for Bangladesh is not a mother but a sister, who struggles there with the disenfranchisement caused by her poverty and her sex. Significantly, Nazneen detaches from both men to act in the best interest of her daughters. Peter Morey reads this resolution as "a conscious disengagement and distancing from a central aspect of community," through a consistent promotion of "individualism." My reading questions both his definition of community and his demotion of sensuousness and affect in his evaluation of her choices.[60]

Sociologically oriented critics have read Hasina as a failed economic actor. She seems finally to choose romance over independence through labor: she runs off with her employer's cook at the novel's conclusion. Emphasis on such oppositions nonetheless reduces important dimensions of Hasina's character and situation. She figures an alter-ego for Nazneen, and of Muslimah agency in a different context of constraint. Poor, unskilled, and unattached in the villages of Bangladesh, Hasina doesn't possess *enough* agency to attain many of the female virtues valued by her culture and religion. Because she is presented entirely through letters, however, Hasina has a voice that her sister, represented in limited third person, does not. The status of Hasina's voice has been the subject of some debate, since the character is not only overdetermined by stereotype but also fantastical in her presentation in English.[61] This suspension of disbelief, however, allows her direct expression as a first-person voice.

Both sisters wage battles with "fate" as an inexorable external force. Both assert agency as desire, but not necessarily as desire for absolute autonomy. They struggle with a matrilineal heritage of passivity that is finally revealed to be annihilating of both self and child. Toward the novel's conclusion, Nazneen learns from her sister the "truth" of her mother's submission: suicide. Nazneen comes to accept that her own prayer for her sick son's life was not sinful in its protest against fate, but rather a beneficent expression of love. This transvaluation becomes linked to her new knowledge and physical experience of God. *Brick Lane* shows Nazneen feel the "charge" of her own will (301). She separates from her lover and finally refuses to depart to Dhaka with her husband because of the misery of her daughters, who know only London and consider themselves British. Nazneen develops a "sense of citizenship"[62] by the end of the narrative. Though she later realizes that she "made [him] up," Karim allows her to realize her potential through prayer as a partnership (382). Dave Gunning observes, in accordance with this view, that "Nazneen comes to an understanding of Islam as supporting, not obstructing, agency."[63] Finally, not an earthly man but God "hear[s]" Nazneen and "provide[s] a way" through recognition and reciprocity (333). The novel's final desire to see her skate in a sari alludes to her retailoring of fate. Chakravorty points out that this is final gesture engages in a "politics of fantasy."[64] I would argue that the central contract of the narrative is honored through such imaginative fulfillment, tied to the remaking of Nazneen's bodily disposition.

Diana as Feminine Assemblage

The popular historical narrative of Diana Spencer follows a trajectory from innocence to knowledge. It is a story of girlish expectation disappointed, but just as potently, a progression of bodily discipline and an acceptance of the power of its display as political and performative. The "shy Di" who appeared at Prince Charles's side during their courtship was slightly plump and primly dressed, an English rose.[65] She was represented visually and discursively as virginal, a childminder, yet a country aristocrat discovered just before she had fully grown up. In *Untold Story*, Lydia's American friend Amber recounts her own princess fantasy as a narrative of revelation and discovery. Amber recalls that in high school, she "walked around in a dream." She explains:

> I was pretty but not spectacular, my grades were nothing to write home about, I had friends but I wasn't Miss Popular, I wasn't on any A-teams …. But it was like I was carrying this big secret around inside of me, that I'd never tell anyone, only one day they would see it because inside I was just so special that the world, when I got out and lived in it, was bound to make me a star. I didn't think I'd even have to try. It would just *happen*.

Though people would initially be "surprised," they would soon realize the inevitability of her ascension, manifested in "the dresses, the houses, the cars, the charming prince who would propose." Lydia responds, "All girls feel like that" (15).

Ali's Lydia has traversed the fantasy that the young Diana held when she became engaged to Prince Charles. As "all girls" do, Lydia and her American friend do not expect that they will need to promote and manage their natural and yet individual aristocratic qualities through competition. Diana's life contrasts in two stark ways with the princess plot. While Amber's description does not feature sexual inexperience as key to her "specialness," Diana was selected because of her suitability as a breeder: the future King's wife had to be a virgin, preferably of aristocratic blood, a woman without a sexual past. Diana's story was in this respect closer to the "archaic" arranged marriage plot signified by Islam and presented in *Brick Lane* than it is to the contemporary ideology of romance. Second, Amber presents continued visibility as central to gratification of the princess fantasy. Amber imagines herself chosen without the requirement of discipline, the work of chastity, reproduction, and beauty maintenance. Diana's life as the historical "prequel" to Lydia's existence illustrates the bodily labor that the postfeminist contract actually requires. Lydia of *Untold Story* attempts to present an afterlife to McRobbie's "new kind of sexual contract," which offers women new modes of visibility, coincident with light itself. In doing so, Ali must rewrite Diana's story of luminosity and mediation, but also the nature and temporality of her labor.

In the legend that emerged, Diana's beauty as well as her compassion resulted from the work of suffering. "Beyond the illusion of every perfect woman there is ... the story of suffering that the transformation demanded," former editor Sarah Benton writes. Benton describes Diana's luminosity as an effect of her relationship to the camera as well as her later training of her body in the disciplines of public performance and appearance: "[W]hen at first [Diana] became famous she was not at all beautiful" but her body was made "radiant by the camera," through a charisma not captured in other media, such as paintings and drawings.[66] Newspapers and magazines in particular chronicled her metamorphosis to slenderness (through bulimia, it was later revealed), through maternity,[67] and into taut athleticism. She progressed from "Sloane Ranger" bows or matronly full skirts to sleek, stylish, and contemporary high fashion. Diana fulfilled her reproductive duty to ensure succession. But the more she fit the postfeminist ideal of disciplined physicality, of sexy but not vulgar display, the more her own romantic injury (and maternal abandonment) entered her public representation. The personal suffering of romantic disappointment became an affective basis for her compassion. Visually and narratively, Diana became a "global caretaker" in a pure whiteness "above and beyond" the body, Shome asserts.[68] Homi Bhabha contends that Diana fashioned "a style of agency" that depended on physical proximity to actual injury and contagion as well as the ability to convey the "intimacy effect" of haptic contact in photographs.[69] She touched the sick and the queer. According to this narrative, Diana was motivated to take physical risks in order to give compassionate touch, her beauty in contact with the affect or recoil signified by visibly imperfect bodies, by dark and queer figures who showed their membership in populations marked for death. Diana herself talked about the importance of touch to her charitable work and described its effect as "'electric,'" one of her mentors reported.[70] Shome adds that Diana's touch became "metaphysical" through the juxtaposition of her image with those of children of the Global South, in a way that nonwhite and nonWestern mothers could not.[71]

In creating this affect, Diana tampered with the "middle distance" of respect[72] for modern royalty upheld by the strictures of discretion and decorum. Mark Cousins argues that consumer identification with celebrity and adherents' identification with saints signal a demand for greater intimacy: both groups are "hungry" and "restless with love."[73] The princess also drew upon an older monarchical capacity to increase regal prestige through touch. The Tudors elaborated on this touch as a "liturgy of state" in Holy Week activities such as foot-washing, which became more "ritualized and performed" in the sixteenth century, Carole Levin contends.[74] Both Mary and Elizabeth used such practices to show that the divine power of the monarch was so great "it could encompass even a female ruler."[75] Mary's Catholicism animated associations with saints as healers. Elizabeth I subsumed the analogy to the Virgin Mary, as well as the aura of priestly sanctity, into the Protestant monarchical formation.[76] In this respect, monarchs broached the proximity of vertical height as well as the later middle space of horizontal respect. During prescribed times and events, the reversal of high and low status or the closing of distance, physical and hierarchical, seemingly created an exchange that appeared to charge common bodies and regal bodies.

In *Untold Story*, Lawrence, the unnamed Diana's former private secretary and accomplice, uses tropes of radiance and obscurity, injury and healing, appetite and purging to describe the princess. "Time after time, over the years, she had come out of the darkness (of her husband's betrayal, of her bulimia, of numerous scandals) and dazzled the world. The deeper the darkness, the brighter she shone" (26). The imagery connects the familiar metaphor of light and dark to an inner psychic state that also signifies invisibility as nonexistence. In time, Lawrence says, "the strictures of royalty, of motherhood, of overbearing fame—those things that should have kept her behavior in check—simply made her progressively more [sic] reckless" (75). As Diana, "Lydia … when she wasn't having her secrets exposed, got busy exposing them herself." Ali attempts to bring the undisciplined appetite of the public gaze into metaphoric alignment with Diana's bulimia when Lawrence recalls:

> Lydia fed the monster that came close to destroying her. At first she thought that she could tame it, train it, make it roll over and beg. It was apparent that it was not so. Yet she was compelled to feed it more and more. Certainly, she liked to see photographs of herself in the newspapers. She looked at them all, more or less everyday, and it was to her chagrin when she did not appear. Certainly, she played tactically when she could, using or creating a photo opportunity to curry favor with the public, or to steal the limelight from her ex-husband. A junkie might shoot up an extra dose to get through a special occasion but that does not, I'm afraid, make him any less of an addict.
>
> (9)

Though the passage describes a cycle of dependency and compulsion, it also registers Diana's increase in symbolic phallic power through her luminosity. She can indulge in serious games and tactical maneuvers as she engages with beasts as equals. She gains masculinity through the figure of the "junkie," coded as male. Unrecognized by both her husband and "the firm," the historical Diana attempted to fill her lack with public adoration. The same attempt to achieve comfort through overconsuming and purging food—a merging of the dynamics of abandon and discipline, as Diana used it also to control her weight—aligns with the light and darkness of recognition and despair or nonexistence in Ali's description. The fictional Diana cannot master the monstrous meeting of appetites within and without herself.

In *Untold Story*, then, both the princess and audience join to make the hunger for love dangerous. The historical Diana's precarity greatly increased after her divorce, when she lost her political station and hence the "strictures" that had protected her physically and semiotically from the consequences of "recklessness." At the same time Diana stoked her own political capital, part of the assemblage of white femininity in Shome's reading, through humanitarian work that touched the global necropolis and conjured an empire of compassion.[77] Ahmed argues that Diana in her day represented the "ideal image of the nation"[78] as well as its racial mother. But Diana also surely anticipated later, multicultural models such as the bronzed, curly haired Genevieve Capovilla, whom Ahmed cites,[79] through her tactile contact with populations marked for death, within the state and its former empire. On this stage, the masochism signified by private self-harm becomes heroic or saintly self-sacrifice in the service of an empire of warm affect. Visually, Diana was proximate to bodies of color, in Africa, India, Pakistan, and other locations; she walked through a field that had been strewn with landmines; she donned a headscarf to visit hospital patients in Pakistan; she appeared as statuesque in a sheath as she stooped to greet the almost comically small Mother Teresa, shot from the back. More semiotically unstable were her love affairs with ethnically different men, such as the British-Pakistani physician Hasnat Khan—a relationship not well known during her lifetime—and finally her relationship with international "playboy" Dodi Fayed. In the narrative of empire that emerged after her death, these romances deepened Diana's affect. The plot came to include romantic merging of races and religions, the fluids of royalty with the subalterns of the past. More recently, the marriage of Prince Harry and Meghan Markel, now the Duchess of Sussex, has fully embodied the mixture, perhaps, in Shome's view, as another iteration of white femininity.

Death completed the plot of Diana's precarious proximity. Ali avoids placing Lydia entirely in the necropolitical realm inhabited by Hasina and Rupban in *Brick Lane*. But Lydia approaches this zone through the masochistic contract that Ali devises for her. To exist, Lydia must abandon her ability to heal, and in turn be healed, through intimate contact, not only with "Diana" but with her own children. As the imagined-dead, Diana stalks Lydia, for the public connection of their identities will actually result in Lydia's biological demise. She acts as the ultimate synthesis of the indifferent, cold mother—she abandons her children—and the maternal martyr—she does so in part to sustain their lives and to complete her biological imperative to supply an heir. Agamben's reading of *bios* and *zoë* become reconfigured in the female consort, who must sustain the next political body through a perpetual deferral of achieving her own status as a "form of life."[80] If such masochism bears the possibility of recognition, as Musser argues, the posthumous Diana assemblage cancels it. Lydia sustains the hope of rebirth only by intensification of masochistic renunciation and confinement to a homogeneous surround *because* she loses the metaphysical status of her white maternal touch and global postfeminist display.[81] The compensatory recognition that masochism might yield is forever postponed in the service of secretly sustaining biological life.

In *Untold Story*, Diana "fabricates" her own body to become Lydia, just as Diana disciplined herself to enhance and increase the yield of beauty created by the camera in images of her. This process does not subvert but rather extends the suffering and labor required of her in managing her body physically and withdrawing from its affect. "Aesthetic practices increasingly constitute aspects of psychic life,"[82] as Elias, Gill, and Scharff observe of everyday beauty demands. Lydia shows the anomie produced by renunciation of them. *Untold Story* attempts to imagine a restoration of a "core" or veridical self at the same time that it illustrates the impossibility of dismantling a "self" that is an assemblage of subject, mediation, and political power. The conundrum manifests in Lydia's self-examination:

> As she stood before the full-length mirror, Lydia shivered. Despite the dark hair, despite the surgeon's knife, despite the wrinkles wrought by the years and a permanent tan, she saw a ghost looking back at her that had long been consigned to the past. Slowly she turned and gazed over her shoulder. The dress scooped low to the waist.

She notices the enfleshment of difference from the image that the ghost still reflects: "The flesh sagged, not much, just a little, beneath the shoulder blades. How horrible that would look in a photograph, where no blemish was ever forgiven" (18). The effects of ageing as well as surgical alteration and a relaxation of bodily discipline enter into this description, as an older Diana would, in spite of beautification regimes, have registered the "blemish" of ageing skin. The gap between self and image closes through sagging flesh, and the veiling-unveiling dynamic is reversed through exposure and disappearance into anonymity.

Surgical alteration becomes a biopolitical technique. It is here that the text reacts to the vulnerability of the celebrity-saintly body stripped of protection. Diana's disciplined presentation acted as a kind of "armor" such as the professional women of *Brick Lane* wore in the city. She was further ensconced in the protection of the "middle distance" of respect, maintained by security guards and other protections. Lydia, in contrast, must be restored to an innocence that still protects her from her assignment to the realm of death, based in Diana's factual demise. Ali restores protection through the imagined geography of white American biopower. Lydia lives in a white American Midwest, a town called Kensington, an Arcadia evocative of Reagan's "morning in America." Narrative logic calls this image into being, though the novel does not mark its fantastic fabrication. The American Kensington is stripped to large extent of commodified images and their electronic circulation. It creates a protective cocoon for the global celebrity princess. If in life Diana became "a focal point for articulations of British national identity, gendered and family identities as well as notions of political belonging,"[83] in America Lydia is a mysterious cipher to her few friends and associates. Though she has developed a circle of women friends and is dating a man, Carson, these relationships are presented as provisional. Her most intimate relationship is with her dog, Rufus. Through him, the text recalls the "fur" so central to the cold Wanda of *Venus in Furs*. Moreover, in Rufus the novel condenses the royal family's canine obsession (which Diana did not share) and American companionability (the dog is a mutt from the shelter).

Through the melodrama of body and representation, *Untold Story* shows a pervasive affinity with *The Picture of Dorian Gray* as a confusion of the very terms that Lydia seeks to keep distinct through her old and new lives. She attempts to separate from the fatal image and enter the healing vision that was synonymous with Diana. Like Dorian, Lydia is a freak, a "multiform ego"[84] constituting a psychic and corporeal assemblage. The text's own fantasy of separating Princess Diana from Lydia, of mediated image from veridical self, postfeminist masquerade from an imagined true being, is countered by Lydia's own production as animate and inanimate. Postfemininity and posthumous desire, regal agency and nonsubjectivity, the life of the object as a past that cannot be abolished or inhabited, dramatize the masochistic contract struck between Lydia and Diana. This is an impossible "becoming." Lydia cannot eradicate her double by murdering a single, magical image. The Diana assemblage, too, unleashes the forces of criminality, through its traffic with impersonation, surveillance, stalking, detection, evasion, entrapment, capture, harassment, and "shooting." In attempting to trade the discipline of celebrity femininity for the discipline of anonymity, Lydia finds melancholy and rage, which McRobbie has identified as emotional undercurrents of the postfeminist masquerade."[85]

The "tragic structure of feeling"[86] associated particularly with the female experience of disempowerment and frustration continues to characterize Lydia, but does not sufficiently promote a melodramatic plot. Ali triggers it by resuscitating the predator-photographer Grabowski's perspective. Homing in on Lydia, he injects an immediate detective element into the gothic situation of immurement and flight. Following her around town, Grabowski imagines himself as a patriarchal rescuer as well as a hunter. He cannot imagine how anyone would "voluntarily incarcerate" herself "in such tedium," an "endless drag of to and fro," in comparison with her former existence, "live[d] ... at dazzling breakneck speed" (152).

No matter how futile the effort to seize the mode of production of her fantasy image, *Untold Story* culminates in such an attempt. Lydia cannot exterminate the "Diana" assemblage, but her desire to do so attaches to Grabowski as a mortal threat to "Lydia," whose exposure *will*, in terms of the book's premise, kill Diana-Lydia biologically. She indulges in aggressive retaliation against Grabowski, coming close at one point to running him over with her car and finally holding him hostage when he invades her house. The protagonist acquires symbolic phallic power by aiming a gun at the camera and contemplating murder. Though she realizes after the first incident that she, not Grabowski, is "torturing" her (213), Lydia flirts with renewed notoriety—and thus her own destruction—through aggression. "'[Y]ou come in [my house] and attack me, try to rape me,'" she says to Grabowski as she holds him at gunpoint. "I manage to get the gun out of my drawer and I warn you, but you just keep coming at me, you leave me no choice" (230–31). Lydia's occupation of the role of hunter, murderer, and spin-master "stages" the possibility of phallic power at the same time that it shows the utter futility of corporeal destruction as an attempt to prevent the resurrection (and then true biological death) of Diana. Grabowski's photographs must be destroyed; his own life or death is secondary, even perhaps irrelevant, to the circulation of Diana-Lydia. She succeeds in humiliating Grabowski and capturing his pictures, but the resolution merely sends them both back into their patterns of flight and pursuit.

Stripped of the possibility of receiving, as well as granting, a healing touch, Lydia is a closed circuit, a suffering organism in need of protection. She exists in a "paranoid temporality,"[87] experienced by dominant populations who feel themselves in danger and so perpetually ward off a future present.[88] Lydia retreats to a cabin in the woods, where she does housework. For the first time she reads literature, Tolstoy's *The Death of Ivan Ilyich*. Rather than plotting her next move, she considers returning to Kensington and resuming her relationship with Carson. The novel leaves her swimming, in the medium of her staged demise. She is an ascetic without a belief, an ordinary housewife without a house, a family, or a purpose. She becomes more isolated than Nazneen was upon her arrival in London.

The Seamstress Resewn

Brick Lane and *Untold Story* disclose the proximity of femininity to fatality. Managing one's specularity is a discipline and a bodily strategy. Ali's interest in representing women who are distanced from their typifying insignia—"the veil" for Nazneen, the status of visual icon for Diana—allows the novelist to investigate the fabrication of women as assemblages, literary as well as social. Her protagonists refashion themselves through occupying different skins or bodies and opening into incorporative flesh. Ali points to such a dynamic when Nazneen "falls" into the body of the female skater. Seeing resonates with the novel's larger project of dramatizing belief as agential and fleshly. The novel must distance Nazneen from the visible and linguistic insignia of Islam in order to insert the invisible and silent Nazneen into the visual field of London. The maneuver allows for recognition of Nazneen as a woman enabled by a female and contemporary mode of Muslim practice. Her future mode of labor figures into this mode of production as well: she in fact seems poised to enter the realm of commodity that Diana of *Untold Story* has fled. Though she retreats from any identification with Islamists, Nazneen reinterprets her belief as potentiality. Upstone argues that Nazneen's "gradual [public] empowerment" is anchored in changes enacted in domestic space,[89] and her new profession anticipates the rise of modest fashion. The novel's resolution touches upon what Gökariksel and McLarney call "the newly emergent 'Islamic' culture industry, a series of images, practices, knowledges, and commodities that are marketed specifically to 'Muslim women.'"[90] Ali gives no indication of the kind of fashion that Razia and Nazneen will design, and the women's own styles of dress certainly point to diversity: the masculinized Razia now prefers to wear jeans and a headscarf, and Nazneen a sari, while her British-born daughters favor jeans of a different style than Razia's and no head covering. But *Brick Lane* does anticipate the discourse of contemporary Muslim femininities that are "increasingly mediated through the market forces of consumer capitalism" as Muslim women produce as well as consume images and goods, and negotiate "a seeming tension between professed Islamic virtues and the logic of consumer capitalism" ... for "the former is often defined as modesty, thrift, otherworldly devotion. spiritualism, and communitarianism" while the latter signifies "self-indulgence, conspicuous consumption, worldly orientation, materialism, and individualism."[91]

Affective merging with others' flesh enables Nazneen. Lydia's new body freezes her in mortal conflict with a fantasy. *Untold Story* challenges the notion that she possesses an individuality separable from her assemblage as the mediated feminine or from her royal flesh as the mother of princes. Ali's revival of Diana through Lydia's biological body forecloses on the possibility of psychic and agential renewal precisely because her subjectivity and power are so intimately produced by fabrications. The "fate" and fatality Nazneen comes to see as the suicidal resignation of her mother, and not the nature of divinity, never diminish in the story of the fleeing princess. The postfeminist celebratory spectacle becomes a gothic narrative of the masquerade's encroachment on the future. The melodrama of Lydia's masochistic contract actually distracts from other eventualities: had she lived, Diana would have faded from view as she aged. Her postfeminist and postimperial luminosity would have dimmed and with it the power that allowed her to heal and nourish globally. Lydia's isolation registers the solitude that results from such youthful bargains. She feels most comfortable among dogs, but even Rufus does not accompany her into the wilderness of the final scene.

Notes

1 Monica Ali, "Simply a Writer," *A Point of View*, 7 June 2019. BBC Four www.bbc.co.uk/programmes/m0005mkg. Accessed October 16, 2019.
2 Monica Ali, "Simply a Writer."
3 See, for instance, Hasan Saeed Majed, *Islamic Postcolonialism: Islam and Muslim Identities in Four Contemporary British Novels* (Newcastle upon Tyne: Cambridge Scholars Publishing 2015), 75–96; Alistair Cormack, "Migration and the Politics of Narrative Form: Realism and the Postcolonial Subject in *Brick Lane*," *Contemporary Literature* 47.4 (2006): 695–721; Nash, *Writing Muslim Identity*, 37–39; Michaela Canepari Labib, "The Multiethnic City: Cultural Translation and Multilingualism in Monica Ali's *Brick Lane*," *La Torre di Babele: Rivista Letteratura e Linguistica* 3 (2005): 205–23; Yasmin Hussain, *Writing Diaspora: South Asian Women, Culture, and Ethnicity* (Aldershot, Hampshire: Ashgate, 2005), 92–94, 109. The representation of Hasina's language in English, and her abjection as a poor, unattached Muslim woman in Bangladesh, have been a particular focus of criticism. Michael Perfect, "The Multicultural Bildungsroman: Stereotypes in Monica Ali's *Brick Lane*," *Journal of Commonwealth Literature* 43.3 (2008): 109–20, argues that such stereotypes call attention to acts of translation; Jane Hiddleston, "Shapes and Shadows: (Un)veiling the Immigrant in Monica Ali's *Brick Lane*," *Journal of Commonwealth Literature* 40.1 (2005): 52–72, contends that the text encourages evaluation of stereotypes and their entanglement in cultural representations.
4 Ana Sofia Elias, Rosalind Gill, and Christina Scharff, eds., *Aesthetic Labour: Rethinking Beauty Politics in Neoliberalism* (New York: Palgrave-Macmillan, 2017), 18.
5 In this concept, a body is constituted by its relationship to other bodies, objects, and images. Relations are privileged over entities. Graham Livesey "Assemblage," in *The Deleuze Dictionary*, rev. ed., ed. Adrian Parr (Edinburgh: Edinburgh University Press 2010), 18–19.
6 Hemmings and Kabesh, "The Feminist Subject of Agency," 32.
7 Spillers, *Black, White, and in Color*, 206.
8 Amber Jamilla Musser, *Sensational Flesh: Race, Power and Masochism* (New York: New York University Press 2014), 19. Brian Massumi characterizes flesh as "a non-conscious, never to be conscious remainder." *Parables for the Virtual: Movement, Affect, Sensation* (Durham: Duke University Press, 2002), 25.
9 Geoffrey Nash, *Writing Muslim Identity* (London: Continuum, 2012), 38.
10 Sa'diyya Shaik, "A *Tafsir* of Praxis: Gender, Marital Violence, and Resistance in a South African Muslim Community," in *Violence against Women in Contemporary World Religion: Roots and Cures*, ed. Daniel C. Maguire and Sa'diyya Shaik (Cleveland: Pilgrim Press, 2007), 70. Also see Carolyn Moxley Rouse for a discussion of the importance of tafsir in Muslim-American practice. *Engaged Surrender: African American Women and Islam* (Berkeley: University of California Press, 2004), e.g., 63.
11 Gilles Deleuze and Leopold von Sacher-Masoch, *Masochism: Coldness and Cruelty* and *Venus in Furs*, trans. Jean McNeil and Aude Willm (New York: Zone, 1989), 128. At the same time Lydia recalls impoverished mothers of the global south who leave their children in order to sustain them through care labor for the more affluent north.
12 Musser, *Sensational Flesh*, 3. After Deleuze, Musser returns to Leopold von Sacher-Masoch's novel *Venus in Furs* (1870) to establish the provenance and dynamics of what became a compound medicalized syndrome. Richard Krafft-Ebing coined the term "masochism" in his foundational treatise, *Psychopathia Sexualis* (1886), based on the case history of a patient. As Deleuze complains, Sigmund Freud's "Three Essays on the Theory of Sexuality" (1906) and subsequent discussions of masochism firmly embedded Sacher-Masoch's formal strategies in a medical symptomology. Further, Freud repeats Krafft-Ebing's appropriation in the conception of "sadism" based on the literary works of the Marquis de Sade and draws it into relation with masochism, calling masochism sadism's "counterpart." Initially understanding masochism as physiological, an excess stimulation of the nervous system that resulted in both painful and

pleasurable sensation, Freud interprets masochism as a "vicissitude of instinct, a result of a primary instinct, aggression, turned inward," according to Arnold Cooper. "A Child Is Being Beaten" (1919) and "The Economic Problem of Masochism" (1924) elaborate on masochism as a "component" of the death instinct, and a "regulatory principle." For Freud "moral masochism" emerges as a universal (that is male) principle in which "[t]he sadism of the superego and the masochism of the ego supplement each other and unite to produce the same effects," that is, "a sense of guilt" and "a conscience … more severe and more sensitive." Instead of directly producing pleasure, masochism becomes a "condition" for producing pleasure. Deleuze and Sacher-Masoch, *Coldness and Cruelty*, 46. Sigmund Freud, "Three Essays on the Theory of Sexuality" (1905), *The Standard Edition of the Complete Psychological Works of Sigmund Freud*, ed. and trans. James Strachey, vol. 7 (London: Hogarth Press, 1953), 123–46. Arnold M. Cooper, "The Narcissistic-Masochistic Character," in *Masochism: Current Psychoanalytic Perspectives*, ed. Robert A. Glick and Donald J. Meyers (Hillsdale, NJ: Analytic Press, 1988), 119–20. Sigmund Freud, "A Child is Being Beaten," *The Standard Edition of the Complete Psychological Works of Sigmund Freud*, ed. and trans. James Strachey, vol. 17 (London: Hogarth Press, 1957–74), 157–70; "The Economic Problem of Moral Masochism" (1924), in *The Standard Edition of the Complete Psychological Works of Sigmund Freud*," ed. and trans. James Strachey, vol. 19 (London: Hogarth Press, 1957–74), 160–61, 70.

13 Deleuze and Sacher-Masoch, *Coldness and Cruelty*, 46, 17–20, 134. Claire Colebrook, *Deleuze: A Guide for the Perplexed* (London: Continuum, 2006), 54. Like Spillers, Musser opens the sexual and racial premises and elisions that feminist and queer theorists have neglected in their desire to interrogate the heteronorm. Both call attention to white androcentrism in queer analyses.

14 Giorgio Agamben, *Means without End: Notes on Politics*, trans. Vincenzo Binetti and Cesare Casarino (Minneapolis: University of Minnesota Press, 2000), 6.7.

15 Raka Shome, *Diana and Beyond: White Femininity, National Identity, and Contemporary Media Culture* (Urbana: University of Illinois Press, 2014), 1.

16 Evelyn Alsultany, *Arabs and Muslims in the Media: Race and Representation after 9/11* (New York: New York University Press, 2012), 57.

17 See, for instance, Richard Lea and Paul Lewis, "Local Protests over Brick Lane Film, *The Guardian*, July 17, 2006, www.theguardian.com/books/2006/jul/17/film.uk; Mario Cacciottolo, Review "Brick Lane Protestors Hurt over 'Lies,'" BBC News, July 31, 2006, http://news.bbc.co.uk/2/hi/uk_news/5229872.stm; Paul Lewis, "Brick Lane Protests Force Film Company to Beat Retreat," July 26, 2006, www.theguardian.com/uk/2006/jul/27/film.books. All accessed July 24, 2014. The film, directed by Sarah Gavron, was released in 2007.

18 For Germaine Greer's much publicized comments, see "Reality Bites," *The Guardian* 24 July 2006, 24. Ali comments in "The Outrage Economy," *The Guardian*, 12 October 2007, 4. The debate and its premises are examined by Mrinalini Chakravorty, *In Stereotype: South Asia in the Global Literary Imaginary* (New York: Columbia University Press, 2014), 151–86, and Rehana Ahmed, "*Brick Lane*: A Materialist Reading of the Novel and Its Reception," *Race & Class* 52.2 (2010): 25–42. Sarah Brouillette argues that the novel itself is an act of gentrification. "Literature and Gentrification on Brick Lane," *Criticism* 51.3 (2009): 425–49. Also of interest is Sara Upstone, "'Same Old, Same Old': Zadie Smith's *White Teeth* and Monica Ali's *Brick Lane*," *Journal of Postcolonial Writing* 43.3 (2007): 336–49.

19 Chakravorty, *In Stereotype*, 154.

20 Sarah Lyall, "A Different, Happy Ending for Diana? Monica Ali Novel Imagines a Future," *New York Times* Arts Beat, 7 January 2011, https://artsbeat.blogs.nytimes.com/2011/01/07/a-different-happy-ending-for-diana-monica-ali-novel-imagines-a-future/.

21 Sara Upstone argues that this rejection of a narrow focus also forwards a particularly British Muslim approach. *British Asian Fiction: Twenty-First Century Voices* (Manchester: Manchester University Press, 2010), 167–70.
22 *Newsweek* occasioned much more comment by publishing an imagined photo of Diana at fifty, aside Kate Middleton. See *Newsweek*, July 4, 2011, cover. Also see, for instance, David Riedel, "Princess Diana Fascination Reaching Creepy Heights?" CBS News, June 29, 2011, www.cbsnews.com/news/princess-diana-fascination-reaching-creepy-heights/.
23 Monica Ali, "No One is Sacrosanct," *Telegraph*, 8 April 2011, http://www.telegraph.co.uk/culture/books/bookreviews/8434547/No-one-is-sacrosant.html.
24 Monica Ali, "What If Diana Had Lived?" *London Telegraph*, January 15, 2011 www.telegraph.co.uk/culture/books/8261683.
25 Lyall, "A Different, Happy Ending for Diana?"
26 Among them are Joyce Carole Oates's *Blonde* (2000), Philip Roth's *The Plot against America* (2004), and Don DeLillo's *Libra* (1988). *Untold Story* also sits with more recent American novels based on the lives of presidential wives, such as Ann Beattie's *Mrs. Nixon: A Novelist Imagines a Life* (2011) and Curtis Sittenfeld's *American Wife* (2008). Joyce Carole Oates, *Blonde* (New York: Ecco, 2000); Philip Roth, *The Plot Against America* (New York: Houghton-Mifflin, 2004); Don DeLillo *Libra* (New York: Viking, 1988); Ann Beattie, *Mrs. Nixon: A Novelist Imagines a Life* (New York: Scribner, 2011); Curtis Sittenfeld, *American Wife* (New York: Random House, 2008).
27 See for instance, British Council Literature, Writers, "Monica Ali" http://literature.britishcouncil.org/monica-ali; Encyclopedia of World Biography, "Monica Ali," www.notablebiographies.com/newsmakers2/2007-A-Co/Ali-Monica.html. Accessed May 28, 2014.
28 Nash, *Writing Muslim Identity*, 38.
29 Lydia Efthymia Roupakia, "Cosmopolitanism, Religion, and Ethics: Rereading Monica Ali's *Brick Lane*," *Journal of Postcolonial Writing* 52.6 (2016): 653; Dave Gunning also discusses Nazneen's struggle between agency and contingency as well as the role of discipline in her depiction. *Race and Antiracism in Black British and British Asian Literature* (Liverpool: Liverpool University Press, 2012), 97, 191–92.
30 Ahmed, *A Border Passage*, 125.
31 For a different reading of *Brick Lane* that treats the material environment, belief, and stereotype with a focus on smell and taste, see Claire Chambers, *Making Sense*, 71–120.
32 Massumi, *Parables for the Virtual*, 35.
33 Diana Taylor, *The Archive and the Repertoire: Performing Cultural Memory in the Americas* (Durham: Duke University Press, 2003), 137.
34 Sara Ahmed, *The Cultural Politics of Emotion* (New York: Routledge, 2004), 133.
35 Ahmed, *Cultural Politics*, 133.
36 Monica Germanà notes that Nazneen's sari "also functions as hijab." "From Hijab to Sweatshops: Segregated Bodies and Contested Space on Monica Ali's *Brick Lane*," in *Postcolonial Spaces: The Politics of Space in Contemporary Culture*, ed. Andrew Teverson and Sara Upstone (Houndsmills, Basingstoke: Palgrave Macmillan, 2001), 77.
37 Noemí Pereira-Ares, "The Politics of Hijab in Monica Ali's *Brick Lane*," *Journal of Commonwealth Literature* 48.2 (2013): 205. Also see Gunning, *Antiracism*, 98.
38 Pereira-Ares, "The Politics of Hijab," 209.
39 Pereira-Ares, "The Politics of Hijab," 205–10.
40 Garrett Ziegler, "East of the City: *Brick Lane*, Capitalism, and the Global Metropolis," *Race/Ethnicity: Multidisciplinary Global Contexts* 1 (2007): 146.
41 Ziegler, "East of the City," 146.
42 Naila Kabeer, *The Power to Choose: Bangladeshi Women and Labour Market Decisions in London and Dhaka* (London: Verso, 2000).
43 Ziegler, "East of the City," 148.

44 Marx, "The Feminization," 20–22.
45 Ali Ahmad, "Brick Lane: A Note on the Politics of 'Good' Literary Production," *Third Text* 18.2 (2004): 200–201.
46 Chakravorty, *In Stereotype*, 166.
47 Roupakia, "Cosmopolitanism," 653–55, sees regular routines such as housework as dull tasks dictated by patriarchy, but associates Nazneen's spiritual belief with an "ethics of care."
48 Monica Ali, *Brick Lane* (New York: Scribner, 2003), 11. Subsequent references to this text will be cited parenthetically.
49 Nash, *Writing Muslim Identity*, 38–39, regards Nazneen's prayer as an "opiate" and her treatment of the Qur'an as akin to that of a "fetish"; in contrast, Roupakia, "Cosmopolitanism," 655, argues that Nazneen recites the suras in search of meaning.
50 Angela Poon, "To Know What's What: Forms of Migrant Knowing in Monica Ali's *Brick Lane*," *Journal of Postcolonial Writing* 45.4 (2009): 426–27.
51 Shao-ming Kung, "'Walking' Experiences and Self-Empowerment of South Asian Female Immigrants in Monica Ali's *Brick Lane*," *NTU Studies in Language and Literature* 27 (2012): 149–50.
52 In her discussion of the relationship of physical space to the affect of "home," Ezra Mirze Santesso calls attention to a passage in which Nasneen fantasizes that changing her dress to resemble such women would change her sense of identity (228). *Disorientation: Muslim Identity in Contemporary Anglophone Literature* (Houndmills, Basingstoke: Palgrave, 2013), 107.
53 Saba Mahmood, *Politics of Piety: The Islamic Revival and the Feminist Subject* (Princeton: Princeton University Press, 2005), 31.
54 Kane, *Conspicuous Bodies*, 11.
55 Frederick Denny, *An Introduction to Islam*, 2nd ed. (New York: Macmillan, 1994), 67.
56 Talal Asad, *Genealogies of Religion: Discipline and Reasons of Power in Christianity and Islam* (Baltimore: Johns Hopkins University Press, 1993), 67, 125.
57 Mahmood, *Politics of Piety*, 29.
58 Ahmed, *A Border Passage*, 121–24.
59 Puar, *Terrorist Assemblages*, 196.
60 Peter Morey, *Islamophobia and the Novel* (New York: Columbia University Press, 2018), 91–92. Morey justly questions the slide of "freedom" into entrepreneurship and material pleasure, but his definition of "solidarity" seems confined to organized identity groups. He interprets Nazneen's burden of care for her daughters as a retreat into domestic singularity. Her somatic experience and her relationship with Razia become narrowly private, lacking the dimensions of feminist praxis that I find.
61 Chakravorty, *In Stereotype*, 178.
62 Upstone, *British Asian Fiction*, 168.
63 Gunning, *Race and Antiracism*, 103.
64 Chakravorty, *In Stereotype*, 183.
65 See Shome, *Diana and Beyond*, 77–82.
66 Sarah Benton, "The Princess, the People, and Paranoia," in *After Diana: Irreverent Elegies*, ed. Mandy Merck (London: Verso, 1998), 90.
67 Pictured with her young children, she appears in an almost celestial light. Shome, *Diana and Beyond*, 58.
68 Shome, *Diana and Beyond*, 84.
69 Homi K. Bhabha, "Designer Creations," in *After Diana: Irreverent Elegies*, ed. Mandy Merck (London: Verso, 1998), 107–109.
70 Qtd. in Tina Brown, *The Diana Chronicles* (New York: Anchor House, 2007), 331.
71 Shome, *Diana and Beyond*, 120–22, 131.
72 Mark Cousins, "From Royal London to Celebrity Space" in *After Diana: Irreverent Elegies*, ed. Mandy Merck (London: Verso, 1998), 83.

73 Cousins, "From Royal London," 84.
74 Carole Levin, "'Would I Could Give You Help and Succor': Elizabeth I and the Politics of Touch," *Albion* 21.2 (1989): 193.
75 Levin, "Elizabeth I," 195.
76 Levin, "Elizabeth I," 198–99.
77 Shome, *Diana and Beyond*, 85.
78 Ahmed, *Cultural Politics*, 124.
79 Ahmed, *Cultural Politics*, 136.
80 Giorgio Agamben, *Homo Sacer: Sovereign Power and Bare Life*, trans. Daniel Heller Roazen (Stanford: Stanford University Press, 1998), 1.
81 Shome, *Diana and Beyond*, 120–122.
82 Elias, Gill, and Scharff, *Aesthetic Labor*, 38.
83 Sofia Johansson, "'Sometimes You Wanna Hate Celebrities': Tabloid Readers and Celebrity Coverage," in *Framing Celebrity: New Directions in Celebrity Culture*, ed. Su Holmes and Sean Redmond (London: Routledge, 2006), 346. Also see Turner, *Understanding Celebrity*, 94–102.
84 Oscar Wilde, *The Picture of Dorian Gray*, 2nd ed., ed. Michael Patrick Gillespie (New York: W.W. Norton, 2006), 119.
85 McRobbie, *Aftermath*, 98–101.
86 Ien Ang, *Watching Dallas: Soap Opera and the Melodramatic Imagination* (London: Routledge, 2013), 50.
87 Eve Kosofsky Sedgwick, *Touching Feeling: Affect, Pedagogy, Performativity* (Durham: Duke University Press 2003), 147.
88 Puar, *Terrorist Assemblages*, 28.
89 Upstone, *British Asian Fiction*, 177.
90 Banu Gökariksel and Ellen McLarney, "Introduction: Muslim Women, Consumer Capitalism, and the Islamic Culture Industry," *Journal of Middle East Studies* 6.3 (2010): 2.
91 Gökariksel and McLarney, "Introduction," 3–4.

3
MUSLIMAH SEEING AMERICA

Local Colors in Mohja Kahf's *The Girl in the Tangerine Scarf*

The Girl in the Tangerine Scarf (2006) again shows the hijabi outside the house or abode of Islam, the *dar-es-Islam* of classical jurisprudence. *Brick Lane* attempts to depict her through indirection. Mohja Kahf does not engage in the politics of masquerade. She explicitly dramatizes the performativity of veiling practices as a politics and as a cultivation of a spiritual disposition. The migrant brown Muslimah covers and discloses not to cite the convention of becoming unveiled, but to forward a conscious claim on feminist agency in belief. Set primarily in the American Midwest of the 1970s and 1980s, the novel develops the idea that belief should be "manifested inside [one's] particular culture and in specific, earth-rooted human bodies."[1] *The Girl in the Tangerine Scarf* consequently endeavors to make brown and black women the foundation of a "new Islam"[2] in America. Black and brown Muslimah are allied in this vision, which the American optic subverts in crucial respects.

This chapter turns to the problem of visual depiction of the Muslimah in America, where the overweening opposition of black and white as binary racial identities dominates the visual field. Phenotypic race trumps religious difference, ambiguously marked unless by dress, in a default Anglo-Christian scene. The opposition of native and foreign interacts with both racial and religious designation as well. Transnational women[3] who are not black-skinned emerge as the necessary "genre" of transmission of Muslim feminism in the novel because of the historical imaginary attached to black women's bodies in America. The hijab becomes a second skin for Syrian migrant Khadra Shamy. The black Muslimah, whether national or migrant, cannot signify in this way. Her skin to is sealed to her flesh because selective unveiling recalls the forcible disrobing and objectifying display of Africa-descended women as property in the U.S.

DOI: 10.4324/9781003189299-4

The difference between settler and native believer complicates the racial semiotic of Islam in America as well. Economic, cultural, and racial differences between transnational and national Muslims characterize practice in the U.S. ummah, historically rooted in an originary black nationalism. A native/settler subtext emerges from the intrareligious strains between African-American Muslims and more recent arrivals from Muslim-majority countries. Jamillah Karim asserts that many transnational Muslims regard Americans of longer standing as "converts" overly focused on antiracism.[4] Zareena Grewal and Sherman Jackson, among others, have contested such groupings of "indigenous" and "immigrant" Muslim communities by attempting to center on a U.S. Islam, as Kahf does.[5] In the novel, the transnational Muslimah comes to figure the imperial settler of a Mecca-centered Islam and the African-American Muslimah as the native other of heterodox origin.[6] The roots of American Islam in black nationalism curb the potential of a African-*American* woman to exemplify Islam, just as the American scene prevents the Kenyan migrant Zuhura from primarily figuring Muslim identity rather than racial difference. The transnational Muslimah registers violence against belief as distinct from violence against race and privileges a Mecca-centered Muslim practice over the "native" or syncretic belief of African-American Islam.

The Girl in the Tangerine Scarf shows that sociogenic and gendered images of domination still permeate techniques of representation in visual media for woman of color in particular ways,[7] just as the New World context troubles the contemporary manifestation of Kahf's "new Islam." *The Girl* displaces African-American "native" women from the central "rahm" or womb of American Islam as a visual presence, even as the narrative acknowledges the evacuation. Kahf finds the most significant configuration of this absence not in a visual figure but in the poetic technique of "standing before" as a witness to the death of an African Muslimah in America.[8] A topos that "permeates all of Arab culture from high poetry to folksong," "standing before" informs Khadra's return to and occupation of the ground of the black Muslimah's death. The author elaborates, "The classical Arab poet always stands figuratively before the old campsite" in order to "call up presences" from the past in the space that forerunners occupied.[9] This empty site acts as a demonic ground, a naturalized absence in a given knowledge system, in Sylvia Wynter's formulation.[10] Only after Khadra has grounded and soiled herself at the site of Zuhura's assault and death can the novel imagine a Muslim "angle of vision" that enables representing the world from "inside" praying.[11] Khadra, the transnational Arab Muslim woman, must mark Zuhura's assault as Islamophobic as well as racist, and racist as well as gendered. But the U.S. "ground" becomes demonic in the disavowal of the native African-American Muslim woman by newer Muslim as well as older Christian "settlers."

In both her prose and her verse collections, Kahf's desire to claim dark Muslimah as producers of vision, creative and spiritual, seems quite distant from the dynamics of masquerade and mediated images that I discuss in the previous chapters. Yet Khadra might be seen as a forerunner of the situational veiling practiced by young women in Europe and America today. Similarly, the figural centrality of photography in *The Girl* may seem dated or quaint in an era of digital simulacrum and transmission, such as Ali presents in the conundrum of Diana-Lydia's identity. Like homemade garments, the narrative's discourse of "self," of a civil rights agenda, and of literary style, may seem bound up in in bygone modes of feminism and U.S. multiculturalism. Yet Kahf also chimes with contemporary feminist concerns in her emphasis on racial identity and nationality within Islam. In conclusion, I introduce recent reformulations of the visual semiotic evidenced in Kahf's novel, primarily in her recent poetry collection, *Hagar Poems* (2016).

Indiana Doesn't Want You

Set next to earlier touchstones of migrant British Muslim feminist narratives such as Adhaf Souief's *In the Eye of the Sun* (1992) and *The Map of Love* (1999) or Leila Aboulela's *The Translator* (1999) and *Minaret* (2005), *The Girl in the Tangerine Scarf* strongly foregrounds the visibility of observant women. The novel employs pop and visual literary elements while delivering racial and gender critique. Late in the story the protagonist unveils as a selective and situational act. Her decision is not a jubilant assertion of self but an almost accidental gesture of exploration, experienced on a safe "home" ground in pastoral Syria. *The Girl in the Tangerine Scarf* often pits visibility against invisibility as a contrast between the recognition and erasure of an identity group. But in white-majority locations, the ontology of a black person lapses habitually to the fixity of an imago, a mirror-stage imaginary. Franz Fanon writes, "Whether he likes it or not, the black man has to wear the livery that the white man has fabricated for him."[12] In contrast, though he too is understood through stereotype, "the Jewishness of the Jew ... can go unnoticed. He is not integrally what he is ... His acts and behavior are the determining factor."[13] Jewish identity is not read, in other words, through "epidermalization." Marriott explains that sociogenic apprehension involves a visual as well as a psychic phenomenology, for blackness is "embodied in skin color, in the color of skin of blacks, their blackness" but is also lived as "a process of psychic internalization of a socially constructed and enforced ideology."[14] The skin in this sense operates as costume and essence, while somatic characteristics do not indicate religious identity.

The female veil and the raced veil, the masquerade and the mask, all bear upon the ground over which Khadra travels. Kahf indicates the interpretive model of demonic ground through multiple gaps in the field of vision that Fanon's sociogeny hides, flattens, conceals, or masks. Wynter explains the "demonic" logic through *The Tempest*, in which "Caliban's woman" cannot be imagined: the plot is "erect[ed] ... upon the 'ground' not only of her absence, but also on the absence of Caliban's endogenous desire for her, of any longing."[15] *The Girl in the Tangerine*

Scarf begins by foregrounding Khadra's affective dispossession from a visual homogeneity. The narrative opens with her drive through a southern Indiana landscape whose churches and box stores barely cover the historical boneyard of racial and religious minorities. "Liar," she responds to a border sign that proclaims the state's welcome. Not only the "unbearable flatness" of the landscape but also its Christian-commercial development illustrates false hospitality (1). Khadra is in Wynter's terms "dysselected"[16] through genres or kinds of being that are not the normative or generic sex, race, or religion.

The biopolitical zone imagined to protect Lydia in *Untold Story* exposes Khadra to danger. Smell alone (later revealed to belong to Turkish cigarettes as well as to manure) connects her to the environment as a specific familiar. Khadra recalls Hardy's Tess crawling like a fly across the landscape, though here the solitary woman is driving and is recognized by God. Significantly, the windshield protects her. The car enables the single female, just as in other locations hijab may. Khadra asserts her "ownership" in, if not of, the landscape. She is a mobile agent with intimate relation to a scene that does not register her kind. Black diasporic struggles can be read, according to Katherine McKittrick's gloss, as "geographic contests over discourses of ownership" that involve the relations of the body to the property of the self as well as to environments and territories.[17] The capacity to act as a geographic subject—one with agency in relation to the wider sphere, rather than merely an object of study within it— diminishes the subordination of racial others and their fictive masks.

The Girl in the Tangerine Scarf challenges norms of relation through graphic as well as linguistic intertexts. At the beginning of each chapter appears a passage between ruled lines that is set off from and inserted into the text. Drawn from world literature in an eclectic mix, these quotations are framed and separated, recalling the sura, or Qur'anic verse, as a "fenced enclosure."[18] Passages from the Qur'an and hadith mix with the writing of Attar, Rumi, Jane Austen, Aisha Taymuria, Soren Kierkegaard, Frances E. W. Harper, Memphis Minnie, James Baldwin, Jo Harjo, Sandra Cisneros, Adrienne Rich, and Michael Wilkerson. The passages may intensify, contrast with, or counterpoint the plot. Within the flashback to Khadra's childhood, intertextual references also open up the homogeneity of Christian white nativism. *A Passage to India*'s Mrs. Moore (1924) and *Bastard Out of Carolina*'s Bone (1993), for instance, crop up in the environs of the town just beyond western Indianapolis.

The rural landscape of the adult Khadra's return to Indiana, where her family has now been long settled, registers her "ontological absence," as I have said. Using the civil rights history of the 1960s, extending it through the idealistic impulse toward spiritual renewal among transnational and other Muslims during the 1970s and 1980s, and concluding with post 9/11 xenophobia and bigotry in the early millennium, the novel chronicles Islamophobia before it existed in its current form.[19] Racialized xenophobia, but not the full-blown Islamophobia connected to the discourse of terror, characterized the area. In the 1970s, midwestern hostility to Arabs was propelled by soaring gas and oil prices, economic recession, and loss of factory jobs—particularly for the automotive industry so important to the region—and farm foreclosures. The seizing of American hostages in Iran during the 1979 revolution also strongly energized anti-Arab sentiment. The Iranian uprising stemmed in part from the broader and longer Islamic revival movement in many Muslim-majority countries. In this and other respects, the Shamy family exemplifies a strain of postwar Muslim migration to the U.S. Muslim émigrés, largely men, "increased more than fivefold" from 1945 to 1965. Students desiring higher education in technical fields and activist religious fleeing persecution from "secular, nationalist regimes … that viewed Islamicist organizations as a political threat"[20] impelled the increase. Like the Shamys, as well as Kahf's own parents, many of these émigrés promoted religious revival. They were inspired by figures such as Abdul A'la Mawdudi of Jama'at-I Islami and Sayyid Qutb of the Muslim Brotherhood. Such activists founded the Muslim Student Association (MSA) in Champaign-Urbana, Illinois, in 1963.[21] From this location the organization spread to other campuses in the Midwest and in 1973 established a headquarters at the al-Amin Mosque in Gary, Indiana. GhaneaBassiri observes: "For MSA activists, adherence to Islamic belief and practices was not only a religious duty but a transformative experience." He continues:

> Qutb's and Mawdudi's writing appealed to them because both of these authors began with the assumption that the religion of Islam is necessarily transformative … for individual Muslims and for Muslim societies, and they went on to interpret Islam as an all-encompassing 'way of life' for the modern world … They went back to the Qur'an and the Prophetic Tradition (the Hadith) as the original and purest source of Islam.[22]

The Shamys fled Syria through Egypt. The novel alludes to American frontier settler narratives in order to characterize their emigration. As members of an ethnoreligious minority, the Muslims push into a nonMuslim "wilderness" chosen without knowledge of or attention to the native locale. Like later ethnic and racially marked immigrant groups, they are inserted into a European Protestant hegemony. The Dawah Center that the Shamys join in Indiana[23] appears to stem from an MSA community outreach branch actually based in Plainfield, Indiana, which became the Islamic Society of North America (ISNA) headquarters in 1973. By 1970s Plainfield, like the "Simmonsville" of the novel, had in some ways become a bedroom community of Indianapolis. It remained in other ways a small town of about 8,000 residents. Basic research almost entirely informed the migrants' decision to settle there: in graduate schools, the Dawah group had chosen from the map. "'There! That's the middle of the country, so Muslims in all parts of the land can find us,'" Khadra relates of her parents' generation. "That Indianapolis … had an international airport, low crime rates, and affordable land, was enough to their minds. None of them had ties to the people there" (44). Even the African-American Muslims of northern Indianapolis who joined the Dawah Center are strangers to "the lives of the small town residents of Simmonsville" and to the farmers in foreclosure in the outlying rural areas. About them, the narrative states, the Muslim students "knew next to nothing, and didn't care to know" (45).

In Indiana the family is screened through racial difference, though one not necessarily registered in terms of their appearance, as Fanon's description of a Jewish stereotype based on behavior suggests. Legally, too, rulings from the first half of the twentieth century in America cast "individuals of Middle Eastern descent" on the dividing line of a binary racial system. Courts classified them as white "by the thinnest of margins" in some cases, while in others they "utilized a performative heuristic that betrayed the constructed nature of the entire race-making enterprise,"[24] John Tehranian states. The naturalization laws at the base of these rulings were dissolved in 1952, but their gestalt informed civil rights cases in the 1960s. The conflation of national origin and religious affiliation with racial identification has since only intensified in the American imaginary.[25]

Though the Shamys understand themselves as Syrian refugees working to transform Islam, they move into a Christian American optic determined by the hierarchy of white over black skin and a provincial suspicion of outsiders. Settler status shapes Kahf's presentation of the religious minority. "In America, you could not be passive about enacting your faith; you had to 'Do for Self,'" the third-person narrator relates. "No one was there to do it for you, like in the Old Country." This task demanded critical discernment of the religious minority (96).

Transnational women foreground the paradoxes of settler/native, white/black, and Christian/nonChristian belief, as well as the frozen signifiers of tradition and modernity. The Muslim community encourages women such as Zuhura to assert their religious identity through veiling practices, seen as traditional but reinterpreted in modernity. Reina Lewis summarizes the insights of Leila Ahmed and other scholars in describing this shift:

> [T]he very identification of the hijab as Muslim can be seen as historically produced and politically intentioned, with Islamic revivalism effectively disavowing the headscarf's pre-Islamic origin and multi-faith regional uses in earlier periods to resignify it as both exclusively Islamic and as the key marker of female piety.[26]

Thus in the U.S. veiling makes a paradoxical visual code, on the one hand proclaiming modesty and piety and on the other group display. As models of the group, women are encouraged to acquire social mobility and prestige through education. At the same time they are expected to accede to their roles as wives and mothers who subordinate their opinions, desires, and activities to those of their husbands and children.

As a racial minority within a religious minority and a woman within them both, the Kenyan-American Zuhura occupies demonic ground. She disrupts white Christian and transnational Muslim norms in her appearance, personality, and action. Zuhura establishes her "unvisible" claim to the territory in which she lives through her bold personality, the territory of her "self," depicted as a "geographic subject rather than an object of study."[27] By virtue of her appearance as well as her self-assertion, her behavior and affect, Zuhura "d[oes]n't fit what the [white] locals think they know about 'someone who look[s] like her,'" that is, an Africa-descended woman. Her body produces "a bristle in the air," as if "her physical presence [is] a challenge to knowledge held dear ... without [the interlocutors] even being aware of it, necessarily" (44). Her speech adds to the dissonant image and aura: "At the sound of her voice, something went 'click' and disconnected between them and her" (44). But Zuhura also shows that racism within the transnational community infuses issues of religious authority and legitimacy. The category "Muslim" is unsettled by the presence of the hijabed black woman, a disturbance of the sociogeny of her race and gender in the patriarchal American scene.

Zuhura is connected to the tensions between "national" African-American and transnational (some, such as Zuhura, more recently arrived African) Muslims. Textually, she acts as a hinge between transnational and national Muslims such as Hakim and Hanifa, friends of Khadra's age, and Aunt Khadija, the secretary at the Dawah Center, all of whom descend from "heterodox" American strains of Islam. The roots of their belief were in the Moorish Temple of Science, founded in 1925 in Chicago by Noble Drew Ali, and its offshoot, the Nation of Islam, founded in 1930 in Detroit by Fard Muhammad.[28] Noble Drew Ali capitalized on African-Americans' exposure to Islam during the 1920s through Masonic lodges, the Ahmadiyya movement, and migrant Muslims, as well as through the allied universalism of Marcus Garvey's nationalist Universal Negro Improvement Association. Garvey "synthesi[ed] ... Islamic and popular spiritualist practices into a prophetic nationalist movement that appealed to African American migrants from the South" who sought jobs in the North.[29] After the death of Nation leader Elijah Muhammad in 1975, his son, Warith Deen Muhammad, began "the Second Resurrection" to bring its doctrines into closer alliance with historical Sunni Islam. GhaneaBassiri notes, however, that W. D. Muhammad and his followers "did not understand their conversion specifically" in terms of mainstreaming with an Arab focus. They placed the shift "in the context of African American history" by "indigenizing mainstream Islamic beliefs and practices" and "reinterpreting the teachings of the Nation of Islam metaphorically in order to resignify them in terms of mainstream Islamic beliefs"—a modification attributed to "reversion" rather than "conversion."[30] In the novel Khadija expresses similar ideas when the young Khadra asks her when she became a Muslim. Khadra has seen photos of Khadija as an average American girl with a beehive hairstyle. She has heard her own father, Wajdy Shamy, say that the "Elijah Muhammad business was nonsense." Khadija asserts that she, like the Shamys, was "born" a Muslim, and says that this is a "natural" state to which she has "*reverted*" (24, italics mine).

Consequently, both African-American and transnational Muslims can lay claim to a more "originary" or legitimate Islam: the migrants through their roots in Muslim-majority locations and "orthodox" practice, and the African-Americans through their nurturing of a "native" American and Afrocentric Islam. In the novel, color prejudice among the migrant Muslims crops up in casually racist remarks. When Khadra and her friends want to get their hair corn-rowed like Zuhura's, Aunt Téta remarks that her niece has "pretty hair, not like that repulsive hair of *Abeed*, all kinky and unnatural" (75). Later, Khadra's brother Eyad explores the possibility of proposing to a Sudanese doctor's daughter who has "piety, character, beauty, and brains, the right language, the right home culture." His father Wajdy responds, "But for heaven's sake, she's black as coal!" and his mother Ebtehaj communicates through silence that she doesn't want mixed race grandchildren (138–39). Structural tensions between national and migrant American Muslims are voiced through Hakim, whose practice acquires a "hard edge" after his sister Hanifa becomes pregnant and is sent away to nonMuslim relatives in the South (136). He argues with Khadra about pronouns: "'You all' is immigrant brothers and sisters. 'We' is black people. I mean, African people, African people of the North American wilderness." When Khadra argues that Hakim is not African in the way Zuhura and her mother are, and that Islam is not racist, Hakim asks, "[H]ow many Dawah Center officers are black? How many immigrants do you know who've married African American? Be for real!" (137).

"Difference is monstrous; it brings death. The sight of real, unerasable difference, face to face, is unbearable," Kahf says in her analysis of Braimimonde's plot in *Chanson de Roland*.[31] Her claim chimes with Sylvia Wynter's analysis of the "monstrous" sexualities of Caliban and of the native mate who she posits for him as an "ontological absence" in the play.[32] Zuhura serves as a primary staging ground for the violence, instability, and beauty produced by and around Muslimahs' bodies, and more specifically around Africa-descended women's bodies. The question is always one of mobility and confinement, safe and demonic territory, for a nonwhite and foreign woman subject.

The Girl in the Tangerine Scarf casts Zuhura as Khadra's role model. Both women are attached to a Mecca-centered geography. Like American-born brown- and black-skinned women, Zuhura and Khadra are subjected to color racism but free from "conversion" or "reversion" narratives, as well as from the Sunni and Shi'a division. Zuhura clears a space for Khadra's development of assertive yet observant feminine practice in the U.S. She anticipates the dilemmas that Khadra will face as a young adult. Like Zuhura, Khadra marries while she is attending college and gets involved in political activities on campus. Zuhura also demonstrates modest and Afrocentric beauty practices. Both the display of beauty and the reception of it are illustrated in the episode of Zuhura's henna party, containing the novel's first sustained physical description of a female figure. In this all-female setting, customs of beauty are transmitted while women's own sight is empowered and extended. From Khadra's perspective, the narrator reports:

> Zuhura was stunning. Her braids, gold-beaded in dazzling constellations, clicked pleasantly when she turned her head. Her lower lip had a mauve sheen that matched her eye shadow. Her body was plump and glowing with health, as if she'd just stepped out of a sauna. Her gown was cobalt blue woven with bronze so that it seemed a different color with every shift of light, like a night sea with schools of fish under the surface.
>
> (80)

Like the later image of Khadra as a developing film, its images swimming up to the surface, Zuhura is rendered beautiful through motion, color, and vitality. To these qualities are added haptic texture and the shine of health. Khadra's admiration of the bride accompanies empowerment of her own eye: during the festivities she receives her first camera and first wears make-up and jewelry. Zuhura acts as a stimulus to the novel's imagination of a reciprocal gaze of women onto one another that is aligned with the divine gaze, "the seen and unseen world" drawn together (161). Yet the protagonist is shown to document defilement rather than celebration in her first photographs. The clubhouse where the party takes place is vandalized while the women are at prayer. Khadra takes pictures of the slogans: "FUCK YOU, RAGHEADS, DIE," signed "KKK 100% USA" (82). Like the car, then, the clubhouse affords an empowered gaze free of sociogenic and sexist objectification. The structure provokes violence, unleashed in Zuhura's later rape and murder.

Zuhura's corpse becomes a bookend to the portrayal of her vitality at the henna party. Empowered vision fails to reconcile the sights. Rather than asking why or even entirely accepting that her daughter has suddenly died, Zuhura's mother, Aunt Ayesha, experiences her shock as a visual illusion:

> What if God was tricking her senses? All she really knew was [that the body] seemed to be Zuhura. What did the Queen of Sheba say in the Qur'an when Solomon showed her the impossible sight of her own throne in his polished court where it couldn't, simply couldn't be—she wisely said, "This *seems* to be it." Your senses can trick you. They are not the final arbiter. Only God, the Unseen, is the final arbiter.
>
> (94)

The Dawah Center first regards Zuhura as a martyr to the faith. But a "gap" between the living Zuhura and her various images opens when the community learns that she did not attend the meeting that she gave as the reason for staying late on campus on the night of her disappearance. The narrator reports: "A small cleft opened between Zuhura's stated plans and her action" (91). The Dawah community begins to doubt her. People speculate that Zuhura was "asking for trouble" in traveling alone at night to her college activities, or had been given the "evil eye" because of her accomplishments. The local newspapers distort her in different ways: the African-American *Freeman* does not mention her religion; the city papers call her a "foreigner" and an "international student," though her family lives locally. A "Take Back the Night" rally featuring white women dominates the front page of one paper, which relegates Zuhura's death to a tiny item on a back page (95). The murder is treated as random rather than a bias crime against a black or foreign woman. (The legal category of "hate crime" did not yet exist.)

Khadra, however, continues to regards Zuhura as a heroic martyr, manifested at the center of Islam. During her hajj, Khadra undergoes the ecstatic experience of swirling and merging with the global ummah as the "circular system" of the body. As the worshippers rotate, "a tall black teenaged girl, rounded-shouldered like Zuhura" whispers into Khadra's ear "*Salamu. Ya Salam*," a message of peace and surrender. Female metaphors for the Ka'ba underscore the association. The black rock is "the Lady of Night," "Islam's Lady in Black," and "Sakina, the serenity within the whirl" (162–63). But Khadra's emphatic installation of black women at the core of Islam's dynamic movement contrasts with a misunderstanding of female mobility in Saudi. Upon arrival, Khadra hears the *adhan* for *fajr* prayer as "the long-awaited invitation," calling her personally. She sets off alone for the mosque (166). She is stunned that she is not allowed to enter. Khadra argues with her parents and the police who drag her back to her residence, that going to the mosque is spiritual participation, citing scripture to support her case. In response, the police regard her as a "joke" or "some kind of bad woman" for being out alone in the morning darkness (167–68). Khadra's anger and shame are compounded by sexual assault by her cousin's Muslim friend (177). Khadra feels her hajj is emptied of meaning because of the two experiences. She returns to Indiana as her "only home" (179), where the humble storefront mosque has a space for women. The realization anticipates her later acceptance of Indiana as an essential element of her own and her parents' identity.

Racial Sociogeny and the Semiotics of Sex-Gender

As I have shown, Zuhura stimulates the novel's imagination of a reciprocal gaze among women that is aligned with the divine gaze, which draws the unseen and seen worlds together. The unseen world also pertains to Wynter's demonic ground. It renders subjects "unvisible" by eradicating them from the landscape of historical representation. Kahf draws on actual events that took place in the 1960s and 1970s to fund her imaginative rendering of demonic ground from the perspective of the early millennium. Recasting distant historical events helps the novel bring into view xenophobia, racism, and sexual violence as continuous with the formation of Islamophobia in the U.S. Yet in spite of these readings of Indiana soil "outside of the received systems of time, space, and knowledge," the racialized and gendered dimension of the sociogenic narrative remains the framing foreground. "Christian terror" is not distinguishable from racist terror, and sexual violence little distinguished as a form of social terror. Only the attack on the clubhouse during Zuhura's henna party registers as an attack on Muslims as a religious identity group. Through it, Kahf makes concrete the protest and accompanying threats provoked by the presence of the Dawah Center, connected to the MSA's acquisition of 124 acres of land in Plainfield in 1976. According to the Polis Center archive, Plainfield "was forced to acknowledge the xenophobic tendencies of some of its residents" during the legal proceedings. Petitions against the planned construction of the mosque failed in a circuit court case. "The protests took on a racist cast" during the appeals process "when a sign at the entrance to the property owned by the MSA was knocked down and painted with the letters KKK."[33] (The mosque was completed in 1983 and the campus now serves as the headquarters of the ISNA.) In the novel the Muslim residents of Simmonsville are "forced" to acknowledge such sentiments much sooner, as Kahf dramatizes through smaller scale acts of hostility not recorded in the few public records.

Zuhura's death later in the novel resonates deeply with the murder on September 16, 1968, of the 21-year-old African-American and Christian Carol Jenkins in Martinsville, Indiana, proximate to the university town of Bloomington to the south, where Zuhura attends college.[34] Jenkins, who lived in a town farther north, was in Martinsville with a group selling encyclopedias door to door. Kahf combines the Jenkins murder with the events of a decade later, when a neo-Nazi group planned but never executed a march in Skokie, Illinois, on June 25, 1978.[35] Skokie, a northern suburb of Chicago with a large Jewish population, among them 5,000 Holocaust survivors, legally challenged the group's right to march. Though Frank Collin, leader of the National Socialists of America, eventually won the case, the group instead held two rallies in Chicago's Marquette Park, a historically significant site of antiracist struggle in the 1960s.[36] On the night when Zuhura is returning late from the Bloomington campus, the narrative reports: "Klansman [are] returning from Skokie, where they'd not been allowed to have the big rally they had planned. Simmonsville, Martinsville, Greenwood, Plainfield, not to mention Indianapolis—all these towns had sent truckloads of bigots to the march." They'd be returning "mad as hornets" (89). Zuhura disappears that night.

Not until 2002 was the Jenkins murder partly solved, and its subtext of sexual violence brought into focus through newly reported details.[37] The daughter of Kenneth Richmond revealed her childhood witness of his murder of a young African-American woman. Shirley Richmond McQueen was particularly convincing to investigators because she remembered that the victim was wearing a yellow scarf, a detail that had never been revealed publicly. McQueen reported that she remained in the car while a friend of her father's held back

Jenkins' arms and her father stabbed Jenkins to death with a screwdriver. The now elderly murderer, who was in declining physical and mental health, died before he could stand trial. His accomplice has never been identified.[38] In the immediate aftermath of these events, defenders of Martinsville were quick to point out that McQueen was from Indianapolis, and local efforts were made to improve the town's image as a "sundown town" with no African-American residents.[39]

Today in the U.S., hijab would be targeted scopically as the offspring of the yellow scarf, a visual marker of ethnic-religious threat that is subtextually racialized. In an earlier era, Khadra's practice of covering calls attention to her racialized foreignness but not necessarily to the threat it encodes through visual alliance with the perverse and dangerous Muslim man. This dimension of the stereotype was revitalized during the first "Gulf War" in 1991, through the doctored, iconic image of a satanic Saddam Hussein that appeared on the cover of a major newsmagazine.

Throughout the novel, the author uses dress to reflect Khadra's *taqwa*, or inner state of devotion, as well as her psychic state.[40] She assumes hijab as a sign of adulthood and of political identity, a desire to exert control over the sexual objectification of female bodies and over the display of class distinction. Annelies Moors, summarizing the work of many scholars, describes the semiotic of Khadra's practice: "[T]he ascendance of an Islamic revival movement in the 1970s and 1980s encouraged a growing number of women to start wearing recognisably Islamic, covered styles of dress." During the era, Moors notes, "this meant a move towards a uniform and sober style, such as full-length, wide coats in muted colors, that many hoped would do away with the sartorial distinctions between the wealthy and the poor."[41] Khadra's understanding of covering fits the description. She feels a "thrill" at her assumption of "the vestments of a higher order." The scarf is "a kind of crown on her head" that sends her forth "lightly and heavily into the world" with "new grace" (112). Later she uses the kind of austere dress that Moors describes as a form of rebellion against what she comes to regard as the more complacent form of Islam practiced by her parents. "Radical Islam" is Khadra's "James Dean" during this period, her dark, stiff garments a kind of leather jacket: she dons a black headscarf and a navy-blue jilbab, which her parents find extreme for a young woman—even though her father, a tailor, made the garment at her request (149). She is "stern" in dress and gaze when they joke about her funereal appearance. Khadra understands her dress as a form of Muslim "action" in the world and her jilbab as a "shield." Her imagination is crowded with representations of the heroic women of history and literature, such as Sumaya, "the first Muslim martyr," who died from being raped with a spear (167).

Khadra does make fashion choices about her public display, but she understands her clothing primarily through a political semiotic rather than as an expression of personal style. Like contemporary U.S. movements promoting identification with blackness and with self-knowledge as crucial to Muslim practice, *The Girl in the Tangerine Scarf* is relatively unconcerned with the relationship of dress to sexual display or to consumer practice. Even the "marriage market," portrayed in *Girls of Riyadh* as an intense arena of scrutiny and surveillance, is minimally scopophilic for Khadra and for the narrative's representation of her appearance. Marriage allows her to stay at Indiana University's main campus, rather than attend a satellite commuter college, and initially affords her physical and social freedoms. Juma, her suitor, whose name resounds with the meaning of Friday as the day of prayer, likes Khadra's Arabic pronunciation, her traditional practice, and her intelligence (223). The narrative pays little attention to any assessment of her appearance. Looking at herself in her wedding dress, Khadra regards herself "almost pretty" in spite of her facial baby fat and her "short-waisted" and "plump" figure (214). After their marriage the narrator reveals from his point of view that Juma is a "breast man" who could see that she was not "flat" even under her "boxy jilbabs" (223–24).

Nonetheless, Khadra's defeat as a self-identified warrior comes from her marriage and the role her husband and community expect her to take as a wife. If Zuhura signifies the reality of nativist, male extirpation of women in movement, Khadra experiences a lesser but similar disciplining from within her community. Initially Khadra "blissful[ly]" enjoys the companionship, sensuality and social prestige that come with her marriage to Juma, a Kuwaiti student. But he soon begins to raise objections to her movements. First he argues that it is "unIslamic" to display her body bike riding, then says that "she look[s] ridiculous … riding a bicycle in hijab" (228). Finally he formally forbids her to ride the bike. His interdiction shocks Khadra—her father would never invoke this right to control her mother, she thinks—but she complies (229–30). Juma's encroachment continues with other expectations of her, to cook for them, though they are both students, and to refrain from speaking to other men without his supervision. But the real crisis of Khadra's marriage occurs when she becomes pregnant, in spite of her careful attention to birth control.

"My life *is* in danger," Khadra insists, as she turns the biological rationale for abortion into an agentic one that emotionally resonates with Zuhura's physical extermination (244). Khadra understands the demands of what she regards as premature maternity to be the death of the possibility of a self that she has not yet borne. The narrative presents this exigency as a spiritual as well as a psychological and educational one. It should not be equated with the shallow pursuit of the "selfish individualism" Khadra and her family connect with mainstream America: "You have to have a self to even start on a journey to God," she thinks (248). The "monster" of difference that Kahf elsewhere links to perceptions of the other now becomes installed within her body as a parasite. Khadra experiences pregnancy as an internal invader, "reaching out its tentacles, even up her throat" (249). Though Islam accepts abortion for any reason until the fourth month of pregnancy, and though she prays repeatedly for guidance, her decision to terminate ends her marriage, estranges her from her parents, and horrifies even her feminist friend Joy, though she does accompany Khadra to the procedure.

Khadra's abortion sends her into crisis. It brings her to an emptiness from which she is forced to reevaluate her goals, expectations, and beliefs. The rupture recalls the "cleft" of Zuhura's representation, coincident with the possession of a female anatomy. Khadra can no longer function as a model member of the community. She becomes the subject of gossip. She feels suicidal. She experiences revulsion for her own life, imagined as elements of her body that she wants to expel, as she did the vomit of morning sickness or the blood clots that fell out of her after the surgery. The narrative in these ways represents Khadra's trauma as an emptying out of her interior, aligned with her earlier study of Islam in the classroom and her encounter with Sufism. The knowledge leads her to the insight that she had previously known Islam from one perspective (231). The blood clots also resonate with sura 96, the "Clinging Clot" or surat al-Alaq, which relates the birth of humankind. Significantly, however, Khadra wants to "abort the Dawah Center and its entire community": "All those hard polished surfaces posing as spiritual guidance. All that smug knowledge … it needed to be cleared out." She decides that it all "ha[s] to go" (261–62). To transform herself, Khadra must examine her practice and knowledge in light of the contradictions of custom and word, apparent clarity and experienced hypocrisy.

It is a topos of exilic and migrant stories that the traveler returns to—conventionally *his*—origin to reconnect with a positive identity and normative experience. In reversals of this trajectory, the returned discovers actual alienation or difference from the homeland as a result of time, distance, change, and idealization of the past. *The Girl in the Tangerine Scarf* presents three such returns. Each represents a major aspect of Khadra's impossible identity. In conclusion, she returns to the home of her actual childhood experience, in Indiana, which creates the present-tense frame. The "drive" toward revising the displaced home as the site of death for the U.S. Muslimah is facilitated by earlier trips to origins, the first to Mecca on hajj with her family, the second to Kuwait with Juma, and the third, after her abortion and divorce, to Syria and the home of her Aunt Téta, the "other mother" who visited Khadra in Indiana during her childhood. In contrast to her Saudi trip, Khadra's journey to Syria as an adult affords her the experience of her birth home, a connection that she feels physically. The "rebirth" of her self as pure and new that she had expected to take place in Mecca takes place here, under her aunt's tutelage. "Who can live without a self?" her aunt asks her. Her aunt distinguishes "ego" from "ego-monster" and counsels her niece to attend to her own needs (270). As she had done before Khadra's marriage, Téta gives her niece valuable old coins as insurance and as a form of independence. In Syria, where Khadra feels safe and acknowledged, in touch with poetry and natural beauty, she purchases a "tissuey" fabric of "brilliant tangerine color" made of Bangalore silk. She has the piece cut and hemmed into matching scarves (293).

The purchase and fabrication signify Khadra's connection to her aunt, but also to a yearning for "beauty" that her family home lacked. She now understands beauty as an aesthetic pleasure rather than a display of style or a "frivolity" (293). Though nowhere explicitly recorded in the novel, the tangerine scarf of course also alludes to Carol Jenkins' yellow one, and to the mixture of red blood with this color, associated with the sun.

The Girl in a Tangerine Scarf more dramatically reimagines Western Muslim women's representation and their prolific binaries when Khadra removes her veil in public. It is the culminating moment of her changes in hijab mode.[42] Out in the country, when her veil slips off, sunlight falls on her as it does on a sheet of film, a blessing of warmth she feels through her body. The narrator relates: "*Sami allahu liman hamadah.* Here was an exposure, her soul an unmarked sheet shadowing into distinct shapes under the fluids. Fresh film. Her self, developing." Significantly, her aunt is watching Khadra at this moment, and her niece imagines that she too is experiencing "*kashf*, the unveiling of light, which stands also for inner radiance" (293). Daphne Grace describes this concept as "seeing with the heart as well as the eyes."[43] The moment of reciprocal look and experience between generations is significant, as is the shared material of the scarf, which she dons in a "non-Arab depata style."[44] Khadra's epiphany disrupts the binary of veiling and unveiling as master signifiers of piety and freedom. In fact, unlike the beautiful tangerine scarf, this action moves the metaphor for the Muslim woman into a register of performative reception, registration, and agency. Fabric is made to align with the metaphor of film and the action of many images developing as they seem to swim up into visibility. Khadra realizes "[h]ow veiling and unveiling are part of the same process, the same cycle," like day and night. Both are essential to "the development of the soul in its darkroom" (309). The actions chime with a later image of the way perception and knowledge are disclosed: "Reality unveils itself for an instant and then just when you think you've got a shot at it, the shutter goes down and the light is evaporated" (421).

"In the novel," Toossi observes, "acts of veiling, unveiling, and reveiling, are treated as different stages in the process of the maturation of the Muslim self and in the light of epistemological aspects of the individual's relationship to the faith."[45] Given Khadra's own history of schoolyard forcible unveilings, the larger violent histories of forced unveiling as part of the secularizing ethos in countries such as Syria and Turkey, and Ghumkhor's reading of "becoming unveiled," such an act is fraught representationally.[46] It must be also be seen in relation to the Africa-descended Muslimah as an epistemological and ontological rupture in "the" Muslim self represented here. Khadra does not decide to institute one mode of dress permanently. Kahf in fact reverses the stereotypical equation of freedom with unveiling by again highlighting the association of fabric with skin and both states with different styles of bodily habitus. Back in the city, Khadra notices the difference between garments "that fit to the line of her body" and those that grant it "freedom and space" (312). Such sentiments are echoed by women who cover such as the American scholar Nousheen Yousuf-Sadiq. She recalls,

> As insecure as I'd been without hijab, I became equally … secure with my hijab, and I felt something I had never felt before: control. Without hijab, society's standards of beauty dictated how I presented myself to the world and, by extension, how I thought of myself when I didn't measure up [physically].[47]

Khadra, too, feels disoriented by her lack of covering. Yet she learns that both kinds of dress have their "moment" corresponding to "modes of being" (32). Khadra does not equate her lack of hijab with a lack of modest appearance, any more than she sees it as the chief indication of her belief or piety. When she is not wearing it, she realizes that she experiences a distinct bodily habitus. Her decisions about dress are intimately bound up in her own bodily comfort, decisions, and flexibility.

The series of visual associations could not work in the same way for the African-American Muslimah. As Saidiya Hartman notes of racial optics in the nineteenth-century, "black flesh itself is identified as the source of opacity," yet must be displayed and humiliated.[48] Auntie Khadija in fact makes the comparison between the unveiled body and the body on the auction block (25). Zuhura's unveiling would not escape the potential for "pornotroping," Hortense Spillers' term for the dehumanized and captive African body as sexualized, powerless, and othered. Such an image frames a body as "a source of irresistible, destructive sensuality" and at the same time a "thing."[49] In Alexander Weheliye's gloss, it "unconceals the literally bare, naked, and denuded dimensions of bare life, underscoring how political domination frequently produces a sexual dimension that cannot be controlled by the forces that (re)produce it" in representations.[50] Thus the image of disrobing or unveiling of Africa-identified subjects connects to "bare life" through affective stickiness, an intractability that impedes the flow of becoming. Because of such scopic fixity, the "disrobed" black woman's body is barred from rendering, even in a linguistic rather than a visual portrayal, a heroic, questing woman. At the same time, the Africa-descended American woman, whether national or transnational, is less suited to display rape as the quintessential racialized violence, in part because the act cannot be rendered starkly and unambiguously legible, as the lynched, chained, or whipped captive body has done historically. In this sociogenic system, Zuhura's skin cannot be detached from her flesh: they are fused. Moreover, her otherness must signify as American and default Christian rather than as transnational Muslim blackness.

Khadra retains her previous standards of modesty in unveiling and of chastity in her single state. She practices without adhering to other customs of her old community. In her move to Philadelphia, where she studies and pursues a career as a photographer, she meets women of different faiths, or lack of faith, as well as Muslim women who differ greatly from her.

Khadra's release into an urban America with cosmopolitan diversity mitigates her own sense of the binary choices that the racial-religious optic forced upon her in the Midwest. Kahf enables Khadra as a model of feminist Muslim-American practice, but she also engages with the discourse of vision through critique *and* exercise of it.

The narrative is alert to the dangers of spectacle and of mobility even as it embraces Khadra's agency through some public visibility. The dialectic of formal associations with various angles of vision and their potential to slide into essentialism, as well as the quick trip from mobile representation into old oppositions, registers most vividly in Khadra's return to the touchstone of Zuhura. The narrative's elegy for the black Muslimah as agent also reveals sensitivity to the problematic category of heroic female martyrdom. She wonders about Zuhura's actual being rather than her exemplary status: "what if," instead, "she had been just a regular Muslim girl trying to make her way through the obstacle course?" (357). Khadra's question coincides with her encounter with Hakim and her realization that she had been part of the disciplinary policing of her own peers. "What could account for such a huge gap?" between her understanding of herself in the past and Hakim's memory of her, she wonders (396).

The "gap" between the living Zuhura and her various images collapses here, just as the opposition between Hoosier and Muslim does in Khadra's late reading of Indiana. The narrative finally produces a larger revision of the Hoosier Muslimah than the eye alone can capture. This presentation involves a performative occupation. At the site, Khadra dreads an approaching man. He turns out to be her brother Jihad. He acts as a bewildered but comforting presence who "sees" and holds Khadra as she keens. As Khadra elegiacally "stands before," and gets into, the site of rape and death, Jihad "stands before" as well, most importantly before his sister as a successor to Zuhura, whose absence remains otherwise "unmarked" as demonic ground.

Prayer constitutes the "secret embedded structure of the novel,"[51] according to Kahf. It is dramatized only after the scene of Khadra's designation and occupation of formerly demonic ground. The episode is delivered through omniscient vision. The narrative makes brief departures from a limited third-person perspective throughout the novel, but does so most significantly when representing Khadra praying in Bloomington, at the Muslim conference she attends in the present-tense narrative. Her perspective is embedded in a vision of the whole scene in Assembly Hall, where the IU basketball team plays. The narrator observes from a high, distanced, third-person vantage before entering into Khadra's perspective from below. "Several hundred Muslim foreheads touch the arena floor in unison, [Khadra's] own widow's-peaked one among them," the narrator observes. "Only a thin bedsheet between the forehead and the hardwood. Palm, palm, knee, knee, points of contact with the ground." But the narration seems to merge the two perspectives in Khadra's own, as she observes, displays, and enacts the prayer among the campus assistants in their red IU T-shirts who observe "with curiosity." In *sadja*, Khadra thinks: "'Here is the way Muslims touch the ground' ... 'Here is the way we shift our bodies daily, and alter our angle of looking'" (54). After she finishes the salam, she considers prostration as an angle of vision for her photography, because in it "one see[s] the underbelly of things." Instead, however, she tries to focus not on the appearance of Muslims praying but on their bodily habitus and epistemology in the photographs that she will take of her old community. "What does the world look like from *inside* this prayer?" she wonders (54). The narrative itself tries to enact such a perspective in its incorporation of various points of view, the divine panoramic perspective, the stare of the uncomprehending outsider, encompassing a "sartorial forest" of hijab, and the experience of the parochial insider.[52] According to Purnima Bose, Kahf wanted "to represent material practices of Islam such as qiyam, ruku, sajda, and juloos," each naming "a specific bodily posture and spiritual stage."[53] *The Girl in the Tangerine Scarf* does not generate an image of the U.S. Muslimah, much as it attempts to incorporate her body into the scene and enact embodied knowledge through enriched affective vision. Finally, in its conclusion, *The Girl* also refigures "racing" to allow forward movement. The African-American native Hanifa, the disgraced Dawah Center friend of Khadra's youth who bore a child out of wedlock, is now training to qualify for the Indianapolis 500. Manifest destiny becomes a recursive loop. *The Girl in the Tangerine Scarf* uses the American frontier narrative to plot the Muslim daughter's movement first eastward—eventually back to Syria—and grafts it onto a circular structure. Circling gives way to collective transformation.

I want to discuss briefly Kahf's verse collections, *E-Mails from Scheherazad* (2003),[54] and particularly *Hagar Poems* (2016), because they imagine paradigmatic embodiment for Muslim women differently. Many of the speakers adapt the stance of the bold termagant or the *mudjadila*, "the woman who argues or disputes," by interrupting or acknowledging her interlocutor. Kahf writes of this figure: "[s]he is both inside and outside the discourse that results from this encounter between herself and others, she both tells the story and is told by it."[55] Both volumes include poems that treat topics of covering and of sexuality, but these are subsumed by the larger project of communal embodiment.[56]

Hagar Poems in particular overcomes the ethnoracial sociogeny that troubles the novel by focusing on a scriptural figure produced at such junctures. The collection insistently interpellates the contemporary American scene into the founding narratives of Abrahamic tradition. Dramatic monologue, rather a visual figure or scenic emphasis, serves as the primary conceit. Sarah and Hajar (in the Arabic spelling) are most often the first-person speakers in a variety of subject positions. Hajar is the younger black woman and the "other woman" in relation to the older brown, and initially nonreproductive wife. The two women detest and embrace one another in different poems, as Hajar is finally cast out of the

House of Abraham (Ibrahim) when Sarah bears a child. In these mostly spare dramatic monologues, Hajar encompasses the posture of the immigrant, the outcast. Christian ethnography casts her as well as the mother of the lost tribe. Islamic scripture elevates her as the revered mother of Ismail. She is memorialized in the hajj as the woman for whom God opened a spring, Zamzam, in the desert to quench her child's thirst. She found it under her heel. Here Kahf ingeniously deploys the significations of Hajar to enfold the problematic that strains at the racial optics of the American setting in the novel.

These themes are introduced in the collection's second poem, "The First Thing," in which Hajar recounts:

> I walked across a razor-sharp horizon/ slates of earth, sediments/ of ancient seas// to stand alone at this frontier:/ where the shape of the cup of morning is strange/ and the dome of sky, mat of earth have shifted,/ where God does not have a house yet/and the times for prayer have not been appointed.

Hajar understands herself not only as a mother of a needy child but also as the "founder" of a people who will "remain unborn" if she does not find water (4).

Kahf describes her work as having "three or four audiences," including American Muslims and "other Americans," "Arabic-speaking intellectuals and scholars, secular as well as the religious, across the spectrum of all religions in the Arab world ... includ[ing] the Arabic-speaking cultural scene in the Arab world and globally," and "Arab Americans." Though she notes the overlaps among these categories, she emphasizes that the last one is "not primarily Muslim."[57] "I can't write ethnically," Kahf has stated, "because my characters don't eat pork and they do use incense."[58] Both news coverage and social media show that Kahf has indeed been received as a Muslim writer in America, particularly among young women. Suzanne Shah, a 21-year-old student at Berkeley in 2007, stated in an interview, "It was refreshing for me to find that there is a poet out there who speaks the same language that I speak and thinks the same way I do." The article reports:

> Ms. Shah, who is unveiled, said she particularly likes a poem castigating those trying to make a battleground out of Muslim women's hair, with Muslims treating the veil as far too sacred and Westerners misconstruing taking off the veil as liberation.

She concluded: "It's not war, it's not freedom, it's just hair."[59]

Kahf's work impeded easy recourse to terms such as "Muslim literati" as new audiences and literatures emerged and as women registered as readers and writers with their own perspectives. An activist and blogger as well as a scholar and writer, she claims visibility on social media and in political commentary without the need for "branding" necessitated by mainstream publishing. Her negotiation of vision and interiority in her public profile, as well as her works, shows the dynamism of popular Muslim feminism (or gender justice discourse) in English, and more particularly an American English inflected by various provincial tongues. Su'ad Abdul Khabeer calls this diasporic epistemology and aesthetic a "Muslim Cool," which is heavily aligned with black expressive culture, a politics of resistance, and a (primarily masculine) aurality. The term describes

> a way of being Muslim that draws on Blackness to contest two overlapping systems of racial norms: the hegemonic ethnoreligious norms of Arab and South Asian U. S. American Muslim communities on the one hand, and White American normativity on the other.[60]

Though the subjects of Khabeer's research often downplayed the centrality of practice as organized, prescribed performance, they shared with the Islam practiced by Khadra and the Shamy family concerns with "self-knowledge," social justice, and related spiritual values. These young Muslims similarly discount material consumption and professional achievement as their paramount aims. Khabeer and others call attention to arenas of self-making. "Cool" techniques are displayed in apparel such as the "hoodjabi," a scarf style tied at the back and associated with African head wraps, or in the dandy style of male dressing. In a different vein, Sylvia Chan-Malik reverses the question of Muslim women's visibility in twentieth-century American history by asking what *African-American women saw* in Islam. She describes Muslim identity as a "contact zone between [working class black women's] bodies and the cultural and political terrains they inhabited" in Chicago and beyond.[61] This change of perspective chimes with Kahf's imagination of a Muslim "angle of vision," enabled by contact with the earth.

Notes

1 Mohja Kahf, "The Muslim in the Mirror, in *Living Islam Out Loud: American Muslim Women Speak*, ed. Saleemah Abdul Ghafur (Boston: Beacon, 2005), 133.
2 Kahf, "The Muslim in the Mirror, 130.
3 Danielle Haque argues that the novel's debt to the U.S. ethnic bildungsroman is overshadowed by its use of Islamic theology and translocality. "The Postsecular Turn and Muslim American Literature," *American Literature* 86.4 (2014): 801–802.
4 Jamillah Karim, *American Muslim Women: Negotiating Race, Class, and Gender within the Ummah* (New York: New York University Press, 2009), 41–42.
5 Zareena Grewal, *Islam Is a Foreign Country: American Muslims and the Global Crisis of Authority* (New York: New York University Press, 2013); Sherman Jackson, *Islam and the Blackamerican: Looking toward the Third Resurrection* (New York: Oxford University Press, 2005).
6 This reading stands in stark contrast to the imperial genealogy that Junaid Rana presents. Rana argues that the Muslim "heathens" of Europe parallel the indigenous peoples of the New World. Many enslaved Africans brought to the U.S. were also Muslim. "The Story of Islamophobia," *Souls* 9.2 (2007): 148.

7 The visual dynamics governing this narrative continue to be evident in such a recent novel as Samira Ahmed's *Love, Hate, and Other Filters* (New York: Soho, 2018), in this instance by virtually eliminating the presence of African Americans from the suburban Midwest. In an Illinois high school a Muslim student of Indian descent—one also fascinated by cameras—is attacked at her high school by a white male student, the brother of an injured veteran. (The fictional incident also recalls the Oklahoma City bombing in 1995.)

8 Here "standing before" might also be seen to signify the space that the dead and black subjects "share" because the black subject is a nonentity and because "the transmutation from enslaved to freed subject never quite occurred at the level of the [American] imagination." Holland, *Raising the Dead*, 6, 15.

9 Mohja Kahf, "Packaging 'Huda,'" in *Going Global: The Transnational Reception of Third World Women Writers*, ed. A. Almireh and L. Majaj (New York: Garland, 2000), 155.

10 Sylvia Wynter, "Beyond Miranda's Meanings: Un/silencing the 'Demonic Ground' of Caliban's Women," in *Out of the Kumbla: Caribbean Women and Literature*, ed. Carole Boyce Davies and Elaine Savory Fido (Trenton: Africa World Press, 1990), 361.

11 Mohja Kahf, *The Girl in the Tangerine Scarf* (New York: Avalon-Carroll and Graf, 2006), 54. Subsequent parenthetical references in the text will be to this edition.

12 Frantz Fanon, *Black Skin White Masks*, trans. Richard Philcox (New York: Grove, 1952), 17, 95.

13 The imago *negre* traps the black subject in an appearance fabricated by racist fantasy. It deprives him of somatopsychic ownership, according to David Marriott. "The Racialized Body" in *The Cambridge Companion to the Body in Literature*, ed. David Hillman and Ulrika Maude (New York: Cambridge University Press, 2015), xv, 163.

14 Marilyn Nissim-Sabat, "Fanonian Musings: Decolonizing/Philosophy/Psychology," in *Fanon and the Decolonization of Philosophy*, ed. Elizabeth A. Hoppe and Tracey Nicholls (Lanham, MD: Lexington Books, 2010), 43.

15 Wynter, "Beyond Miranda's Meanings," 361.

16 Wynter, "Beyond Miranda's Meanings," 361. Also see Sylvia Wynter, *On Being Human as Praxis*, ed. Katherine McKittrick (Durham: Duke University Press, 2014).

17 Katherine McKittrick, *Demonic Grounds: Black Women and the Cartographies of Struggle* (Minneapolis: University of Minnesota Press, 2006), 4.

18 Aminah Beverly McCloud, *Transnational Muslims in American Society* (Gainesville: University Press of Florida, 2006), 28.

19 Sophia Rose Arjana, *Muslims in the Western Imagination* (Oxford: Oxford University Press, 2015) discusses the racial anxieties provoked by Islam but also their bearing on sex and gender.

20 Kambiz GhaneaBassiri, *A History of Islam in America: From the New World to the New World Order* (Cambridge: Cambridge University Press, 2010), 264.

21 Gutbi Mahdi Ahmed, "Muslim Organizations in the United States," in *The Muslims of America*, ed. Yvonne Yazbeck Haddad (Oxford: Oxford University Press, 1991), 14–15.

22 GhaneaBassiri, *A History of Islam*, 267.

23 Kahf's mother and father came to work there in 1971, after completing degrees at the University of Utah. In the novel, Utah becomes Nebraska and Plainfield Simmonsville. The term *da'wa*, from the Arabic verb meaning "to call" or "to invite," defines their mission, directed in the novel at fostering submission to Allah, an injunction that has taken different forms historically and internationally.

24 John Tehranian, *Whitewashed: America's Invisible Middle Eastern Minority* (New York: New York University Press, 2009), 64.

25 GhaneaBassiri, *A History of Islam*, 81.

26 Reina Lewis, "Introduction: Mediating Modesty," in *Modest Fashion: Styling Bodies, Mediating Faith*, ed. Reina Lewis (London: Tauris, 2013), 4.

27 McKittrick, *Demonic Grounds*, 11.

28 Fard was known variously as David Fard, Wallace D. Fard, and Muhammad Fard. GhaneaBassiri, *A History of Islam*, 81, 223. See Moxley Rouse, *Engaged Surrender*, 81–104, for a short summary of African-American liberation movements and Islam.
29 GhaneaBassiri, *A History of Islam*, 218.
30 Louis Farrakhan split off from the new leadership to continue what he regarded as the legacy of the Nation under Elijah Muhammad. GhaneaBassiri, *A History of Islam*, 284–87.
31 Mohja Kahf, *Western Representations of the Muslim Woman: From Termagant to Odalisque* (Austin: University of Texas Press, 1999), 31.
32 Wynter, "Beyond Miranda's Meanings," 361.
33 Indiana University at Indianapolis, Polis Center, "Plainfield," n.p. www.polis.iupui.edu/RUC/Neighborhoods/Plainfield/PlnfldNarrative.html.
34 Carol Marie Jenkins' alleged murderer, arrested in 2002, was declared incompetent to stand trial and died that year. Yaël Ksander, "Martinsville and Diversity," January 15, 2007, *Moment of Indiana History*, http://indianapublicmedia.org/momentofindianahistory/martinsville-and-diversity/. Accessed June 12, 2015. For a brief history of the Klan in Indiana, see Jordan Fischer, "The History of Hate in Indiana: How the Ku Klux Klan Took over Indiana's Halls of Power," December 8, 2016 www.theindychannel.com/longform/the-ku-klux-klan-ran-indiana-once-could-it-happen-again. Accessed April 27, 2018.
35 The march was first slated for Chicago, in response to Martin Luther King Jr. Coalition marches in the summers of 1976 and 1977. The park had been the site of an attack on Martin Luther King, demonstrating for open housing, on August 5, 1966. Police refused the National Socialist application. R. T. Reid and Bob Warden, "3,000 Protest against Nazis in Chicago's Loop" *Washington Post* 25 June 1978 www.washingtonpost.com/archive/politics/1978/06/25/3000-protest-against-nazis-in-chicagos-loop/b21c5ab5-2775-4d97-963b-acddc0a440f2/?utm_term=.cadb5ab5c379; Ron Grossman, "Flashback: Fifty Years Ago: MLK's March in Marquette Park Turned Violent, Exposed Hate," *Chicago Tribune*, July 28, 2016 www.chicagotribune.com/news/opinion/commentary/ct-mlk-king-marquette-park-1966-flashback-perspec-0731-md-20160726-story.html.
36 Phillipa Strum, *When the Nazis Came to Skokie: Freedom for Speech We Hate* (Lawrence: University of Kansas Press, 1999), 5; Ron Grossman, "Flashback: Fifty Years Ago: MLK's March in Marquette Park Turned Violent, Exposed Hate."
37 Richmond reportedly was a domestic abuser who also asked a wife to castrate him; he succeeded in castrating himself. Diana Penner, "Suspect Faces Murder Charges for the Third Time." *Indianapolis Star* May 9, 2002, 1, 11.
38 The foregoing information is drawn from Sandra Chapman, *The Girl in the Yellow Scarf: One of Indiana's Cold Case Murders Solved as a Town Tries to Leave behind Its Past* (Indianapolis: Prince Media Group 2012); Mark Singer, "Who Killed Carol Jenkins: What a Thirty-three year old Murder Has Done to a Town," *New Yorker* 77.42, January 7, 2002: 24–28; Don Terry, "34 Years Later, Sad Secret Surfaces: Childhood Memory May Solve Slayings," *Chicago Tribune* May 12, 2002: 1 chicagotribune.com/2002-05-12/news/0205120236_1_black-man-new-yorker-magazine-arrest; Sara Rimer, "After Arrest, Town Shamed by '68 Killing Seeks Renewal" *New York Times* May 17, 2002: A18; "Old Murder Case Moves Forward," *Indianapolis Star* May 10, 2002: A22; Penner, "Suspect," 1, 11.
39 Will Higgins, "'We Need to Acknowledge It': Martinsville Tries to Remake Its Racist Image," *Indianapolis Star* November 2, 2017 www.indystar.com/story/life/2017/11/02/martinsville-remakes-racist-image/775258001/.
40 Purnima Bose, review of *The Girl in the Tangerine Scarf*, by Mohja Kahf, *Indiana Magazine of History* 105.1 (2009): 90. Bose notes that the novelist is also interested in recording the material culture of the era, including specifics such as "the rage for Kuwaiti headties."

41 Annelies Moors, "Discover the Beauty of Modesty: Islamic Fashion Online," *Modest Fashion: Styling Bodies, Mediating Faith*, ed. Reina Lewis (London: Tauris, 2013), 19.
42 Katayoun Zarei Toossi, "The Conundrum of the Veil and Mohja Kahf's Literary Representation of Hijab," *Interventions* 17.5 (2015): 650.
43 Grace, *The Woman in the Muslin Mask*, 123.
44 Toossi, "Conundrum," 652.
45 Toossi, "Conundrum," 652.
46 Mohja Kahf, "From Her Royal Body the Robe Was Removed: The Blessings of the Veil and the Trauma of Forced Unveilings in the Middle East," in *The Veil: Women Writers on Its History, Lore, and Politics*, ed. Jennifer Heath (Berkeley: University of California Press, 2008), 27–43.
47 Nousheen Yousuf-Sadiq, "Half and Half," in *I Speak for Myself: American Women on Being Muslim*, ed. Maria M. Ebrahimji and Zahra T. Suratwala (Ashland, Ore: White Cloud Press, 2011), 21.
48 Saidiya Hartman, *Scenes of Subjection: Terror, Slavery, and Self-Making in Nineteenth-Century America* (Oxford: Oxford University Press, 1997), 20.
49 Spillers, *Black White and in Color*, 206.
50 Alexander G. Weheliye, *Habeas Viscus: Racializing Assemblages, Biopolitics, and Black Feminist Theories of the Human* (Durham: Duke University Press, 2014), 90.
51 Qtd. in Bose, review of *The Girl in the Tangerine Scarf*, 90.
52 Toossi, "Conundrum," 653.
53 Bose, review of *The Girl in the Tangerine Scarf*, 90.
54 See Al-Sawy, Amany. "Revolutionizing Scheherazade: Deconstructing the Exotic and Oppressed Muslim Odalisque in Mohja Kahf's Poetry, in *Memory, Voice and Identity: Muslim Women's Writing across the Middle East*, 234–46.
55 Mohja Kahf, "Braiding the Stories: Women's Eloquence in the Early Islamic Era," in *Windows of Faith: Muslim Women Scholar-Activists in North America*, ed. Gisela Webb (Syracuse: Syracuse University Press, 2000), 155.
56 For discussions of Kahf's poetry, see, for instance, Samaa Abdurraqib, "*Hijab* Scenes: Muslim Women, Migration, and Hijab in Immigrant Muslim Literature," *MELUS* 31 (2006): 62–68; Amal Talaat Abdelrazek, *Contemporary Arab American Women Writers: Hyphenated Identities and Border Crossings* (Youngstown, New York: Cambria Press, 2007); Al-Sawy, Amany. "Revolutionizing Scheherazade: Deconstructing the Exotic and Oppressed Muslim Odalisque in Mohja Kahf's Poetry, in *Memory, Voice and Identity: Muslim Women's Writing across the Middle East*, 234–46; and Lisa Suhair Majaj, "Supplies of Grace: The Poetry of Mohja Kahf," *ArteEast*, www.arteeast.org/artenews/artenews-articles2006/september06/artenews-mohja-kahf.html. Accessed September 15, 2014.
57 Hilary E. Davis, Jasmin Zine, and Lisa K. Taylor, "An Interview with Mohja Kahf," *Intercultural Education*, 18.4 (2007): 385.
58 MacFarquhar, Neil. "She Carries Weapons; They Are Called Words" *New York Times*, May 12, 2007. www.nytimes.com/2007/05/12/books/12veil.html?pagewanted=all&_r=0.
59 MacFarquhar, "She Carries Weapons."
60 Su'ad Abdul Khabeer, *Muslim Cool: Race, Religion and Hip Hop in the United States* (New York: New York University Press, 2016), 2.
61 Sylvia Chan-Malik, *Being Muslim: A Cultural History of Women of Color in the United States* (New York: New York University Press), 43–44.

4

SURFACE VIOLATION

Parastou Forouhar's Domestic Sublime

The insignia of the veil and its attributes have posed an obstacle to be overcome as well as a creative opportunity for Muslim women makers who have entered mainstream media in Europe and America. As I have argued, critics attended to a manifest content defined by Western visuality, without discerning the works' other coding. Phenotypic and epidermal race, with their commitment to simple visual binaries, complicates the essential narratives of sex and gender, belief, and culture. I turn now to an artist who addresses received ocular epistemologies themselves. Parastou Forouhar calls into question *how* an audience sees. In this, the German-Iranian artist closes the gap of women's spectatorial distance from other women that allows, in Doane's theorization, for a sense of control over the cinematic image. Forouhar shows that what viewers see depends on their position, perspective, and quality of attention. Her aesthetic implicitly calls for a dialectical and mobile "female" gaze on *tawhid*, the Muslim concept of the unity of God's creation.[1] In this the artist dispels postfeminist enchantment with "luminous"[2] surfaces. At the same time, Forouhar treats the intricate surface as a sensuous lure that is not false or artificial.

Forouhar makes ornamental design central to her politics of representation. Here ornament[3]—conventionally linked to nonEuropean modernity, to the female, and to ephemeral or minor aesthetic categories—enacts a critique of unified perspective and its offer of clarity and transparency. Meaning is mobile. In Forouhar's estimation, the audience only misunderstands through a first glance as the second, sustained gaze produces recognition of ambiguity and dislocation.

DOI: 10.4324/9781003189299-5

She asserts, "The viewer is thrown back on himself and forced to reevaluate his perception."[4] Elsewhere she observes:

> [a]ll surfaces are covered with the vibrations of patterns. They represent the harmony of the world, of God's all-embracing power and beauty ... But this untouchable harmony can only be appreciated from a distance, as it conceals a great potential for brutality.

She compares the "ornamental order" to the "preset patterns in Islamic miniatures"[5] that dictate the realm of the representable and function therefore as repression, or even as "totalitarian"[6] demand. She challenges conventions that unite the state with terror in a default male mode, and patriarchal violence with Islamic or even Muslim-majority states while she uses Muslim concepts and Persian aesthetic vocabularies in conversation with digital modes and European high art.

Forouhar's popular and professional reception, as well as her own commentary, has diminished both the feminist orientation of her work and her significance as a feminist theorist. Her own tragic experiences have understandably trained attention on her critique of state terror, exemplified by the practices of Republic of Iran and addressed more particularly to the assassination of the artist's parents. Dariush Forouhar, founder of the Pan Iranist Party and a leader of the Iran Mellat, or Nation, and Parwaneh Eskandari Forouhar, his wife and fellow political dissident, were murdered by state security in their Tehran home in 1998.[7] The autobiographical context of much of Forouhar's iconography, while central to it, has also obscured its relevance to theories of violence against women. The field she often uses is domestic and feminized. Her figures are genderless and faceless. Yet her lyrical compositions disclose the exemplary violated body as female and the exemplary invasion of bodily intimacy, security, and everyday comfort as sexual violation. J. M. Bernstein posits the fusing of "the moral and physical body" that make rape and torture possible. In both, degradation is enabled by "compromis[e] of the human standing."[8] He argues that "torture and rape are paradigms of moral injury."[9] Forouhar realizes this paradigm as a totality of design. The spectacle of individualism, evidenced in *Sex and the City 2* and *Girls of Riyadh*, and the precarity of feminized bodies, foregrounded in the works of Ali and Kahf, become the crux of epistemological shifting in Forouhar's designs. Domesticity appears as the actual weaving and embroidery of violence and torture into the fabric of women's zones, routine and abominable, seen and unrecognized, beautiful *and* sublime.

"Commemorations": Figure and Furnishing

"When I arrived in Germany, I was Parastou Forouhar. Somehow, over the years, I have become 'Iranian,'" says the artist in the catalogue of her work.[10] After attending the University of Tehran, Forouhar studied at the Hochschule für Gestaltung Offenbach am Main in Hesse, Germany, and has remained in Germany since then. Her experience of transformation from an individual to a national and ethnic-religious identity crystallized when her elderly parents were murdered in their Tehran home.[11] Dariush Forouhar, imprisoned by the Shah for a total of 14 years, became Minister of Labor under the interim government of the revolution in 1979. He resigned later that year and was arrested in 1982.[12] He was imprisoned for 14 months. The Forouhars afterwards resumed their calls for reform, advocating for a democratic Iran in which church and state are separated. They became the first victims of what came to be known as the "chain" or "serial" murders of the late 1990s, during which four other activists were killed by the Iranian Ministry of Information.[13] (It is widely suspected that many more extrajudicial killings took place before and after the Forouhars' deaths.[14]) The artist and her brother have tirelessly campaigned to expose those responsible for their parents' death. Her art productions often explicitly refer to the state apparatus that authorized their murder.[15]

Forouhar notes that after her parents' murder, "[p]olitical correctness and democratic coexistence lost their meaning in [her] daily life."[16] Such comments provoke a number of questions about her identity and concerns. What does it mean to "become" Iranian through the violent reinscription of state power, and how do the terms "political correctness" and "democratic coexistence"—problematically yoked in themselves—bear upon traumatic loss? Forouhar may mean that her unceasing attempts to expose her parents' deaths as state-authorized assassinations have met with authoritarianism, doublespeak, and despotism. She may mean that a world that perpetrates such violence has no claim on freedom anywhere. She may mean that the concepts have lost meaning for her on an intimate psychic and physical level, a capillary shift in which the grip of power over her renders such abstract values remote experientially. Wherever her intentions lie, Forouhar makes clear that the conjunction of subjection, agency, and identity have profoundly shaped her art.

In her interviews, catalogues, and other written statements, the artist inserts herself into a discourse about state violence against citizens, as I have said. Her art frames it as a particularly feminist issue, in which the "domestic" plot of violence pertains to the intricate relationship of interiors to terror. The implements of daily life at home—forks, knives, and scissors—converse with guns and whips as features of lyrical patterns; male and female genitals are interwoven with wires and other constraints, whose constitution as elegant design and intimate brutality reveal themselves only through examination. Figures become instruments and tools, crafted as, by, and through exchanges of utility. Is this knife for preparing dinner to nourish me, or is this knife meant to butcher me, her compositions seem to ask. It is in either case the same utensil. In her controversial meditation *The Body in Pain*, Elaine Scarry contends that torture is "world-destroying":[17] torturers annihilate everyday existence by transforming the implements of home into tools of bodily destruction. Forouhar suggests that torture is in equal measure world-*making*, or to use her frequent visual idiom, home-making. Through her presentation of perspective and position, the artist sets out a very different reading of the suffering body than those offered by theorists of spectatorship on torture, usually modeled on masculine interactions.[18]

Central to Forouhar's optical strategy is the instability of *tawhid* as an aesthetic. In this she presents a very specific and individual adaptation of the "*tawhidic* paradigm," the principle of God's "unity and incomparability," or oneness with creation.[19] From this standpoint, to assert that any human beings possess God's traits is to commit *shirk*, or idolatry. Feminist and gender equality theorists draw on *tawhid* to argue against gender hierarchy, which places men as intercessors or intermediaries for women. Such authority belongs God alone.[20]

Forouhar adapts *tawhid* to an authority over vision that produces totalization. In her aesthetic, the *mashrabiyaa* offers alternate perspectives that oscillate with authoritative vision and total pattern.[21] In architecture, the screen conventionally opens light and space while also obscuring and separating areas.[22] Reina Lewis argues that the *mashrabiyaa* "opens a mutuality of the gaze."[23] In many two-dimensional fabric and wallpaper patterns, Forouhar manipulates the optics of the screen to distract, deceive, and entangle the eye in mise-en abyme or other paradox. The insistent flatness of surfaces, their field of ornamentation, and their often narrow or muted palette seduce the glance, and then coerce the gaze through particularities revealed only after the viewer has been drawn in by the beautiful, hypnotic repetition and interplay of elements. The *mashrabiyaa* acts as a psychic, social, and cultural, as well as a spatial, scaffolding in such pieces. It aims to cancel erotic scopophilia through paradox and symbol. The screen's logic extends as well to the signification of Islamic patriarchy in Western Christianity. What is unrepresentable in the West becomes representable in an Islamic visual idiom, here with a different twist. Iranian women make "visible" the cultural scaffolding of bodily production and violation that operates just as pervasively in other cultures, countries, and locations, through different as well as similar formations.

Forouhar uses synecdoches of the body most dramatically to draw a relationship between suffering and state power. The installations, which appeared in various exhibitions from 2003 to 2010, use the iconography and epigraphy of popular religious banners to unleash significations of her parents' assassination. Here as elsewhere in her work, the artist employs Shi'a Muslim practices and aesthetics to contest absolutist appropriations of Islam. Through chairs covered in commercially printed fabrics, the artist shows "home" as a space of loss and bodies as absent yet material presences. She nonetheless highlights the structures of political and religious history rather than focusing on individual affect.

Ingvild Flashkerud observes that the Shi'a have a long and rich tradition of sensory appeal to vision.[24] In "Trauerfeier" (The Funeral," Figure 4.1) and in "Countdown,"[25] Forouhar evokes the performative bodies of Shi'a practice with a specific emphasis on pious vision[26] and its potential challenge to the state. The

FIGURE 4.1 *Trauerfeier* (The Funeral), 2003. Installation at Kunstverein Aschaffenburg, 2006. 3624 cm. x 2448 cm. Courtesy of Parastou Forouhar.

master signifier of this challenge is Hussain, the grandson of Muhammad, the son of his cousin and brother-in-law Ali, and, according to the Twelver Shi'a interpretation, the third imam. Shi'a Islam observes the commemoration of his death in the battle of Karbala, in 680, as the climax of Muhurram. "The Funeral" and "Countdown" feature chairs upholstered in banners sold during 'Ashura, the tenth day of the period, during which Hussain's martyrdom is enacted.

According to many religious historians, the passion of Hussain is the founding event of Shi'ism. The battle of Karbala itself was part of a second-generation power struggle waged between the Umayyad caliphate, established in Damascus, and the circle of the Prophet, led by his relatives. Vali Nasr observes, "Husayn's defeat ended prospects for a direct challenge" to the Umayyad caliphate, "but also allowed his party to gain ground as a form of ethical opposition to it." Nasr continues, "Military defeat paved the way to a deeper appeal to Muslim consciousness." Through the defining events of 680, "Shi'ism ... evolved not as political sedition against Umayyad authority but as a moral and religious resistance to what that authority based itself upon and represented" in its brutal slaughter of the Prophet's family.[27]

Hussain condenses a multitude of meanings. He fights injustice. He epitomizes opposition to brutal state power.[28] Forouhar's chairs similarly call upon Hussain as a figure for an oppositional community. Her works also refer to the group failure signified by 'Ashura. The Shi'a concept of sin "is not [humanity's] 'original sin,'" as in Christian doctrine, but rather "a historical failure of the entire 'party' in a concrete situation," Heinz Halm says.[29] Self-flagellation and mortification with swords or knives, weeping, and other acts repent for this failure. Significantly, Forouhar chooses not to feature the iconography of needles, knives, or ropes here, though they appear prominently in her two-dimensional works of the same era. Instead, the banners belong to a public act of mourning while registering a fierce challenge to the government of the Islamic Republic of Iran as the sole arbiter of Shi'a meaning.[30] Claiming popular support, the government dictates. Claiming authority, it represents the killers rather than the defenders of Hussain. Against the frozen master narrative of Islam that the government enforces, "The Funeral" and "Countdown" suggest various, even paradoxical, aspects of the "furniture" of home, as bureaucratic and comfortable, fragmented and embracing, celebratory or showy in mourning. By archiving these installations as "Commemoration"[31] in the catalogue of her work, the artist underscores polysemic allusion to the death of Hussain as a collective narrative of grief and an avowal of culpability, a repository of visual as well as narrative representation[32] and an occasion of garish display—shot through with bureaucratic control of the "representable"—as well as of piety.

State leadership similarly directs the meaning of sacred time and the ways in which bodies enter into it. Mass-produced rather than unique artifacts indicate the historicity and sensuality of religious practice, especially Shi'a practice. The popular banners used in these pieces are related to embroidered *parchams*, or wall hangings, displayed in spaces of worship, and to pennants, hung under a hand, carried in procession. The textiles encode visualization as "part of [the] complex ritual aesthetics" of Shi'a practice, with an emphasis on bodily sensuousness.[33] Parchams often feature portraits of Hussain, his father Ali, his brother Hasan, and their compatriot Abbas, all of whom died in the campaign; Qur'anic verses; and images of the grave-mosques at Karbala and Nasf. The banners that the artist employs feature epigraphy and nonfigural patterns in bold colors. Forouhar notes: "The banners look very ornamental, very oriental with their religious verses. It's an exotic trap that continues to function: it attracts us, but it is full of aspects that we do not fully perceive."[34] The 'Ashura banners used to upholster the chairs of "The Funeral" and "Countdown" similarly feature epigraphy as their major decorative element, though they may incorporate architectural and bodily images as well, such as the one, presumably the mosque at Karbala, shown on the back of a chair in "The Funeral." The chair in the foreground of the 2003 National Gallery Hamburger Bahnhof installation[35] features the greeting "Hello Hussain" in Farsi, rendered in white and yellow, in the panel stretched over the seat and arms of the chair. In green against a black field, Arabic script appears in panels around the top back. A side panel displays a minaret.

Installations of "The Funeral" in particular call to mind the spaces in which 'Ashura prayers take place, their walls hung with parchams. Here, however, the swivel chairs, backs usually turned to one another, suggest the antithesis of community and performative practice. This ordering of space is otherwise processed and rationalized. Combined and stretched, the banners cover office chairs that are made to "stand for" figures through synecdochal replacement. The chairs evoke "robing" because the coverings do not conform to the contours of the chairs, but stretch over the arms. Bodies cannot occupy the chairs. But even if they could, the swivel base and wheels would allow movement while proscribing it. In broad horizontal bands, the script, often in yellow or green, stands out in contrast to black, red, or another contrasting color and may be juxtaposed with ornamental fields on the sides or back of the chair. The home that has been excised is made visible in the commemoration of martyrdom in pop fabric that "turns" around the absence of actual bodies, of the martyrs and their mourners. Bulky and sculptural over the pedestal of the base, the covered shapes might also be read as funerary monuments or shrouds. The angular base of the chair is drawn into an almost calligraphic relationship to these lines of bold, curved script: the base echoes or counterpoints its strokes.

The epigraphy of "The Funeral," in its combination of languages and patchworked banners, alludes to the cosmopolitan milieu of the elder Fohourars. "Countdown" stresses to greater degree lost intimacy. Soft forms and their arrangement suggest sociability and ease. Beanbag chairs face one another. Their central portion often consists of a field of jewellike color. Largely vertical in orientation, the banner upholstery may also incorporate Arabic and Farsi, but the epigraphy becomes an element of the decorative patches rather than their dominating feature, as in "The Funeral." Over a bulb-shaped cushion that sits on the floor, the chair back rises into a spoutlike form and may be curved down or forward like a neck inclined toward the other chairs. Often their arrangement in a circle suggests casual conversation. Sitters would alter the chairs' attitudes.[36] Yet the comfort of the low chairs could in fact impede sitters from rising again.[37] "Countdown" marks a moment of the community, but one in which mourning and soft control are operating.

Forouhar states that she is "fascinated by the transformation ... these ['Ashura] fabrics have undergone." She continues: "Years ago, they were black and white, or perhaps key colors like red and green. And now they are totally colorful, garish even. It's a mixture of pop culture and religiosity."[38] Such specular display suggests the dynamic of transcultural influence and ritual signification. It contrasts with performative revision through everyday religious practice such as *Brick Lane* suggests. At the same time the Shi'a theocratic state legislates against such mixing. Forouhar observes:

> At some point ... it became popular in the Islamic Republic to paint the portraits of the twelve imams [recognized by Shi'a Twelvers]. Over the course of time, they increasingly mutated into Indian actresses. They really looked like Shahrukh Khan and Bollywood, with sensuous, full lips,

bedroom eyes, bushy eyebrows, and silky hair. These portraits were sold as paintings, posters, and as buttons, and they became more and more beautiful. At some point the regime noticed that something was going wrong, that it wouldn't do, and they banned these images. They issued a prohibition on icons—it's forbidden to show them even during the mourning ceremonies for the Third Imam. At the same time ... [i]f you take a look at Ahmadinejad's election campaign or election campaigns in general, you can see how colorful they've become, with all these little pictures.[39]

The installations represent Iran as a religious state infused with pop media, its version of disciplinary belief deeply engaged with global culture. The contemporary references mingle with, and draw upon a Shi'a history of visual representation. With their multiple allusions to the contexts of belief, their visual tools and symbols, and their scriptural basis, the "Commemoration" installations display various kinds of syncretism and popular engagement while illustrating the Shi'a state's failure to regulate dynamic performativity. "Hello Ali" and other references typologically align the Forouhars and other victims of extrajudicial killings with the slaughters that act as inaugural events of Shi'a identity.

Figure and Book

As in "The Funeral" and "Countdown," much of the artist's oeuvre in both two- and three- dimensions uses script, fabric, and pattern to represent bodies. The focus on "interior design" and its public display establishes the micro relations of violence and home. Domiciles, public buildings, and spaces of worship frequently evoke the human corpus. Foregrounding the intimacy of her media, the artist suggests script through geometry and figure through bodily parts and small implements. Unlike the colorful, mass-produced fabrics of the installations, Forouhar's two-dimensional works of this era often manipulate viewers' perception of figure and ground, embellishment and structure, hand-craft and technological production. The lyricism and organic allusiveness of pattern turn into an obsessive idiom of conventional forms. Straight lines, in diagonals or grids, often constrain them. Only with scrutiny does the seemingly nonrepresentational surface reveal its allusion to objects and its use of digital technology. Here the relationship between the book and the figure translates the architectural idiom of the *mashrabiyaa* into a simultaneous realization of harmonious *tawhid* and compulsively controlled *horror vacui*.[40] Like the Persian miniatures that they recall, Forouhar's two-dimensional compositions create an "atmosphere of dissimulation"[41] enhanced by repetition. Oleg Grabar remarks of Persian manuscript paintings: "Each rock, each figure, each gesture, may be nothing but a cliché that is repeated once again, or it may conceal an iconographic secret."[42] Forouhar herself acknowledges the "openness and ambivalence of the beautiful Persian patterns that the old masters of past centuries have left to us," particularly in writing as a visual, tactile, and aural art.[43] Begum Ozden Firat calls this engagement with the miniature an "intimate encounter" in which the image "looks back" at the viewer and so changes the affect of intimacy.[44]

Though she rarely "marks" the figures as male or female, Forouhar's media and vocabulary constantly show feminization as the ground of the beautiful and sadistic, woven into the everyday environment as well as its master signifiers. She has been associated with Alfred Loos in her strong critique of the decorative.[45] Yet her deep engagement with its idioms and her awareness of its gendering strongly distinguish her from his theory. In "Ornament and Verbrechen" (Ornament and Crime [1908]), he links decoration to commercialism, superficiality, waste, alienated labor, and femininity, embedded in a framework of ethnologic degeneration theory: "As there is no longer any organic connection between ornament and our culture, ornament is no longer an expression of our [contemporary, Austrian] culture," he states.[46] Forouhar clearly represents a more complex relationship to design as a cultural-aesthetic repository, one that emerges from a very different conception of "home."

She creates two-dimensional patterns, rather than using mass-produced materials, to suggest variations on fabrics, books, and wallpaper. Though they are not presented as clothing, fabric swatches, whether on paper or fabric, also bear this association. The "Eslimi"[47] series (2003–10) evokes Persian miniatures and textile designs through abstract patterns, which often call to mind epigraphy or calligraphy. The design and presentation of the material highlight cloth, digitally or conventionally printed. The series appears in bound swatches of fabric, on rolls and as loose sheets. The term "eslimi" itself refers to an element of floral patterns that, along with geometric and calligraphic designs, constitutes a major genre of Islamic and pre-Islamic decoration found in manuscripts, fabric, painting, ceramic, goldware, carpets, and architecture. According to Etemad, Samavati, and Prusinkiewicz, "the patterns are characterized by curved shapes that are abstractions of plant elements such as flowers, stems, buds and leaves." "Eslimi" designates the decorative leaf itself. Compositionally, these designs, which incorporate spirals and arabesques, "have both *translational* symmetry, repeating the elements using rotation, translation, reflection, and *dilational* symmetry, using scaled repetition" of elements.[48] Analogy, "a more subtle form of repetition in which similar elements are used to induce a pleasing unity of forms," is also a salient strategy in the floral patterns.[49] Eslimi conventionally incorporate gold and rich blues.[50] Forouhar's adaptations often narrow the neighborhood of colors in order to enhance the dominance of line. Other variations employ simpler forms and higher contrast, emphasizing a screen effect. Notably, the "Mahrem" pattern book uses basic shapes, predominantly in low contrast between field and pattern, and nonfigural designs, in which one color is set against another, without intricate outlines or ornately defined individual elements.[51] The title of the series refers to the system of Muslim practices that governs marriage and social relations. They primarily encode incest taboos, but also define the relations of male guardianship over women. The relative simplicity of the basic elements and their links suggests clearly defined separations and connections, easily read from a distance. For instance, in one iteration,[52] circular patterns, resembling flowers, accompanied by smaller diamonds of the same color, compose a panel. In it decorative shapes are lime green and the background a light blue. These are set against a panel on the same sheet in which the shapes are white against the same pale-blue background. In both their white and green versions, the larger flower forms align horizontally and interlock vertically with the smaller diamond shapes appearing amid any set of four larger flower forms. Each inset diamond extends four lines diagonally to connect it to a petal of the larger flower form.

Deriving in part from the decorative marginalia of Qur'an manuscripts, eslimi share with other broad genres of Islamic and Persian art close relations with script. Such forms and their import draw upon the history of the illustrated manuscript, in which the pictorial grew out of a governing calligraphic art. As Grabar states,

> The Iranian tradition [which includes pre-Islamic art], and the Islamic tradition in general, consider painting only one aspect of the art of the book, with writing playing the principal role. In many written sources, this cohabitation of painting with calligraphy may well have been an excuse to get around the opposition to representation of living beings latent in the Muslim world. The paintings would have acquired a right to exist by virtue of their association with calligraphy.[53]

The more prestigious of the two media, "calligraphic art required the artist to relinquish his own impulses and accept the rules already laid down for composition and design," including "the overall determination of spaces for and arrangement of the pictorial, in the lozenge or the square."[54]

Forouhar also gives primacy to ornamentation in her use of the pictorial space and recalls the historical flexibility of ornamentation as *mediation*. She restricts tone to emphasize the mediation between structure and pattern, the "architecture" of the image and its elements. She continues ornament's role in "facilitat[ing] access to the image by establishing the adjacent structures and controlling the surfaces."[55] On a macro level, this negotiation also occurs between the book and bodies, between fabric and living spaces, between the contemporary digital and the historical cultural aesthetic,[56] and, perhaps most strikingly, between traditionally female and male media.

The exchange of similar shapes in the "Eslimi" group (2003–10) suggests another method of mediation, in which the implied signifiers of sexual social relations figure into the semiotics of genitals and weapons. In the "Mahrem" pattern book, one sheet features what resemble fork tines set next to another in horizontal lines of light green, against a cerulean blue background. Another sheet juxtaposes a five-pointed shape resembling a stylized razor or blade, colored a

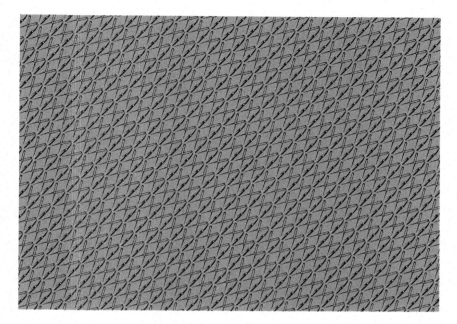

FIGURE 4.2 *Guns*, from the series *Eslimi*, 2003–2010, detail. Digital print on fabric, 594 cm. x 420 cm. Courtesy of Parastou Forouhar.

light pink and outlined in red, with a pale green background.[57] The tines resemble the fork-forms in a swatch of "Guns"[58] and the blade in another swatch included in the series (Figure 4.2).[59]

That similar shapes appear in different designs, all of them belonging to the "Eslimi" series, suggests interrelations among the disparate categories. For instance, male and interlocking female genital forms revise the clear, basic separations and connections of the "Mahrem" sheet. "Genitals" gives the five-pointed, curved blade shape of "Guns" exaggerated, bulbous points that resemble nipples. "Genitals"[60] features elaborate patterns of arcs (Figure 4.3). On one sheet, pictographic dark-pink, curved forms bordered in tan lines, set against a black background, resemble fattened commas and parentheses. The simplified clitoral and scrotal representations intertwine and repeat to compose the basic element of the design. Each scrotal shape culminates in a textured shaft, so that the unit has three extensions, one perpendicular, the other two inclined toward one another. Inside this larger scrotum and shaft is another, smaller outline in light tan, a dilational symmetry. It describes the black form as if revealing the background within the shape. The triangular arrangement of the male genitals is both separated and joined by two labial, liplike forms paired in between the inclined shafts. Threadlike outlines also loop through another set of labia, one on each side, strung like beads connecting the basic elements and forming a modified diamond shape in the center. The fundamental elements in

FIGURE 4.3 *Genitals*, from the series *Eslimi*, 2003-2010, detail. Digital print on fabric, 594 cm. x 420 cm. Courtesy of Parastou Forouhar.

turn interlock through statement and reversal, one version next to another horizontally and vertically. From a slight distance, the shapes look both jewellike, as if enameled metal, and calligraphic, through their bowed and looping lines. In its relative subordination of the perpendicular, this piece contrasts with others in the "Genitals" iterations, many of which incorporate strong geometric shapes such as diamonds, squares, rectangles, and radiating starlike forms.

Similar disruptions and merging of categories appear within "Guns." The series features swatches with designs based on objects such as pincers, blades, scissors, cutlery, and penknives or switchblades. One[61] displays a pale pink background and light gray-green forms that resemble open pincers, inside which a cut-out shows the pink background emerging from the form. This inset pink shape suggests the spring of a clothespin, with a rounded top and two legs, cut into or lying atop the pincer legs that they echo in dilation. Heavily outlined inside and out, the pincer shapes are arranged in horizontal rows of the figure and, right next to it, an upside-down version of the figure. Adjacent rows also present the pincers so that upside-down pincers align vertically with right-side up ones. One leg of the pincer meets with an extending leg of the pincer above or beneath it, an arrangement that creates strong diagonals from the top to the bottom of the page.

The forms resemble domestic tools and implements while alluding to the human anatomy. The curved grips of the pincer's head also read as arms, and the sharpened bottom handles as legs. Almost pictographic when understood as human figures, the outlined forms appear to be splayed and headless, the clothespin shape inside each one a description of a chest and thighs. The juxtaposition grants figural depth and turns the background pink shade into a highlight. The page or swatch in this way condenses a common domestic tool and an instrument of torture, and both with bodies that may use or be subjected to the implement. Its interior form might be read as a reinscription or dilation of the implement as a human figure. That figure may be cut out or modeled through light that unites tonally with the background. The implied figures are not distinguished as men or women; they share instrumentality. Gendering operates more strongly through the association of fabric with women and embroidery or cloth-making with female arts. Pattern may be dictatorial in Forouhar's reading, but the elements of the patterns that she employs allow for multiple readings of form and hence of meaning.

Many sheets of the "Guns" series of "Eslimi" do not present forms resembling human figures. The designs resonate with human flesh only through association. They feature tools for cutting cloth and food, for protecting and sustaining bodies, that become instruments for puncturing, stabbing, and ripping skin. The prominence of sharp points constantly highlights the potential of everyday objects to threaten and injure. In this way, the instruments represent both tortured and torturer. A page of pinlike shapes,[62] which uses a strategy similar to that of the pincer design, acquires this resonance through more ornate and lyrical forms that resemble safety pins. In a muted turquoise, set against a light olive-green field, these shapes are twinned with one another horizontally, as they touch in groupings of the right-side up and upside-down formations. One leg of each element of the pair extends sharply to meet with the leg in the horizontal band beneath it, again juxtaposing statement and reversal. But this pattern substitutes for the diagonal movement of the sheet of pincers a strong horizontal thrust accented by the arc of touching extended legs, which thin and bend to cross the space between rows. These "pin" shapes further suggest traditional embellishment or even tracery through the intricate lozenges and angled circles, which form the interior of each element, and the intersection between the paired shapes. Particularly at the top of each form, where the "head" of the safety pin would be, the shapes meet in two arms of pincerlike points, seeming to overlap one another. They are echoed by thornlike points that break out from the body of the pin, and are met by a crossed, angular butterfly shape, consisting of two triangles, at the base. Heavily outlined in black, the basic element communicates organic, lyrical linearity and architectural embellishment. At the same time the form resembles a piercing and pinching weapon or a calligraphic detail, through swooping lines and interlocking rows.

Other "Guns" sheets show kitchen knives that suggest pocket knives, one paired with the tines of forks (Figure 4.4),[63] and the other with scissors.[64] In each, the pocket knives and scissors bear a cut-out circle in the center, at the axis, and the handle breaks into a second, sharp leg to resemble the needle of a drawing

FIGURE 4.4 *Guns*, from the series *Eslimi* (2003–10), detail. Digital print on fabric, 594 cm. x 420 cm. Courtesy of Parastou Forouhar.

compass. Both images present strong color contrasts, as the knives and fork tines, arranged diagonally and alternating with one another in each row, are a very light green, outlined in black, against a muted grass-green background. The forms contrast highly with the background. The curve of each blade is emphasized by the compasslike sharp foot and reinforced by the three points of the tines next to it. The tines emerge from a thin horizontal base, and lack handles, which appear absent or broken off so that the background of green seemingly underneath them shows. The sheet featuring scissors, as well as one featuring a similarly shaped penknife fabric, is more unusual in that the forms are solid blocks of color without outlines. Alternating from top to bottom and side to side, the featured element is set at an extreme diagonal, each iteration close to another in both directions. The lack of linear outline increases the pictographic quality of the forms, as does the contrast between their solid blue color and their light olive-green background. The handles of the scissors are elongated and lozengelike. The points of the blade and the compasslike leg of the knife are highlighted in white at their tips, in a very thin line that suggests a glint of metal.

The Figure as Architecture

Forouhar's presentation of the suffering form uses dissimulation as a technique of revelation through spectatorial distance and intimacy, but also through types of attention. Hilary Neroni reads the alibi for state torture as a regard for the body

Surface Violation **107**

as a receptacle of "truth" and the victim's sole motive as biological survival. In Deleuze's interpretation of Sade, which I mention in Chapter 2, sadism reinforces republican institutions and legality, and drains the ego for the energies of the superego psychically.[65] Both positions invest in the reason of violence, of violence as a form of reason. But Neroni additionally suggests the enjoyment that underlies the alibi of political torture as a desire precisely to reveal the unconscious and libidinal energies released *through* the victim of torture.[66] In focusing on torture as a derivative of the scaffolding of patriarchal structures, Forouhar recasts this libidinal energy into aesthetic regulation and repetition. Its effects oscillate with the proximity of viewer position and a mutuality of the object's and the subject's gaze onto ideological structures. The representation is infused with a divine conception of totality as well as with "reason" as a neoclassical principle.

"Tausendundein Tag" ("A Thousand and One Days" [2003])[67] in many ways exemplifies Forouhar's aesthetic and political adaptation of *tawhid* through its depiction of tortured bodies on wallpaper (Figure 4.5). The broader series includes digital drawings and flash animation, rendered primarily in pink, white, and black.[68] The constant among them is a pink figure, outlined in black, joined by curving or straight black bands that signify whips, gags, ropes, binds, prison bars, poles, or gallows. Like the "Eslimi" series, "Thousand" is preoccupied with the human figure as a product of *tawhid*, but here the human form dominates and creates the pattern that in turn makes it: the alliance of figure, pattern, and

FIGURE 4.5 *Tausendundein Tag* (A Thousand and One Days), 2003, detail. Digital print on wallpaper, 2657 cm. x 1772 cm. Courtesy of Parastou Forouhar.

calligraphy again suggests the human agent as a derivative of a larger, implied scaffolding. The aestheticization of torture even more explicitly speaks to the home as a site of violence and affective "ties." Forouhar treats both beauty and brutality as effects of totalization. Here regulated practice produces not just a way of knowing, but also a habitus of living, in the body and in the domicile. The digital production of the wallpaper, like many of the two-dimensional designs I have discussed, enters into the signification of agency and power as well. "A Thousand and One Days," in setting pink figures against a white field, recalls neoclassical unity and variety through serpentine line, idealized figure, and strict geometry, as well as intricate decorative stylization derived from Persian miniatures and related media.

Invoking calligraphy through black ribbonlike bands that transform function while joining the figures, "A Thousand and One Days" connects the narrative to lyrical repetition. From a distance the design of some sections might evoke a floral pattern on wallpaper, an association invited in many panels by pink coloring and prominent serpentine undulations. Against a white background, the pink figures appear almost to dance as they tumble and fall in groups, hang in a line from black ropes, kneel under black, comblike whips, or stand on columnar pedestals.

The elegance of their placement gives way to dense interconnection in pieces such as "Panorama" (2006, Figure 4.6).[69] The black background and amassed pink shapes highlight a larger pattern while nearly dissolving it. In another series of digital drawings, "A Thousand and One Days I" (2007),[70] also featuring pink figures on the black background, the artist takes the opposite approach by subordinating the pink forms to dominant shapes allied with geometric and floral designs. The white or black field on which the figures appear particularly evokes latticework. The pieces installed as wallpaper actually become architectural elements in their mimicry of a *mashrabiyaa*. Whether lightly or densely patterned, the screen actually composes a room.

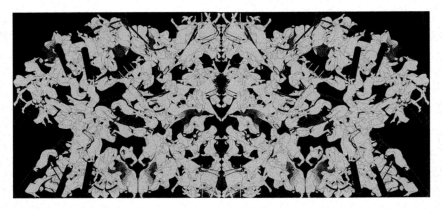

FIGURE 4.6 *Thousand and One Days—Panorama*, 2006. Digital print on paper, 145 cm. x 326 cm. Courtesy of Parastou Forouhar.

The pieces' lyricism and pink coloring suggest an intimate feminine space. Indeed, as I have mentioned, critics quickly assumed that Forouhar takes specific aim at oppressive practices against women justified by sharia. It seems important to observe, given these contexts, that the figures themselves are not sexed in any obvious way. Both torturers—such as those wielding whips—and victims are represented through the same basic pictographic form, in different postures and arrangements. This figure has a head but lacks a face; has somewhat powerful shoulders and a rounded chest that is not defined into breasts; usually lacks hair or any other head covering; and wears a tunic that falls over the knee. In their lack of specific sexual assignment, the figures recall the symbolic or typed human forms of Persian miniatures, just as their interaction with architecture recalls the preeminence of textual layout over the space allotted to illustration. They modify Deleuze and Guattari's bodily facialization by distinguishing parts of the anatomy while refusing to distinguish central categories of identity. To note the seeming ambiguity or inclusiveness of the figure is not to mitigate Forouhar's feminist critique, but rather to stress the alliance of a feminized position with derivation and vulnerability. The "screen" in the piece might also be read as a psychic one, onto which Christian fantasies of a frozen, despotic Muslim patriarchy are projected. Such an interpretation does not erase patriarchy justified in the name of Islam, but rather illustrates both the ubiquity and the cultural and social particularity of patriarchies, using specific narrative and visual idioms. It seems especially telling, given this projection, that Forouhar installs the pieces as wallpaper, a decorative method historically associated with middle-class EuroAmerican architecture and interiors.[71] "A Thousand and One Days" portrays bodily vulnerability as a cultural scaffolding of home, in reference both to private spaces of domesticity and to such spaces' formation by larger and interpenetrating structures of enforced violence. In this the piece connects obviously to the stabbing of Forouhar's parents in their home. Such acts may be carried out against men as well as women, cis or trans identities.

Forouhar's direct evocation of Scheherazade, a virtual touchstone for women artists of or with ties to the subcontinent and the Middle East, alludes to the power of the female storyteller or artist: this association is usually foremost in works by such female artists. At the same time Forouhar points to the female artist's involvement with death and torture as constant threats. She represents "an indigenous myth," according to Feroza Jussawalla, who writes that the character is "the speaking subject, with agency" who is also "symbolic of the moment of decoloniality."[72] Forouhar transforms the emotionally injured and consequently ruthless king Schariar and his bride Scheherazade, who forestalls her own death and that of other women, into a system of perpetual violation and suffering without a designated villain or heroine. Forouhar's choice of "days" rather than "nights" further suggests the labor and confinement of the figures in mundane time. In contrast to the fictional enchantment and potential eroticism of the night, the daylight shows the routine inevitability of torture as well as the variety of its effects on suffering bodies—bodies that nonetheless do not open or bleed, as in fairy tales.[73] Deleuze and Guattari's facialization pertains to the distinct head, but it is featureless and without individuation of sex assignment. The absence of eyes erases the "circuit of gazes"[74] that Grabar describes as a cue to the narrative illustrated in Persian miniatures. Here, sense comes primarily from skin, a canvas for pain. The figures act as Cahill's "derivatives" of a system that is both endless and encompassing, a social *tawhid* in which unity and submission act as the space of living that is at once claustrophobic, predictable, and catastrophic. "Unrepresentable" as a system, torture nonetheless ceaselessly grips bodies that perpetrate and suffer violence in the daily labor of terror. Forouhar reimagines Kant's mathematical sublime as representable through the infinite variation on the small and the embodied.

Most of the works in "A Thousand and One Days" and related series illustrate the connection between the torturer and the tortured, though some depict only the victims. The joining of persecutor and victim, like the androgyny of the figures, might seem to suggest equivalence between the parties, as one body transforms into another, or the thick line from a binding of a victim bisects the torturer who wields it. My reading instead highlights the system of practices that remakes subjects, not a cancellation of differing levels of agency or positions of intersectionality. The series exposes Gavey's scaffolding by revealing the "patterning" of torture as connective, pervasive, and circulating, while entirely corporeal. It constantly confuses and restates the relations of decoration and structure. Even in the most densely populated of these works, however, such as "Panorama,"[75] individual figures are discernable upon close inspection, and black ribbons are traceable through their undulations.

In "A Thousand and One Days I" (2007)[76] the artist uses pink figures to compose shapes that suggest the female genitals. Often arranged around one large and one small opening, the drawings may use the legs of tables, binding ropes, and scaffoldings to protrude into the gaps in the designs created by the dense bodies (Figure 4.7).[77] One features a geometric crisscross[78] that tangles into scaffolding in the smaller aperture. These lines are echoed in perpendicular gallows that emerge from the outside of the larger opening. Another pair of images[79] produces more delicate effects through the protrusion of thin table legs, alternating with human legs, into the black center of the design. It creates a reversal of the vagina dentata, in which needle-thin lines actually seem to poke into the clitoral form. In each instance the left and right sides of the pattern perfectly mirror one another. Angled arms and legs, bound or straining in contorted postures, puncture the geometric symmetry of the central black fields, alternating with objects or not.

Forouhar introduces other colors and shapes into this concept in related works. They share the dominant sense of struggle and coalescence between figure and pattern. Notable among these is a series that employs the shape of butterfly wings with depictions of prison. The butterfly alludes to the meaning of Parwaneh, the artist's mother's name, and to the bars of the prison that incarcerated her father.

Surface Violation **111**

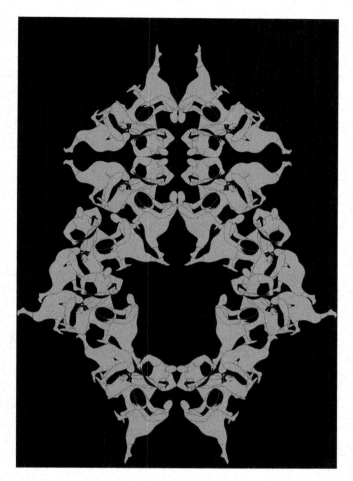

FIGURE 4.7 *Thousand and One Days, I*, 2007. Digital print on paper, 297 cm. x 420 cm. Courtesy of Parastou Forouhar.

In the "Papillion Collection" (2010),[80] the wing governs the postures of slumped bodies that arrange themselves around an orange-red field. In "'Ashura Day" (2010) red and orange drips on the bodies suggest targets as well as blood splatters; the entire shape is set against a black field.[81] "Ewin Prison (2010),"[82] where Dariush Forouhar was jailed for 14 months by the Iranian Republic, features asymmetrical patches on the black wings. Individual bodies are crossed with vertical or horizontal lines, so that the figures appear doubly trapped, by the shape of the wing and the shapes of the prison cells themselves, irregular six-sided forms that seem to be cut out from them. The black wings are further juxtaposed against a light-green hue, on which are traced standing versions of the figures. In outline only, they suggest ghosts or shades that have escaped entrapment through their loss of substance.

112 Surface Violation

Recalling the "Eslimi" series, "Red Is My Name, Green is My Name I" (2007, Figure 4.8)[83] allows dense patterns actually to swallow the figure. In a full convergence of the intricate small designs of the "Eslimi" series and the figures of "A Thousand and One Days" variations, this series allows replications of weapons such as guns, clubs, and blades completely to absorb figures.[84] Heads, hands, or feet become metonyms of the pattern. Simultaneously the human figures create disturbances—bends, arcs, and diagonals—in the strict horizontal and vertical urges of the designs. Forouhar's own recombinations of these techniques and patterns in pieces that employ the pictographic figure, some with more dramatic colors but many featuring the pink and black palette, investigate and restate the problematic of the cultural scaffolding. Intimate physical violation belongs to the structure of home. Such violation becomes fundamental to the figures that it produces, without entirely describing them.

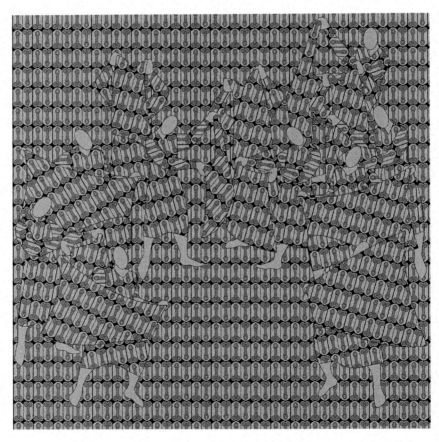

FIGURE 4.8 *Red is My Name, Green is My Name,* 2007. Digital print on paper, 40 cm. x 40 cm. Courtesy of Parastou Forouhar.

Figuring Women

Forouhar's most explicit representations of women appear in her photography of this period. Here the artist renders figures in celebratory, ironic, and even comic scenes. Themes of torture and punishment are absent from these works, which remain preoccupied with the figure's relationship to fabric and fabricated environments. They often incorporate epigraphy. Bodies' interactions with surfaces appear as a major interest, and skin as well as walls, floors, and cloth become surfaces on which Shekasteh script is written. In some of these pieces, the dynamic performativity of veiling challenges the fixed signifier of "the veil" defined both by Muslim patriarchy and by EuroAmerican reading of it as the insignia of Islamic misogyny. Forouhar is particularly engaged with veiling not only as an oppressive practice when enforced on women, or conversely as a EuroAmerican signifier that erases women's agency (especially when chosen by women) but also as a bodily and material code of unstable signification. Her pictographs and photographs frequently focus on the capacities of fabric as analogous to those of her rendered figures. The cloth dislocates and designates bodies and body parts through context, focus, arrangement, and selective revelation. Fragmentation liberates limbs from the conventions of erasure and disclosure.[85]

Forouhar shares with a number of other feminist artists of the period, many of them Iranian nationals or migrants, an interest in depicting the veil as another kind of surface. The refusal of scopophilia unfailingly registers in Western contexts as a cancellation of female agency. Exhibitions such as *Veil* (2003)[86] and *Masques of Shahrazad: Three Generations of Iranian Women Artists* (2009)[87] as well as the Robert Adanto documentary *Pearls on the Ocean Floor* (2010)[88] examined, celebrated, and critiqued the veil as a totalizing metonym of Muslim women. After the French-Iranian graphic artist Marjane Satrapi, author of *Persepolis* (2000–03) and *Embroideries* (Broideries, 2003), American photographer and filmmaker Shirin Neshat became the most prominent figure in this visual discourse. Her controversial photographic series *The Women of Allah* (1993–97), her video installations *Turbulent* (1998), *Rapture* (1999), and *Fervor* (2000), and her film adaptation of *Women without Men* (2011)[89] treat covered woman as agents of violence and eros.

Forouhar shows veiling as a practice that allows for resignification of limbs and parts, a *mashrabiyaa* or screen for seeing and not seeing, for projecting and marginalizing. In "Freitag" (Friday [2003]),[90] a digital print on vinyl, cloth, and limb interact to dislocate readings of the female anatomy (Figure 4.9). The devotional act implied by the title and the decorum observed in bodily covering become unmoored, without any direct transgression of propriety. The artist uses the hand as a particularly rich signifier, presented as a sign of agency as well as of erasure. As I have noted, the hand is an emblem of Hussain in Shi'a iconography. It also functions as an amulet, usually understood as female. The hand of Fatima, or the "hamsa," enjoys popularity in the Middle East and North Africa. "Friday" shows

FIGURE 4.9 *Freitag* (Friday), 2003, central panel. Digital print on vinyl, 6 m. x 2 m. Courtesy of Parastou Forouhar.

the capacity of the hand to manipulate cloth, as the artist does, to protect, and to figure multiplicity.[91] "The veil" fails to control women's meanings externally. The apparent split created by the opening between forefinger and thumb makes the cascade of cloth, woven in a subtle eslimi design, appear produced by the woman's body. The cloth in fact makes this hand female. Nothing that appears of the limb sexes it.

Digital manipulation of the figures of "Blind Spot" (2001–10 [Figure 4.10]) and "Rorschach Behnam" (2008) imply technical fabrication as well as artistic manipulation of the figure, which presents photographic verisimilitude while showing the impossibility of the figure's derivation from a single pose of a single body. "Blind Spot,"[92] a series of digital photographs, displays a figure seated

Surface Violation **115**

FIGURE 4.10 From the *Blind Spot* series, (2001–10). Digital print on paper, 110 cm. x 150 cm. Courtesy of Parastou Forouhar.

upright, in profile and in full frontal views. The frontal image displays what appears to be a smudged thumb, in a slightly whorled pattern. The figure's hands seem to be turned backward, as they lie on the robe in an unnatural or even broken position at the wrist. The outward-turned palms of "Blind Spot" are both anatomically impossible and reminiscent of the wrists' painful dislocation, made to display empty palms. Here is the genesis of the insignia of "the veil" as the Muslim woman shown in reverse, a time lapse that ends in a large blot on the ground. In "Rorschach Benham," a digital print on plexiglas, the smudged, thumblike ovals of the featureless face were actually taken from photographs of the back of a balding man's head.[93] The substitution depicts anonymity as well as identification, as the face reads as a male idea or a smudged thumbprint of a police blotter. Expressive "character," assumed in the Western portraiture tradition to be lodged in the face, is replaced with patriarchal projection or criminal anonymity. The two positions of the figure might suggest the postures of worship or of judicial proceedings, yet the figure inside the robe is entirely backward to the plane. The robes flow out before figure's head, bent back and foreshortened as the figure seems to sink back through the four images. Depth is created through the juxtaposition of black veil and light tan "face," but the black can also resolve into a large, flat plane barely articulated in the blank white environment. Two of these images appear in an installation of billboards,[94] indicated by the language of the street signs, as if the faceless robed figure might be a commercial advertisement or even a directional sign. The billboard itself is difficult to "read" in space, as it appears at some points to combine with the environment, of poured cement apartment blocks with scrubby grass in the foreground. Other cues suggest they are illustrations on an independent, free-standing structure.

Forouhar shows the performative potential of the robed woman in "The Swanrider" series (2004–10)[95] by using the shape of the robe to grant agency to women through pattern (Figure 4.11). Internationally, these photographs constitute her most well-known pieces, as they turn black fabric into a completely malleable and expressive medium. Bob Duggan observes that the series conveys "multiple layers of allusion—from Hans Christian Anderson's ugly duckling to the legend of Leda and the swan to even *Lohengrin*."[96] Draping the black robe to make angular edges against the white of the molded swan boat, the artist suggests that the figure belongs to the swan as a design. Yet the

FIGURE 4.11 From the series *Swanrider*, 2004–10 Digital print on paper, 80 cm. x 80 cm. Courtesy of Parastou Forouhar.

figure rides and also guides (perhaps peddles) the vehicle, shot variously from the back and from the side. Some images show the figure's face. The photographs in various ways suggest reciprocity between the bird and rider. The robe implies wings in one photograph, an analogue in another, as the rider pictured in profile answers the curve of the swan's neck. The black of the fabric reads as a property of the swan's design, its black set in rhythm with the black of the cygnet. At the same time, the artificiality of this seemingly organic pattern is highlighted by the size and material of the boat, its concave seats, numbered hull, or hold visible.

"The Swanrider" series offers primarily celebratory representations of women's bodies associated with Persian culture and art and with hijab. The series "Bodyletter"[97] (1995–2010) similarly shows the performative agency inherent in the interaction of figure, pattern, and script. White walls and floors oscillate optically between two and three dimensions. Shekasteh script, applied through digitally cut plastic transfers, suggests pages. In some images[98] a black-robed figure dances in the space between the transfers, enlivening the inert blots of a work such as "Blind Spot" with the figure's artistic agency: the dancer produces this textual and poetic architecture and script. "Written Room"[99] emphatically casts the page into three dimensions. In one image, a woman dressed in a white shirt and black pants—the white scarf with an intricate design at the border around her neck, a black purse slung over one arm—has just released a green balloon into the air. She looks up as it floats off.

Forouhar's wittiest work at this time appears in the "Villa Massimo" (2006)[100] series of photographs, which combine Roman classical and Catholic allusions with 'Ashura fabrics, and figures in hijab with Italian architectural and urban scenes. Like "Blind Spot," some of these photographs use digital manipulation and collage to create ambiguous spatial effects. Juxtapositions of planes may flatten depth and produce the effect of a two-dimensional design, a surface divided into separate areas like a manuscript page. Unlike Persian miniatures or Forouhar's fabric patterns, however, a single figure dominates the scene here, as in much of the artist's photography. In many of these images, Forouhar calls attention to hijab as drapery by setting it in a series that includes togas and other types of robing as well as contemporary kitsch and ephemera. In "Ping Pong Caesar,"[101] for instance, a man stands in an alcove. Clothed in a white toga, he assumes a somewhat wooden classical pose, as in a Roman copy of a Greek statue, one arm bent up and away from the torso, the other hand placed on his chest. He wears green laurels studded with white ping pong balls. "Roman Martyrs"[102] suggests the similarities between Christian and Shi'a emblems of suffering while including props such as women's wigs and an umbrella. Shot from above, the fallen figures are covered in 'Ashura fabrics dominated by epigraphy. The image features bright fields of red and yellow. In a street scene from the series,[103] a figure draped in black fabric, suggesting a burqa but lacking a netted panel for vision, straddles a motorcycle that appears to be emerging from a stall of 'Ashura fabrics, to the left, and from a stone building, to the right. Though the figure's face is completely covered, a pair of bare legs clutches the bike: it is unclear visually whether these legs belong to the black-robed figure or to another figure, one otherwise blocked from sight by the front of the cycle. The effect of depth changes throughout the image, as recession is often created primarily through the overlap of planes. The indeterminate figure drives blind, yet does so on a metallic vehicle that signifies individual mobility, speed, and sleek engineering.

Even in the images that refer to martyrdom, the "Villa Massimo" series accents theatricality. In one image[104] that exemplifies this attitude, Forouhar herself appears facing the camera in black hijab, her head crowned in a laurel of yellow and pink forms that appear to be made of paper, like a string of decorations for a party. Her mouth is open, her head tipped back, her eyes inclined upward. The figure appears to be licking a lollipop, which is actually a circular fan printed with the figure of Pope John Paul II. What might be the confluences and fabrications involved in such an image? Her drapery suggests associations between Catholic saints or nuns and women in hijab, between a Fellini movie and the frozen signifier of the veiled Muslim woman, between belief and its emblems, including their kitsch versions. How does a Muslim woman signify amid the architecture of empires that vanquished and absorbed other belief systems? Forouhar highlights in these images the spectacle of visual cultures of belief and of classical antiquity as they play out in contemporary popular culture—just as the contemporary pop 'Ashura fabrics do. The confluences disrupt univocal signifiers. Through such work Forouhar lampoons what Allison Donnelly calls the "engineer[ing] of a representational equivalence between the Islamic woman and the cloistered, apolitical, even ahistorical victim."[105] The images play with artifice and wit, disrupt assumed essences with surface confusions, and juxtapose depth and perspective. In this series, Forouhar answers the system of facialization with affective ambiguities and irreverence.

Forouhar has compared the given patterns of Islamic miniatures to dictates on the realm of the representable, as I have said. At the same time, Persian miniatures, like Shi'a visual culture, constitute a rich and source of pattern and design for the artist. What functions as "repression" in classical Persian art in her interpretation supplies her with a vocabulary for articulating the presumed inseparability of bodily violence and female space, somatic and architectural as well as social and political. Forouhar's compositions reflect less the notion of the personal as political than they do the constitution of both as intricately braided. Her critique of embellishment as a vehicle of state brutality applies differently, but significantly, to the postfeminist optic, which contains, detaches from, denies, and imagines personal mastery of the cultural scaffolding. This disposition screens out the dictates of oppression of home and assigns it to "foreign" women, off in the distance or blotted out by cloth.

Notes

1 To be clear, interpreters of *tawhid* also argue for reciprocity; I describe Forouhar's adaptation, which uses the concept but does not forward theological claims. See, for instance, Amina Wadud, "Foreword: Engaging Tawhid in Islam and Feminisms," *International Feminist Journal of Politics* 10.4 (2008): 435–38.
2 McRobbie, *Aftermath*, 59–62.
3 For the association of the ornament and the "yellow" or Asian-American woman, see Anne Anlin Cheng, *Ornamentalism* (New York: Oxford University Press, 2019).
4 Brigitte Werneburg, "'You Have to Have Faith in People': An Interview with the Iranian Artist Parastou Forouhar," *Deutsche Bank Art Magazine* 55 (2009) http://db-artmag.com/en/55/feature/an-interview-with-parastou-forouhar/. Accessed August 2, 2014.
5 Rose Issa, ed. *Parastou Forouhar: Art, Life, and Death in Iran* (London: Saqi, 2010), 17.
6 Werneburg, "You Have to Have Faith," n.p.
7 Kazem Alamdari, "The Power Structure of the Islamic Republic of Iran: Transition from Populism to Clientelism, and Militarization of the Government," *Third World Quarterly* 26.8 (2005): 1294; Fariba Amini, "It Happened on Hedayet Street: The Forouhar's House, November 23, 1998," *The Iranian*, November 22, 2002 http://iranian.com/Arts/2002/November/Forouhar/index.html. Accessed June 12, 2016.
8 J. M. Bernstein, *Torture and Dignity: An Essay on Moral Injury* (Chicago: University of Chicago Press, 2015), 172.
9 Bernstein, *Torture and Dignity*, 2.
10 Issa, *Parastou Forouhar*, 8–9.
11 For Parastou Forouhar's own extended account of the murders and their aftermath, see *Das Land, in dem meine Eltern umgebracht wurden: Liebesklärung an den Iran* (Freiburg: Herder, 2011).
12 Michael Rubin and Patrick Clawson, "Patterns of Discontent: Will History Repeat Itself in Iran?" *Middle East Review of International Affairs* 10.1 (2006): 105–21; Reza Afshari, *Human Rights in Iran: The Abuse of Cultural Relativism* (Philadelphia: University of Pennsylvania Press, 2001), 211–15.
13 Mir M. Hosseini, "Assassination of Dariush Forouhar," www.fouman.com/Y/Get_Iranian_History_Today.php?artid=22; Reza Afshari, *Human Rights*, 211–15. Accessed July 22, 2015.
14 Parastou Forouhar, "Documents relating to the investigation into the politically motivated murder of Darius and Parwaneh Forouhar," www.parastou-forouhar.de/english/Documents-Parwaneh-and-Dariush-Forouhar.html. Accessed May 28, 2014. Also see Forouhar, *Das Land*, and Ali Akbar Ganji, *L'eminence rouge* (Tehran: Tarhno, 2001), 8–16.
15 Forouhar, "Documents."
16 Issa, *Parastou Forouhar*, 9.
17 Elaine Scarry, *The Body in Pain: The Making and Unmaking of the World* (New York: Oxford University Press, 1987), 29, 44.
18 Hilary Neroni observes that torture is by nature an act that occurs in private or hidden spaces. *The Subject of Torture: Psychoanalysis and Biopolitics in Television and Film* (New York: Columbia University Press, 2015), 6, 84. She draws on Agamben's concept of the state of exception as a mobile category. State or "sovereign" power moves to allow or disallow certain practices. As women have usually resided on the periphery of political life, their torture has long been altogether occluded. Cf. Giorgio Agamben, *State of Exception*, trans. Keith Attell (Chicago: University of Chicago Press, 2005).

19 Hidayatullah, *Feminist Edges*, 110.
20 See, for instance, Barlas, *Believing Women*, 94–96; Aziza al-Hibri, "Divine Justice and the Human Order: An Islamic Perspective," in *Humanity before God: Contemporary Faces of Jewish, Christian, and Islamic Ethics*, ed. William Schweiker, Michael Johnson, and Kevin Jung (Minneapolis: Fortress, 2006), 247; Wadud, *Inside the Gender Jihad*, and "Foreword," 435–38.
21 In this, Forouhar is in interesting dialogue with critics such as Zygmut Bauman, who contends that empathy depends on proximity and mutual recognition, and Hartman, who discusses the replacement of empathy by the (white) viewer's own immersion in self through witness of black slaves' suffering. Though Forouhar does not aim for empathy, her oscillations between proximity and distance bear upon the optics of witness and the oppositional gaze. Zygmunt Bauman and Leonidas Donskis, *Moral Blindness: The Loss of Sensitivity in Liquid Modernity* (Cambridge, UK, Polity, 2013), 213; Saidiya Hartman, *Scenes of Subjection: Terror, Slavery, and Self-Making in Nineteenth-Century America* (Oxford: Oxford University Press, 1997), 20; bell hooks, "The Oppositional Gaze: Black Female Spectators," in *The Feminism and Visual Culture Reader*, ed. Amelia Jones (New York: Routledge, 2010), 94–105.
22 David Bailey and Gilane Tawadros, eds., *Veil: Veiling, Representation, and Contemporary Art* (Cambridge, MA: MIT Press, 2003), 22.
23 Reina Lewis, Preface, *Veil: Veiling, Representation, and Contemporary Art*, ed. David Bailey and Gilane Tawadros (Cambridge: MIT Press, 2003), 8–16.
24 Ingvild Flashkerud, *Visualizing Belief and Piety in Iranian Shiism* (London: Continuum, 2012), 2.
25 Issa, *Parastou Forouhar*, 4–5, 34–37; for some of these images, in different arrangements, installations, and details, see "Funeral," 2003, www.parastou-forouhar.de/english/Works/funeral-site-specific-work/; "Countdown" 2008, www.parastou-forouhar.de/english/Works/countdown-2008/.
26 Flashkerud, *Visualizing Belief*, 75–81.
27 Vali Nasr, *The Shia Revival: How Conflicts with Iran Will Shape the Future* (New York: Norton, 2006), 42.
28 Heinz Halm, *The Shi'ites: A Short History*. 2nd ed., trans. Allison Brown (Princeton: Markus Wiener, 2007), 16.
29 Halm, *The Shi'ites*, 19.
30 Britta Schmitz, "Tausendundeine Macht," in *Tausendundein Tag* (Berlin: Walter König Hamburg: Nationalgalerie Hamburger Bahnhof, 2003), 15–16.
31 Issa, *Parastou Forouhar*, 33.
32 Flashkerud, *Visualizing Belief*, 75–81.
33 Flashkerud, *Visualizing Belief*, 2.
34 Werneburg, "You Have to Have Faith," n.p.
35 Issa, *Parastou Forouhar*, 35.
36 In fact, photographs of some installations show viewers sitting in the chairs.
37 Lutz Becker, "Art, Death, and Language," in Issa, *Parastou Forourhar*, 19.
38 Werneburg, "You Have to Have Faith," n.p.
39 Werneburg, "You Have to Have Faith," n.p.
40 Schmitz, "Tausendundeine Macht," 16–17.
41 Oleg Grabar, *Mostly Miniatures, An Introduction to Persian Painting* (Princeton: Princeton University Press, 2000), 149.
42 Oleg Grabar, *Mostly Miniatures*, 149.
43 Issa, *Parastou Forouhar*, 17.
44 Begum Ozden Firat, *Encounters with the Ottoman Minature: Contemporary Readings of an Imperial Art* (London: Bloomsbury, 2015), 2.

45 See, for instance, Annette Tietenberg, "Vom Verschleiern und Enthüllen oder Warum Parastou Forouhars Arbeiten ein Kontextuelles Gewand-tragen," in *Tausendundein Tag* (Berlin: Walter König; Hamburg: Nationalgalerie Hamburger Bahnhof, 2003), 54–61. More recently, Forouhar has mounted a show at the Kunsthalle Göppingen called "Im Zeichen des Ornaments [In ornamental signs]." The catalogue documenting the exhibition includes many of the pieces I discuss here, as well as newer work. Werner Meyer and Melanie Arjah, *Parastou Forouhar: Im Zeichen des Ornaments* (Stadt Göppingen, Germany: Göppingen Kunsthalle, 2018).
46 Alfred Loos, *Ornament and Crime: Selected Essays*, trans. Michael Mitchell (Ariadne Press, 1998), 171.
47 Issa, *Parastou Forouhar*, 42–47; www.parastou-forouhar.de/english/Works/eslimi/patternbook-2003/.
48 Katayoon Etemad, Faramarz Samavati, and Przemyslaw Prusinkiewicz, "Animating Persian Floral Patterns," *Proceedings of the Fourth Eurographics Conference on Computational Aesthetics in Graphics, Visualization, and Imaging*, ed. Paul Brown et al., (Aire-la-Ville, Switzerland: Eurographics Association, 2008), 25–26.
49 Etemad, et al., "Animating," 25–26.
50 Etemad et al., "Animating," 25–26.
51 Issa, *Parastou Forouhar*, 42–43; "2008 Kunsthalle Vienna," and "2007 Santralistanbul," www.parastou-forouhar.de/english/Works/eslimi/patternbook-2003/.
52 Printed fabric-pattern book. Issa, *Parastou Forouhar*, 42; "2008 Kunsthalle Vienna," www.parastou—forouhar.de/english/Works/eslimi/patternbook-2003/.
53 Grabar, *Mostly Miniatures*, 23–24.
54 Grabar, *Mostly Miniatures*, 131.
55 Grabar, *Mostly Miniatures*, 121.
56 Alexandra Karentzos, "Tausend Tode Sterben: Erwachen aus dem Märchentraum," in *Tausendundein Tag* (Berlin: Walter König; Hamburg: Nationalgalerie Hamburger Bahnhof, 2003), 37–38.
57 Digital prints on fabric, each 594 cm. × 420 cm Issa, *Parastou Forouhar*, 42–43; www.parastou-forouhar.de/english/Works/eslimi/patternbook-2003/.
58 Issa, *Parastou Forouhar*, 44.
59 Issa, *Parastou Forouhar*, 47.
60 Issa, *Parastou Forouhar*, 46; "Genital 12," www.parastou-forouhar.de/english/Works/eslimi/patternbook-2003/.
61 Issa, *Parastou Forouhar*, 44; some images appear at www.parastou-forouhar.de/english/Works/eslimi/patternbook-2003/.
62 Issa, *Parastou Forouhar*, 44; "Gabel 12," www.parastou-forouhar.de/english/Works/eslimi/patternbook-2003/.
63 Issa, *Parastou Forouhar*, 44.
64 Issa, *Parastou Forouhar*, 45; "Gabel 17," www.parastou-forouhar.de/english/Works/eslimi/patternbook-2003/.
65 Deleuze and Sacher-Masoch, *Coldness and Cruelty*, 18–19.
66 Neroni, *The Subject of Torture*, 84.
67 Issa, *Parastou Forouhar*, 86; Maura Reilly and Linda Nochlin, *Global Feminisms: New Directions in Contemporary Art* (New York: Merrell and Brooklyn Museum, 2007), 263–64; "Wallpaper," www.parastou-forouhar.de/english/Works/tausendundein_tag/wallpaper/.
68 Issa, *Parastou Forouhar*, 60–63, 70–73, 78–79, 87; www.parastou-forouhar.de/english/Works/tausendundein_tag/drawings/.
69 Digital print on paper, 145 cm. × 326 cm, 2006. Issa, *Parastou Forouhar*, 78–79; www.parastou-forouhar.de/english/Works/tausendundein_tag/drawings/panorama/.

122 Surface Violation

70 Eight digital drawings on photo rag, each 297 cm. × 420 cm, 2007. Issa, *Parastou Forouhar*, "A Thousand and One Days I," 60–63; "Drawings Series I, 2007" www.parastou-forouhar.de/english/Works/tausendundein_tag/drawings/zeichnungen/.
71 Alexandra Karentzos, "Tausend Tode Sterben," 35.
72 Jussawalla, Feroza, Introduction, in *Memory, Voice and Identity: Muslim Women's Writing across the Middle East*, Feroza Jussawalla and Doaá Omran, eds. (New York: Routledge, 2021). But in the same volume, also see a complex assessments of Scherherzade by Naila Sahar, "Feminist Ethnography, Revisionary Historiography, and the Subaltern in Assia Djebar's *Fantasia: An Algerian Cavalcade*," in *Memory, Voice and Identity*, 69–80 and by Brigitte Stepanov, "Djebar and Schehherazade: One Muslim Women, Past and Present," in *Memory, Voice and Identity*, 211–22.
73 Alexandra Karentzos, "Tausend Tode Sterben," 36.
74 Grabar, *Mostly Miniatures*, 133.
75 Issa, *Parastou Forouhar*, 78–79; www.parastou-forouhar.de/english/Works/tausendundein_tag/drawings/panorama/.
76 Issa, *Parastou Forouhar*, 63; www.parastou-forouhar.de/english/Works/tausendundein_tag/drawings/zeichnungen/. In later black and white prints, these typographic figures actually compose heads with suggested features. See Portrait I-III (2014), Meyer and Ardjah, *Im Zeichen*, 42–45. Patterns of black and white lidded eyes also come to overwhelm and absorb limbs in "Augen" (2018). Meyer and Ardjah, *Im Zeichen*, 66–70.
77 Issa, *Parastou Forouhar*, 62–63; www.parastou-forouhar.de/english/Works/tausendundein_tag/drawings/zeichnungen/.
78 Issa, *Parastou Forouhar*, 62; Z.nr. 10, www.parastou-forouhar.de/english/Works/tausendundein_tag/drawings/zeichnungen/.
79 Issa, *Parastou Forouhar*, 63; Z.nr. 15, www.parastou-forouhar.de/english/Works/tausendundein_tag/drawings/zeichnungen/.
80 Digital print on photo rag, each 100 cm. × 100 cm, 2010. Issa, *Parastou Forouhar*, 56–59; www.parastou-forouhar.de/english/Works/Papillon/2010-Papillon-Collection/. For stunning later installations that use the butterfly shape with images of violence, see Meyer and Ardjah, *Im Zeichen*, 32–38.
81 Issa, *Parastou Forouhar*, 58; "2010 'Ashura Day," www.parastou-forouhar.de/english/Works/Papillon/2010-Papillon-Collection/2010-papillon-collection-'Ashura.html/.
82 Issa, *Parastou Forouhar*, 59; "2010 Ewin Prison," www.parastou-forouhar.de/english/Works/Papillon/2010-Papillon-Collection/2010-papillon-collection-ewin.html.
83 Digital print on photo rag, each 40 cm. × 40 cm, 2007. Issa, *Parastou Forouhar*, 64–65; www.parastou-forouhar.de/english/Works/the-color-of-my-name/red-is-my-name-green-is-my-name1/. Also see Meyer and Ardjah, *Im Zeichen*, 57–58. Meyer notes that the colors evoke those of the Iranian flag, "On the Role of Ornament in the Work of Parastou Forouhar," in *Im Zeichen*, 85.
84 Meyer, "On the Role of Ornament," notes the "sexualization of violence" in the pieces, 85.
85 Also see later work that actually blurs the black-robed figure in movement or makes it appear to float, in empty rooms or streets, Meyer and Adjah, *Im Zeichen*, 8–12, 22–23.
86 New Art Century, London, 2003.
87 Candlestar and Day, Tehran and Mall Galleries, London, 2009.
88 *Pearls on the Ocean Floor*, dir. and prod. Robert Adanto, 2010.
89 *Women without Men* [Zanan-e bedun-e mardan], dir. Shirin Neshat and Shoja Azari Essential Filmproduktion, 2009.
90 Digital print on vinyl, 6 m. × 2 m, 2003. Issa, *Parastou Forouhar*, 100–101; www.parastou-forouhar.de/english/Works/freitag/Friday.html.
91 Also see Meyer and Adjah, *Im Zeichen*, 6–7, for this piece in a later exhibition.
92 Issa, *Parastou Forouhar*, 102–103; "2001 Second Berlin Biennale," www.parastou-forouhar.de/english/Works/Blind-spot-series/2001-blind-spot/.

93 www.parastou-forouhar.de/english/Works/Blind-spot-series/2001-behnam/.
94 Issa, *Parastou Forouhar*, 104–105; www.parastou-forouhar.de/english/Works/Blind-spot-series/2001-blind-spot/2001-2nd-Berlin-Biennale-2.html. Also see Meyer and Adjah, *Im Zeichen*, 30–31, where the piece is simply entitled "Rorschach/Benham."
95 Photographs, digitally printed, each 80 cm. × 80 cm, 2004–10. Issa, *Parastou Forouhar*, 108–109; www.parastou-forouhar.de/english/Works/2004-swanrider/. See further images from this series in Meyer and Adjah, *Im Zeichen*, 26–27. This 2018 show also features photographs of black robes immersed in water and merged with a tree in a field. Their status in relation to the figure is ambiguous. See "Das Gras ist grun, der Himmel ist blau, und sie ist schwarz" series ("The grass is green, heaven is blue, and she is black," [2017]), 14, 17.
96 Bob Duggan, "Black Swan: Uncovering Iranian Women Artists," *Big Think*, January 30, 2011 http://bigthink.com/Picture-This/black-swan-uncovering-iranian-women-artists. Accessed August 15, 2016.
97 Installation of digitally cut plastic foil, 2008. Issa, *Parastou Forouhar*, 22–25.
98 Issa, *Parastou Forouhar*, 22–23; see "Tripartite 1" and "Tripartite 2" www.parastou-forouhar.de/english/Works/written-room/bodyletter_series_of_photog/.
99 Acrylic paint, 2009–10. Issa, *Parastou Forouhar*, 26–27; for images of various similar installations, see www.parastou-forouhar.de/english/Works/written-room/schrift_raum/.
100 Slide show, 2006. Issa, *Parastou Forouhar*, 112–19; for some of these images, see www.parastou-forouhar.de/english/Works/2006-dolce-vita-slide-show-projection/.
101 Issa, *Parastou Forouhar*, 114.
102 Issa, *Parastou Forouhar*, 114.
103 Issa, *Parastou Forouhar*, 118–19; www.parastou-forouhar.de/english/Works/2006-dolce-vita-slide-show-projection/dolce-vita-1.html.
104 Issa, *Parastou Forouhar*, 128; "Lolly Pope 2008," far left image, www.parastou-forouhar.de/english/Works/lolly-pope-2008/.
105 Allison Donnelly, "Visibility, Violence, and Voice? Attitudes to Veiling, Post-11 September," in *Veil*, ed. Bailey and Tawadros, 134.

5
THE MOTHER MARK AND OTHER TONGUES IN *NYLON ROAD*

Parastou Forouhar's work of the early twenty-first century moves us back to the gaze discussed in the first chapter. The gap between the female spectator and the screen image becomes elastic and variable in Forouhar's formulation, in part because viewers can move physically and optically as they regard the image and actuate its potential. Forouhar's treatment of surfaces offers a compelling exchange with the revisions of neoliberal individualism in dialogue with Muslim belief, practice, and culture. Significantly the artist does not dismiss the surface as false or shallow. It is complete, its manifest and latent meanings available. Forouhar's direct representations of veiled women offer exchanges of bodily and sexed parts with things, as we have seen in the objectification of women in the literary works I discuss in the first three chapters. In these ways the artist surmounts disclosure and revelation as opposite activities and restates the dynamism of bodily habitus. Just as Monica Ali illustrates a latent dynamic of collaborative somatic exchange and internalization of the prophetic body, and Mohja Kahf understands hijab as a second (though racially limited) skin, Forouhar bypasses, plays with, and consistently disrupts the conventions of representing Muslimah identities.

Nylon Road[1] (2006) also engages with the Lacanian fragmented self that Ghumkhor argues is granted coherence by the robed religious other, and also does so through digital stylization and typification. But unlike Forouhar, the Swiss-Iranian Parsua Bashi uses the face as a site of subjectification. Its recognizable commercial traits allow for multiplicity of form, perspective, and emotional expression. The face's novelty consists not in its distinctive properties but in its attachment to a Muslimah. Through a large and highly stylized visage, Bashi hails the European viewer as part of a global pop audience. The graphic narrative works through the facialization of the full figure in movement without engaging with "veiling/unveiling" as the central axis of display and identity. The singular

DOI: 10.4324/9781003189299-6

figure, presented in full-frontal view in the first panel, splits off and never fully coheres again. The many constituent subjects who emerge align with moments of the protagonist's life narrative. While showing herself as complicit with the forces of commodity that she comes to lampoon, Bashi subjects the conventional signs of the Muslimah to critique and deflation. In conclusion the subject is envisioned as an ongoing collaboration of agents. Bashi illustrates the messiness and necessity of coalition among the women produced by seemingly incompatible identity groups by aligning them with her own life stages.

Parastou Forouhar shifts the focus from individual female bodies as the necessary vehicles of agency to the perceptual and epistemological field of feminization. The assemblages of abstracted forms create total fields that ensnare the gaze through oscillation.[2] Bashi, too, capitalizes on the resources of her medium to move the audience's eye. Her designs illustrate and interact with the dialectical structure of the protagonist's production. Yet Bashi differs profoundly in her political aims and mode of address, locating herself firmly in the world of personal beauty and style, shot through with strong self-mockery. A multimodal vehicle, *Nylon Road* explicitly sets itself apart from both trauma[3] and from high aesthetic theory. The author-protagonist presents herself as a privileged, middle-aged émigré in the European cosmopolis, one who left Iran because of a broken heart rather than the situation of precarity in which many transnational graphic memoirs are set.[4] Figures of past selves quickly disrupt the placid if aimless diegetic present of 2004. They appear as strangers. The first, a child, has a birthmark that the adult also bears. The child's sudden manifestation forces the adult to recognize the girl as herself at six. The "mark" of origin and identification— that is, the imago of the past as a fully materialized being—overcomes Bashi's "misrecognition" of herself as a coherent figure, reversing the operation of the Lacanian mirror stage. Bashi develops a maternal relation to her abandoned younger identities. Soon the narrative reveals her status as a biological mother to a daughter who was taken from her ten years before, in Iran.

Eleven past selves eventually come to occupy the space of the present. In so doing they fragment and mottle the container of one body and the form of one story as a continuous development. The "Muttermal" ("birthmark"), etymologically in German the mother's "instance" or "mark," and in Farsi the "alamat tavalod" ("birth sign") or "nesha mathar zadi" ("birth mother sign")[5] comes to signify the mother-daughter relation as paradigmatic. It represents the physical absence of the author's daughter as well as the absence of Farsi, the mother tongue entirely erased from the "original" German text. Bashi could not comprehend much German at the diegetic time in which the narrative is set, yet the language of the original edition is German. The graphic mark, associated with the birthmark, must serve as the medium of representation fully available to the artist. Lingering in the visual realm of the imaginary because the symbolic is unavailable as a mode of communication with the past, *Nylon Road* installs the other in the subject and brings a temporally disparate "circuit of gazes" onto a single plane. The "Muttermal" recaptures the "female" line while it shows the process of working through losses. Through graphic marks, too, the memoir installs the primary significance of maternity, including Bashi's biological mother and previous generations of feminists in Iran and elsewhere.

The citation of a recognizable and commercially circulated face in *Nylon Road* counters the EuroAmerican reduction of the stereotypic Muslim woman's face and the capture of her body in a black blot. This sign deprives subjects of agency and even substance because it suggests that there is no corporealization at all without exhibition of the figure underneath, as I have said. Here both the figure and the face draw on the typification from which the cartoon draws its idioms.[6] The face features large eyes in an expanse of the white flesh of the base paper, again recalling the white wall/black hole system of facialization that Deleuze and Guattari describe.[7] Bashi's self-portrait resonates most strongly with a stripped down, plainer version of mid-century fashion illustrations and comic strips such as *Brenda Starr* and *Mary Worth*, as well as animated Disney princesses and heroines of the 1980s and later.[8] In this sense the use of the Western mediagenic face reinforces critiques of Muslimah representation entering the mainstream only through the replication of white femininity. Contradicting conventional vehicles of white prettiness are the distortions caused by fear, grief, anger, shock, and confusion. In addition, some panels use insignia and emblems to represent the human figure. The paratext features puppets, silhouettes, and dolls. Movement among these visual idioms is animated by the interplay of panel and page design and the openness of reading sequence, both of which contribute to the varying "pulsions and affects"[9] of the visual plane.

Nylon Road now exists in a visual pop field that features a number of comic book Muslimah heroes, as it did not at the time of its original publication in German or its translation into English. The most well known is Ms. Marvel, introduced in 2013 as Kamala Khan, a 16-year-old Pakistani-American Muslim who lives in New Jersey.[10] She replaced Dust, who emerged in 2002.[11] A Sunni Muslimah, Sooraya Qadir appeared as a refugee from Afghanistan to the U.S. who struggled with American norms, particularly in relation to her religious practice and belief.[12] Also attracting major attention is Naif al-Muttawa's *The 99*, launched in Kuwait in 2006 and globally in 2007. The transnational superhero group is named for the numerous attributes of God. The band consists of male and female members whose powers derive from the Noor Stones, bearers of medieval Islamic wisdom literature. The first woman to appear was Dana Ibrahim/Noora, who with the assistance of the stone can see the light and dark in people, a power associated with Muhammad.[13]

Figure and Design

Nylon Road evokes the Silk Road as a trade route as well as the garment stockings, also originally made from silk. Like many of the producers I have discussed, Bashi uses fabric and clothing as the conceit for Muslim female identity, beauty, labor, and exchange. And like Forouhar in particular, Bashi bases elements of her style on the intricate exchanges between Persian manuscript illustration and contemporary media. Here the material and psychological struggle between text and image renders dynamic the hierarchy of text and image in Persian manuscripts. The story consists of nine chapters. Each begins with a small emblem in a square, resembling a woodcut or collage. The figures, in black, resemble shadow puppets or cut-outs and are strongly two-dimensional. These small paratextual images relate to the content of the chapter in various ways. They pick out an element, such as a boom box, which is featured as a consistent device or visual element in the chapter: the boom box draws together news reports about the Iran-Iraq war and the music played at a dinner party in Zürich. Another section highlights a thematic, as in the first chapter overleaf, which features a woman in flight, complete with zip lines and hair trailing behind her, her foot protruding through the black frame to the bottom right corner.

While they are in many respects identical, the size of the original German (10.6 in. × 7.6 in.) and the later English (9.3 in. × 6.4 in.) editions differ. The larger format of the German edition suggests the presentation of an art book or exhibition catalogue, as it gives more scope to the images themselves. The enlargement especially enhances figures who appear in full panels or, more frequently, a half-page panel running horizontally.[14] The panels that comprise the main pages of the story use fields of brown, gray, and tan. Few of them accord with the graphic standard template,[15] of nine or twelve panels in arrangements of three panels across and three or four tiers down. Often a grid constructs the page design, but does so with great variety, such as in the layout of the opening page. It installs a strong vertical axis on the left through a single panel, then divides the right column into five boxes of text and image. The temporal movement of the frames varies accordingly. The typical eye movement from left to right is invited to proceed down first, before it moves up and across.

To highlight emotion and psychological intensity, the artist also uses large panels: in two column pairs of one or two images; in two column panels answered by a single horizontal panel that stretches across the bottom of the page; or in single-panel "splash pages" that coincide with sweeping iconic variety or temporal sequence contained in one image. Very characteristic is a horizontal band that spans two columns left to right combined with two paired panels in other areas of the page, in a modified grid. Neil Cohn calls this a "staggered" layout, in which the two left panels are exactly the same size and the two right panels different sizes. The gutter drops between the two columns.[16] *Nylon Road* also modifies "overlap"[17] lay-outs by allowing one panel to intrude into another without using a gutter between them. Such visual strategies may interrupt the conventional "Z" movement of the eye across the graphic page, by, for example, arranging the layout to invite two "Z" eye movements through the stacking of texts and panels.

Design elements also bear upon the memoir's organization, which does not follow a conventional chronology of flashback to childhood and then forward to join with the present. Instead Bashi constantly shows disjunctions between narratological "story time," or chronological order, and "discourse time," presentational order.[18] For example, the last two selves to appear to Bashi in the present story time are herself at 13 in 1979, and at 33 in 1999. The 36-year-old, from 2002, has already manifested some time before.[19] The last two selves to appear serve to emphasize disagreements that cannot be reconciled. The 13-year-old revolutionary delivers an unresolved Marxist and cultural critique of "freedom" as an alibi for privilege and consumerism. She stomps off in disgust at the end of her encounter. Nonetheless, the conversation provokes a structural illustration of the manufacture of young women in parallel ideologies: Western consumer, state Islamic religious, and Marxist. The 33-year-old recalls her attempt to synthesize Iranian or Persian cultural affinities with the world of fashion, advertising, and pop imagery. The extremes of such combinations appear in imagined trivializations of Western traumas. The panels illustrate the impossibility of any synthesis between fashion quotations and historical traumas such as imperialism. Even mother-daughter collaborations do not overcome aporias.

The memoir begins in the present of 2004. A vertical panel that runs the length of the left border of the page shows Bashi frontally as a complete figure (Figure 5.1). She wears a longish white blouse, unbuttoned at the bottom and hanging over the waist of her grey slacks or jeans, slightly flared at the knee, and laced, flat shoes that might be sneakers. Her arms are crossed and her gaze out to the viewer is steady and neutral. One foot points out and penetrates the panel frame, interrupting the bordered cut line at the bottom; the other foot parallels the horizontal bottom border of the frame. "Ich lebe seit dem 23. April 2004 in Zürich," says the top text strip. The page uses a "blockage" layout, which Cohn describes as the horizontal gutter abutting and stopped by a panel that takes up the entire right column.[20] The text box moves horizontally to the right, in tension with the vertical thrust of the left panel. Two texts boxes, interspersed with three smaller panels in the right-hand column, continue: "Wiese ich hierher gekommen bin, ist eine Geschichte, die ich jetzt nicht erklären will" ("I've been living in Zürich since the 23rd of April 2004. The reason why I came here is another story that I won't explain now.")[21] The bottom panel in the right vertical column begins a sentence that is completed through the bottom text panel on which the vertical figure stands, but runs across the gutter between right and left established above: "Ich beschlossen, den Iran to verlassen, ... und in die Schweiz zu gehen 'eine weiterer Iranerin in Zürich' zu werden."[22] In the English version, the sentence syntax is not strung between the panels: "I decided to leave Iran and come to Switzerland. To become 'eine weitere Iranerin' in Zürich." Notably, the English translation preserves the German phrase, but its translation below the panel erases the German's use of the feminine article: Bashi calls herself

The Mother Mark and Other Tongues **129**

FIGURE 5.1 *Nylon Road*, 2006, p. 6. Courtesy of Parsua Bashi and Kein & Aber AG.

"just another Iranian in Zurich," in English but the German actually indicates "another Iranian woman (or female) in Zurich."[23]

The illustration emphasizes not the figure's acquisition of a new or European identity but rather the apparel of a youth uniform that also serves as modest dress. At the same time the text designates her as another sexed but anonymous member of an implicitly foreign mass of migrants. The "story" (the German word carries a resonance of "history") that the narrating-I does not want to relate points to the *bildungsroman* that will burst upon her after the text establishes her position in Switzerland. Bashi at 38 is settled if undirected. She narrates her attempt to follow a disciplined program of self-improvement and adaptation: she tries to acquire the languages of her new location, she practices calligraphy, she exercises, and she socializes with other émigrés. But she becomes demoralized and abandons this program. Instead she smokes cigarettes, eats, sleeps, and surfs the Farsi Internet. The three representations of her engaged in these activities, of escape or boredom, are crammed into one bottom panel.[24]

In the next sequence, a full splash page shows a haggard Bashi during her morning toilette, surprised to encounter there a smiling, curly-haired girl in sandals and shorts (Figure 5.2).[25] The scene visually echoes but also modifies the previous splash page, in which the imagined calligrapher Bashi floats over the Zürich promenade on a cloud while she inks a page in lyrical fantasy.[26] This metalepsis, or fantasy world presented as such, gives way to an actual merging of storyworlds or actualities. In the present-tense Bashi has recently abandoned her self-imposed improvement regime. Her subsequent manifestation as her six-year-old self appears as part of a two-page blockage. Each two-page folio contains a single splash page (one verso and one recto) next to a page of strong tabular panels running across the layout on the page facing the image. Though in the bathroom they occupy the same space—of private cleaning, excretion, and arrangement of public presentation—the adult and child are separated by a strong though staggered verticality. A towel hanging from a rack, the edge of the sink, and the cabinet underneath it suggest the line.

The adult, narrating Bashi, first calls the figure "eine Fremde" ("a stranger," gendered female)[27] and doubts her own sanity through scenes of cartoonish psychiatric scenarios, until she notices the "Muttermal" on the child's arm and wonders what it means. The adult Bashi displays the same mark on her arm. A full splash page then presents the child in the open air, staring directly out and smiling. She holds thistles and wildflowers in one hand, a bag with rocks and a lizard in the other.[28] Only small boxes toward the right-hand border of the frame punctuate the silent, natural scene. "Sie erinnerte mich an mich selbst in Alter von sechs Jahren: ein unbekümmertes kleines Mädchen," says the first box. "Wie hatte ich sie so lange vergessen können?" says the second. The box at the bottom of the panel concludes "Ja, sie muss ICH sein. Wie hatte ich MICH vergessen können?" ("She reminded me of myself at age six: a happy-go-lucky little girl.

FIGURE 5.2 *Nylon Road*, 2006, p. 13. Courtesy of Parsua Bashi and Kein & Aber AG.

How could I have forgotten her for such a long time? Yes, she must be ME. How could I have forgotten me?"). The child's carefree status comments upon the adult's confined and undirected one, as her alienation and use of "ICH" recalls "das Ich," or the ego.

The juxtaposition of the two figures in the same space shows a reversal that is also a restatement of the mirror stage's premises: where does the "ich" find its location when the gaze sees a stranger as well as the mark of similarity? The image of the little girl resembles a snapshot, depicting the full figure complete with bandaged knee and birthmark. It "braids" with the opening image of Bashi, for both full figures gaze directly out at the viewer. Yet the child's body language is open and un-self-conscious, in contrast to the 38-year-old figure's crossed arms. The child also appears in the natural landscape of home, on a beach with small hills or dunes in the background. Groensteen defines braiding as a "network" that lends density and multivocal connection to the graphic narrative. The term generally refers to a cue that calls different panels into relationship, whether through image or language.[29] Here, the six-year-old Bashi braids not only with the gaze of the narrator and adult "I" but also portends the appearance, in the fourth chapter, of Bashi's own daughter. The daughter appears when the 29-year-old Bashi is a young mother in Tehran. The toddler also gazes out at the viewer,[30] though she does not otherwise strongly resemble the six-year-old Parsua here or elsewhere.[31]

The "Muttermal" dramatizes this braiding when Bashi witnesses a child, harshly scolded by a mother, crying on the street over a lost ball.[32] The Swiss child, airborne because of her mother's yanking, appears in the next panel enlarged, right next to a discomfited Bashi. The speech balloon containing the child's cry for her ball becomes the hilt of a knife that pierces the present-tense Bashi's heart. The 29-year-old Bashi appears in the next panel, her face in profile as she pokes into the frame under the withdrawing knife, which splashes drops of blood. Holding a book with the scales and the sword of justice on it, the 29-year-old Bashi, her face growing larger and more anguished as the scene continues, tells the 39-year-old Swiss émigré about her long ordeal to obtain her child. The daughter was legally awarded to her husband because she asked for the divorce.[33] The present-tense Bashi yells, in a horizontal panel that takes up the bottom half of the page, "Hallo! Wach auf! Hör bitte auf damit! Das is jetzt zehn jahre her!" ("Hey, wake up! Listen, dammit! That was ten years ago now!").[34] The mournful mother appears full-faced frontally toward the plane. Every line that describes her expression moves down; her eyes are bloodshot from weeping. Nonetheless the older Bashi winds up comforting herself as a young mother by pointing out her terrible isolation as a divorced woman in Tehran, where she was socially censured and economically trapped. She reminds her younger self that women "im Herzen Europas" ("in the heart of Europe," linked to the bloodied maternal heart) also suffer in the legal and economic system. At the same time, the page shows the younger mother wallowing in self-pity, her shroudlike garment patterned with the words "Trauer," "Tranen," "Leid," "Schmerz," and extending a bowl of tears to others for contribution ("Suffer," "Tears," "Sorrow," "Pain").[35] The images recall the practices of 'Ashura, the Shi'a rites of mourning for Hussain, as well as the hamsa, which I discuss in the previous chapter. Here the imagery satirizes the young mother for seeking an audience for her agony while depicting her inconsolable grief. The younger self is finally portrayed in the lake, drowning and calling for help, her head tipped back while the observers on land express pity. After grabbing a log, the fingers of each hand prominently displayed as the bowl floats away, the 29-year-old looks back at the shore with a glare on her face that braids with the older, angry Bashi's. She too appears in profile, facing in the opposite direction, her scowl forming a single eyebrow. The older Bashi, returning from the symbolic drama to the present day, consoles her younger self. She then throws the shroud into the washing machine of her Zürich apartment. The figure's empty hand appears at the horizontal center of the panel. She narrates: "Erst danach würde ich mein Leben in den Griff kriegen können" ("Only afterwards could I get a grip on my life").[36] Both graphically and rhetorically, the "hand" and the "grip" stress the association of loss with the curative of drawing and of self-direction. But the same knife stabs her again when she hears a child crying, in the last panel of the chapter.[37]

In the first chapter, Bashi withdraws from her six-year-old self in order to consider what reality she is occupying. The focus returns to her face in a single panel with the thoughts in a block within the panel: "Einseits könnte ich nicht recht verstehen, was da vor sich ging, anderseits sah ich die ganze Szene in einem einizigen Augenblick: Ich war alleine, hoffnunglos, verzweifelt" ("One the one hand I couldn't quite understand what was going on. On the other hand, I could see the whole scene in one instant. I was alone, hopeless, desperate, and apparently unable to deal with the situation").[38] This description in itself scans the operation of the psychomachia to follow, in which a single instant or instance encapsulates the unfolding of the subject as a scenario with the image, particularly the figure, as its vehicle. The Muttermal acts as a mark and a temporality, an absence and a generative tool.

In the prior scene in the Zürich bathroom, the child says that there are more former selves waiting to meet the adult. Bashi decides that she has to "höre sie auf" ("listen to them") because the adult is "das Ergebnis iherer Lebens" ("the result of their lives").[39] Yet it is the six-year-old who has pointed to this multiplicity of selves. The present-tense Bashi leaves her apartment only to discover six of her past selves (including the six-year-old) seated on a bench on a Zürich promenade, across from the bench where the adult sits by herself.[40] A garbage can ("Abfall") stands in the gap between the benches.

These figures are personifications arranged as a psychomachia, a fourth-century form devised by Prudentius. It represents an epic of inner space divorced in its manifest text from recorded history and identifiable territory. Bashi renders the subject as multiple agents, rather than relating a conflict of virtue and vices, as the original *Psychomachia* in Latin does. The *Psychomachia* conducts its struggle only on "the field of semantics," Malamud observes,[41] rather than through heroic characters. Notably, however, by creating iconographically clear allegorical figures out of words and giving them the ability to act, the poem endows abstractions with all the inconsistencies and ambiguities of human language.[42] *Nylon Road* translates this linguistic intensity, with its strong visual allegiances, into a primarily visual idiom interacting with narrative and drama. Here the relations of the narrating- and narrated-I, a distinction central to narratological theory of the autographic, multiplies and narrows through the proliferation of figures. In this Bashi's device bears affinities with what Diana Taylor calls the performative scenario: the present changes not *the* past, but pasts, which modify the crowd of imagos and understand the present as dialogic, as if Doane's spectator engages and interacts with the images on the screen who emerge from it.[43]

Mother Tongues and Other Mouths

Unlike *Persepolis*, as well as less well known and later portrayals of turmoil produced by religious-political difference, *Nylon Road* presents a life profoundly shaped by political repression and war but not directly experienced as a threat to her life. In this the work contrasts with trauma and witness graphic narratives works of the era such Lamia Ziade's *Bye, Bye Babylon* (2011) and Zeina Abirached's *A Game for Swallows* (2012), both set in 1970s Lebanon; Amir and Khalil's *Zahra's Paradise* (2011), about the Iranian suppression of protests against the 2009 elections; or Riad Sattouf's *The Arab of the Future* (2015), partly set in Libya and Syria. Bashi loses family members and friends to emigration, is whipped by the Revolutionary Guard for walking on the street with a man unrelated to her, and so is pressured socially to marry. Yet her life in Tehran also includes graduation from art school and a career in graphic design. *Nylon Road*'s psychomachia breaks open the master sign of Muslim women as the materialization of masquerade or the blot of bodilessness, and of Muslim men as their despotic oppressors. Bashi's life story continually renders ironic binary readings and fixed identifications. Her own status as a body and a subject, much less as an Iranian, a Muslim, and later as a migrant, is fluid, relational, and multiple. Julia Watson praises this approach: as a witness to the Iranian revolution and its aftermath in everyday life, the narrator "constantly negotiate[s] with her memories as embodied subjects in creative tension with her migrant 'I,' rather than consolidating them into a coherent post-migration identity." Such strategies of self-presentation "provide a prismatically multi-sited account of her pre-migration past in Iran, giving *Nylon Road* an experiential authority closer to that of an eyewitness."[44] The memoir installs the "I" as itself migrant, under the pressure of displacement. Experience diminishes the certainty of younger selves. For example, at a party, when a Swiss woman asks Bashi if she is homesick at hearing Persian music on the radio, Bashi says no, a response that concludes with the appearance of a young adult Bashi in a flashback scene.[45] Back in Tehran, the younger self argues with her departing family and friends that one shouldn't abandon one's birthplace—as she now has.[46] The same sense of isolation and abandonment haunted her in Tehran that now haunts her in Zürich. The strident criticism of those who abandon the project of revolution for a life of ease and alienation turns on her migrant present, as she engages in her own Marxist-derived "Selbstwerdung" process, in part through group "Selbstkritik" ("self-building" through "self-criticism").[47] The subject constantly oscillates between the relations of older and younger versions of being, themselves mother and daughter surrogates.

The "Muttermal" centrally installs the significance of maternity to the semiotic of *Nylon Road* through its narrative episodes and its refusal of synthesis. Its graphic and rhetorical presentation of language itself, as I have mentioned, focalizes maternity as an affective space. The paradox of language is illustrated when the narrating-I recalls the absence of her "tongue" in Switzerland early in her residence there. A panel that spreads horizontally across the bottom of the page and more than half of its vertical span shows this loss of tongue symbolically, at the same time that the artist renders it as entirely somatic. On the left, in an area of the panel dominated by white and tan, stands a pavilion or gazebo with "Farsi" and "Persisch" written on the lintels, amid calligraphic script. The pavilion itself appears under "Die Farsi Sonne." Inside the structure is a small rendering of a young woman, arm propped on a pillow, her eyes closed in enjoyment as she both basks in and is protected from the sun. On the right, in the half of the panel dominated by gray, stands a castlelike structure. Its door, barred and closed by a huge padlock, is further guarded by a sentry with a pike and a sculpture of a guard dog. "Deutsch" reads the placard over the door. Snow fills the entrance of the building, and stops at the center, where Bashi stands holding up a placard over an umbrella. She is naked and shivering between the two structures. Her sign designates her condition as "Meine Fremde Sprache verkentnisse" ("my knowledge of foreign language").[48] A zigzag pattern of the gray and tan separates the fields of color over her. "Oh Mutter, wo bist du?" the thought balloon to the left says ("Oh mother where are you?").[49]

Farsi becomes a maternal architecture that allows movement in and out as well as warmth and protection. The use of German to portray the narrating-I's previous thoughts and current narration becomes a physical and psychic gap over which communication takes place. Related instances occur when near-present selves appear in conversations with Swiss nationals, even in the presence of other Iranian migrants. The conversations take place in a German that Bashi cannot yet comprehend, and yet she participates in the talk. The moments in which her past selves appear might well also be regarded as neither quite external nor internal, as the dialogue of selves also takes place in German (not, as it could, in Farsi) and yet is rendered as distinct from the present-tense scene among German speakers in which Bashi participates.

The physical presentation of the base script compounds the dynamic of the mother mark and the mother tongue that I am arguing is central to *Nylon Road*.

The German "original," which was produced with the assistance of a translator, as well as the later English translation of *Nylon Road*, uses a digitally generated font that resembles hand-lettering. The text, particularly in speech balloons, may be centered rather than blocked and appears in a squared off rather than a rounded balloon format. This particular effect is created by the author's method of composition, which she related to Julia Watson:

> First I draw quick pencil sketches on paper, then draw them again in a final form by ink on paper, scanned the outlined versions, and colored them in computer by a drawing software. The bubbles with the text was the last layer.[50]

The squared off containment of text in the dialogue balloons helps propel words that break out of the balloons or even appear to press or shove figures to the margins of a panel. At times the speech text escapes any balloon or tail at all. Prominent among these scenes of linguistic break-out are panels that illustrate Bashi's past selves while they criticize her current life, pointing out its ease, its triviality, its small cruelties, and its gender inequities.

The graphic appearance and arrangement of text contribute a visual element to the "metafocalization" of language itself in *Nylon Road*. Horstkotte and Pedri summarize the concept of focalization in narratology, first identified by Gerard Genette, as "the filtering of a story as prior to and/or embedded in its narratorial mediation." It allows distinctions to be made between, for instance, a character's consciousness and the narrative perspective.[51] Recent critics, recognizing the premises of either rhetoric or image in narratological theory, have sought a semiotic tool that can encompass both elements and their interplay in the medium of graphic narrative. The "multimodal" text operates beyond the lens of perspective and character, on the one hand, and ocularization as synonymous with perception on the other.[52] Horstkotte and Pedri present shifts in visual vocabulary, shading, and form, as well as multistage braiding, as vehicles of focalization.

Bashi uses the psychomachia to exploit the capacities of graphic focalization. Internal experiences of her past appear and act as external presences, but at the same time challenge the distinction between them, particularly when they appear side by side. Focalization's engagement with perception in graphic narrative, according to Mikkonen, uses "an extremely rich and complex scale of potential intermediate positions between ... subjective or internal focalisation, on the one hand, and clearly non-character bound perspective or external focalization on the other," two of the major categories that Genette defines. Unlike purely literary narrative, graphic texts can reflect shifting relations between character point of view and the storyworld narrative by representing two perspectives simultaneously.[53] In one instance, two figures of Bashi at different ages look down at a common scene or speak in tandem as they look out to the viewer. The configuration might be described as creating a new storyworld on the margins of two past probabilities. Such an instance occurs when Bashi's 33-year-old self returns to show the present-tense character her hyperbolic retort to EuroAmerican fashion's advertising of "Colonial Girl" as a clothing line, a spoof of Banana Republic. The younger Bashi comes to show her older self designs such as "Suisse Sklavinnen" ("Sweet Slaves"), who are women in chains or stocks, and "Hot 9/11" with shardlike metal earrings.[54] No such incident took place in the past. The new incident arises from the encounter of a past self with another past self who has been mesmerized by the world of fashion made available first hand to Bashi in Europe.

In one of the most vivid instances of metalepsis and focalization, *Nylon Road* effaces the mother mark, Farsi. The protagonist's encounter with her past selves on the promenade bench braids with this later episode of linguistic erasure and visual domination. Here, a Swiss friend introduces Bashi to another Iranian woman. The three gather in a horizontally oriented panel, in which they sit, same sized, together on a park bench.[55] Though the Iranian woman greets Bashi in Farsi when they are introduced,[56] the conversation among the three proceeds in German to include the Swiss friend. Large speech balloons at the left and right illustrate the change in the discussion topic—to mathematics—as Bashi's image shows two faces, as if she rapidly switches her attention between the speakers to each side of her. The panels also beg the question of linguistic confusion: Bashi's knowledge of German is presumably still budding at this point, so that the intellectual content and the rapid pace of the discussion would in themselves overwhelm her.

The Iranian woman lights on the subject of Persian mathematician Hakim Omar Khayyam, who proved one of Pascal's theorems 500 years before Pascal did. The woman's face, in profile, moves from the right margin to dominate the next frame. Throughout the monologue the acquaintance aggressively asserts her Persian identity against both European ethnocentrism and Arab-Muslim conquest. The faces of Bashi and the mutual Swiss friend shrink and move back to the top left of the panel, crowded out by the new acquaintance's speech. The woman's face, in profile and then three-quarter profile, appears three times in the bottom horizontal panel. Each one has a sequential speech balloon, placed in front of a silhouetted black background, evoking Persian architecture. On the next page, the woman's face and speech come to dominate the panels, without any speech balloons at all (Figure 5.3).[57]

In the next four panels, her words crowd out the two other figures as they are very distantly seated in the background of the frame. Her speech and face finally eliminate the other two entirely. A full-frontal profile leads to close-ups of part of her face, in the panel with her text. The bottom panel at left includes her ear and eye as she tips her head back and then finally contains, at the bottom right, only her speech and her mouth, open grotesquely so that her vocal chords lie at the center of the image: "WIR, die pazifistischen Arier in PERSIEN, genossen unsere eigene Religion, genossen es, auf unseren himmlischen Teppichen

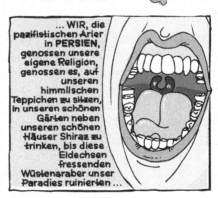

FIGURE 5.3 *Nylon Road*, 2006, p. 53. Courtesy of Parsua Bashi and Kein & Aber AG.

zu sitzen, in unseren schönen Gärten neben unseren schönen Häuser Shiraz zu trinken, bis diese Eideschen fressenden Wüstenaraber unsere Paradies ruinierten" ("WE, the pacifist Aryans of PERSIA, enjoyed our own religion, enjoyed sitting on our heavenly carpets, drinking Shiraz wine in our beautiful gardens, beside our great buildings, until those lizard-eating desert Arabs ruined our paradise").

The recto facing page allows the monologuist a nearly full-sized splash page (Figure 5.4). A text block of Bashi's narration runs across the layout in a thin rectangle at the top so that the woman appears as a conjurer looming over the two figures on the bench at the bottom left.[58] One hand dances, bent over her own head. The other extends as if she is producing emblems and insignia of Persian art and architecture—flying carpets, winged lions, and Shiraz wine—while she continues to enumerate accomplished Iranians. The woman's eyes are closed and her belly exposed while she speaks, her words a full element in the composition, placed under her lower extended arm. She concludes the speech on next page.[59] Her face is back in a horizontal panel at right with the two others, in three-quarter size, at left. Her visage, enlarged and foregrounded, takes up the same amount of space at right that the other two figures do at left. In three-quarter profile she scowls, mouth open and finger pointing into the speech balloon that dominates the center of the panel. Bashi cowers. The Swiss man holds his palms out before him as if to prevent an accident. Throughout the rant, Bashi shares the startled reactions of her Swiss friend. A very small speech balloon of Farsi, on the following page, which presumably delivers her farewell to the departing woman, registers its absence from the conversation.

The presentation of the dialogue of the Iranian Persian chauvinist braids with other panels in the work, such as the speech of hectoring mullahs in a satirical panel, and the endless monologues of Bashi's husband-to-be[60] (which appear just before she is married at 23, though the husband's torrent is a stream of water that also braids with Bashi's drowning in a body of water made by her tears). The scenes show repeatedly the sheer power of a self-righteous monologist to foist a "storyworld" on the audience All of these episodes use language that invades the panels by breaking free of the balloon constraints and dominating panels as if they are material elements of the scene that can exert physical force.

The Persian chauvinist is soon revealed to be an element of Bashi herself, as well as of other characters who pontificate on absolutist positions. Her most "patriotic" self, who existed in 2004, when she was 35, wants to know why Bashi did not agree with the other woman's diatribe, considering the damage that patriarchal Iranian laws had done to her. The 35-year-old's face, in profile, at the top of the recto page, braids with the acquaintance's in expression (though Bashi's profile is flat and so does not display the interior of her mouth).[61] Bashi's 38- and the 35-year-old iterations repeat the aggressive dynamics of the previous scene, though visually the figures remain the same size: the younger patriot appears in profile at left while the present Bashi appears in a full-frontal position. Nonetheless the patriot takes up more of the actual space of the panel as she

FIGURE 5.4 *Nylon Road*, 2006, p. 54. Courtesy of Parsua Bashi and Kein & Aber AG.

asks: "Seit wann verteidigst du die Religion?" ("Since when are you religion's defense attorney?"). The younger self continues, though in a less insulting vein, to criticize the Islamic regime as Muslim. On the next page, a small image of a sculpture of a king's head, actually a balloon held by a small, scowling and turbaned mullah, appears between the two women, portrayed in full length. The head appears under an inset, in a slightly darker color than the background block, that reads "2500-Jahre-alte GROOOOSSE ZIVILISATION" ("2500-year-old Grrrreat civilization") and under the mullah who is labeled "27-jährige Bastard" ("27-year-old bastard"). [62]

As the narrator of the text block overhead, the present-tense Bashi challenges wholesale conflation of Islam with the current regime. She also recalls that she, as a recent emigrant from Iran, was poisoned with anger ("Vergiftet vom Zorn") at hypocrisy that she projected wholly onto the state religion ("projizierten wir alle fälschlicherweise alles auf die Religion").[63] The older Bashi continues on the next two pages by explaining (without dominating the panel, as the younger self still does by occupying the top left in three-quarter or full profile) that belief is an alibi for a regime that aims at totalitarian control. The younger Bashi is persuaded. With three lightbulbs glowing over her head like a crown, widely open eyes, and raised eyebrows, the 35-year-old realizes how the alibi operates. The text block over the bottom panel continues her statement, which began in a speech balloon: "Unter dem Mantel der heiligen Mission nehmen sie dann exklusiv Besitz vom nationale Wohlstand" ("Under the cover of this sacred mission, they get exclusive hold of the national wealth").[64] The box of text continues: "Sie lieben es geradezu, wenn alle sie eine streng religiöses Regime nennen" ("They love it when everyone calls them a strict religious regime"). The full single panel below shows the two Bashis as very small figures in the foreground at the left and right bottom corners, as they witness comically rendered but serious acts of violence. In the speech balloon she is given within the panel, the present-day Bashi continues to elaborate that the regime profits from the conflation of politics and religion. Critics who represent Islam as monolithic also benefit. They use it to justify racism and xenophobia, activities shown even more fully in a single-panel panorama on the following splash page.[65]

The younger and older Bashis appear atop this spectacle. In it, other figures stand on brown and gray jagged patches that suggest anger and violence. The peace activists, crowded down to the bottom right of the panel, are silenced and disappointed by right wing and conservative responses in America and Europe. These critics gloss over the tactics of immigration police, skinheads, and xenophobes. Tellingly, bans on religious symbols do not include crucifixes or yarmulkes. The two women return to profiles on the left and right of a full splash page that follows. The older Bashi insists: "Siehst du jetzt, warum ich sage, unsere Regierung liebt es, wenn die Westen sie hasst? Sie haben den eine gute Entshuldigung, Menschen zum Schweigen zu bringen, die neben Demokratie

142 The Mother Mark and Other Tongues

FIGURE 5.5 *Nylon Road*, 2006, p. 61. Courtesy of Parsua Bashi and Kein & Aber AG.

soziale Unterstutzung, Bildung, Frieden, and Sicherheit benötigen" ("Now do you see why I'm saying that our regime loves it when the West hates them? They have a good excuse for silencing people who advocate for social democratic structure, education, freedom, and security as necessary").[66]

On the facing recto page the two figures stand side by side, both full frontally posed, in a frame that takes up two-thirds of the page (Figure 5.5).[67] They look much alike except for their clothing. They stand before the river and Alpine mountain background of Zürich, as if posing for a photograph. In two speech balloons set next to one another at their waists, they participate in a single discourse, stating that Iran's problems don't have much to do with alcohol or scarves or even the current regime. Instead the country needs Iranians who have the energy and education to forward the historical progress underway and to change the country's image in the world. "[S]hale Patrioten" ("Shallow Patriots") are in charge of that image now. Notably, the concluding panel does not graphically incorporate the past into the present figure, or fold the narrated- into the narrating-I, even though the present-day Bashi has changed the mind of her former self. They stand side by side, looking out to address the reader.

The closest and most frequent visitor among Bashi's new "Freundinnen" ("female friends") is the 36-year-old. Only two years younger than the narrator in the present, and one year older than the so-called shallow patriot, she possesses many of the same characteristics, but now leavens her absolute judgments. The present-tense Bashi describes her slightly younger self as "aktiv, erfolgreich und unabhängig" ("active, successful, and independent") and therefore "sehr stolz ... fast arrogant" ("very proud[,] almost arrogant").[68] She owns her own graphics studio and is an ardent critic of the consumerism of Western advertising, which she regards as humiliating ("erniedrigend") to Western feminist pioneers such as revolutionary Rosa Luxemburg, painter Käthe Kollwitz, and writer Virginia Woolf.[69] A full top-page spread is devoted to Iranian feminists such as judge, lawyer, and human rights activist Shirin Ebadi, who won the Nobel Peace Prize and defended the Forouhars; writer and publisher Shahla Lahiji; lawyer and feminist activist Mehrangiz Kaz; writer Scharnusch Parsipur; and photojournalist Zahra (Ziba) Kazemi.[70] Many of these women went into exile or spent time in prison. Kazemi, whose corpse occupies the central panel of the page above the gravestones of known and unknown members of the opposition in 1988 and 1989—a reference to the chain murders—was raped and died in prison.[71] The younger Bashi takes to task the stock imagery of the Muslim woman that appears on Western book covers. The present-day Bashi hears her younger self out and agrees with elements of her complaints. "Sie hatte recht" ("She was right"). "Aber sie erinnerte mich an meine eigen Fehle, wenn ich false Elemente zur Gestaltung von Buchumschlägen verwendete, an meine Unkenntnis des Westens" ("She was right. But she reminded me of my own mistakes when I used inappropriate elements designing book covers and my own ignorance of the West").[72]

Repetition affectively "binds" images and blocks flows, as in the hijabed woman in the European metropolis, or the scantily clad one in Tehran. Bashi unravels, breaks open, or reweaves without blending individual elements. The Iranian woman who advocates so unilaterally for Persia prompts an internal conflict that is temporal and historical within and without Bashi. It allows the memoir to display the ideological manufacture of the religious alibi as well as the Edenic gardens that are associated with Farsi in Bashi's migrant experience and in the Persia advocate's historiography. Most frequently Bashi claims affinities through her past identities so that political binaries break down through multiplication. The single person contains performative, often agonistic scenarios that enable dialogue and some understanding. The assignment of stances to political, cultural, and geographic binaries is thus constantly dislodged and lampooned. The "bildungs" plot is sent up as well through the alterations that past subjects may exert on the present, a present that has developed from them. In the opening, Bashi appears as a coherent self. In the story that emerges, she must again defend and compromise with the material eruptions of the past.

Fashion and Figuration

Bashi reserves perhaps the harshest critique of her present self for a late manifestation of her past, her own adolescent self at 13. As I have said, narrative order is determined by a prompting event or connected affect rather than by a chronological progression from childhood to adulthood. She is a Marxist-Leninist full of political righteousness. She assists in delivering a metacritique of Bashi's career as an art student and fashion designer, on the grounds of commodity and class as well as betrayal of feminist ideals and cultural sensitivities. Because the memoir itself deploys the visual vocabulary of design and fashion as its lingua franca, this critique strikes at the heart of *Nylon Road*'s own technique: the "Muttermal" of drawing in this mode and medium.

The provoking scenario occurs on the Zürich street in warm weather. Couples kiss in public and women are minimally covered, with plenty of midriff-baring tops in view. Bashi encounters her self right after the 1979 revolution, when the overthrow of the Shah was associated with anticapitalist fervor. As the child of "an old leftist," the adolescent embraces Marxism-Leninism and shows her immersion in dialectical materialism. She trains physically and psychically for the struggle. One panel shows the "self-criticizing" and "self-building" exercises practiced among similarly inclined female comrades.[73] Comically, Bashi takes action by staging a living-room sit-in against her parents to get her own room, a protest undeterred by condemnation of their bourgeois ways.[74]

For all her affectionate satire of adolescent stridency, Bashi shows its deep shaping of her current mode of thought. Structural critique allows her now to see the ways in which young women are produced as consumers, whether of commodities, religious doctrines, or Marxism. In stacked, friezelike panels, each on a facing page in a two-page spread, she illustrates for her 13-year-old self the means of production of initially identical naked young women, who resemble somewhat bewildered paper dolls (Figures 5.6 and 5.7).

In each strip a disembodied hand, index finger pointing, accompanies an imperative. "Du hast keinen Namen, Du bist ein Konsument" ("You don't have a name. You are a consumer"), the top strip begins at left. The hand, engaged in different activities, accompanies each stage of the process: "Trag das," "Höre das," "Kauf das" ("wear this," "listen to this" ["be like this" added in the English translation], and "buy this") while the doll is made-up, dressed in a cropped top and capri pants, and given a shopping bag. "Du hast keinen Namen, Du bist ein Schaf," says the second strip ("You don't have a name. You are a sheep"). "Trag das," "Liese das," "Folge dem" ("wear this," "read this," "follow this") the figure is instructed as she is draped in a long cloak and given a Qur'an and beads. The third strip begins, "Du hast keinen Namen. You bist ein Genosse" ("You have no name. You are a comrade"). "Trag das," "Liese das," "Sei so" ("wear this," "read

The Mother Mark and Other Tongues **145**

FIGURE 5.6 *Nylon Road*, 2006, p. 110. Courtesy of Parsua Bashi and Kein & Aber AG.

146 The Mother Mark and Other Tongues

FIGURE 5.7 *Nylon Road*, 2006. p. 111. Courtesy of Parsua Bashi and Kein & Aber AG.

this," and "be like this"). The Marxist doll is clothed in knee socks, shorts, and glasses and given a book of ideological theory and a picture of a male "Idole" ("idol"). The hands wield a measuring tape against the figure in each, as the implied voice intones, "Gut, jetzt passt du. Geh!" ("Good, you fit, now GO!").[75] Through each strip, behind each figure, runs a gray line that ends in an arrow at the right. It points to the result on the facing page. Against the protests of trivialization from the adolescent Bashi, her present-day self insists that the processed girls all suffer, like fighters, but in different ways. The result in each case is an emptiness, of head, heart, pockets, or freedom.[76] On the following page, the beneficiaries, each one wearing a small crown and clutching a fat fold of money, appear: a well-established fashion designer, a mullah, and Stalin.[77] Though the older Bashi says it is all about "Macht und Wohlstand" ("power and wealth") and the irate younger subject protests that Lenin says "der letzte Kampf" ("the last struggle") is near, their positions are not as far apart ideologically as the younger self thinks. Yet Bashi cannot come to any agreement with the adolescent, who stomps off angrily at the offer of ice cream and companionship.

The following, final chapter returns to the time of Bashi's emigration and her enthrallment to fashion and design in Tehran, which I mention above. It culminates in a crisis between "die Prinzipien der Pressefreiheit" and "die Gefühle anderer respektieren" ("freedom of expression" [actually "the principles of freedom of the press"] and "respecting others' sensibilities").[78] Bashi's 33-year-old self appears, eager to see the magazines and store windows. But the 33-year-old is shocked to disgust by the ad for "Colonial Girl." Bashi remembers her own creations of modest fashion inspired by local sources and her hunger for seeing garments other than "Manteaus," which are long-sleeved coats, or "Schals," shawlike scarves.[79] The subject who longed for such variety now confronts the migrant Bashi with a number of horrifying appropriations of traumas. "Ich wollte dir nur zeigen, wohin diese Freiheit führen kann" ("I just wanted to show you what freedom can lead to"), the 33-year-old Bashi asserts against the ire of the present-day subject.[80] The chapter ends in a mise-en abime panel in which the 33-year-old, her full figure in profile curled along the right panel, points her finger angrily down at the present-day Bashi, a much smaller figure jumping back in fear, her eyes enlarged, her head topped by three exclamation marks. Behind the figures is an image of the open book in which they appear, centered on this panel, but extending beyond it. Responding to the present-day Bashi's struggle over the offensive designs, the younger self scolds, in a large balloon at the top left of the panel:

> Stop! Warum hast du den diesen Comic hier gezeichnet? ... Warum hast du zu all dem nicht die Klappe gehalten? ... Du hast doch dieses Buch gemacht und uns hier hineingezeichnet, oder? ... Du wolltest doch mit dieser Geschichte deine Meinung sagen, nicht? Du hast doch auch

sonst immer gesagt, was du wolltest. Und jetzt behauptest du, du hältst dich zurück? Du zensierst dich? Ich muss sagen: Ich glaube dir diesen BULLSHIT nicht!

Oh please! Why bother writing a book? ... Why not just shut up? ... You've drawn us in your comic book, haven't you? ... By telling your story, you're expressing your opinion, right? You've said whatever you've wanted to say in every other chapter. And you think you're censoring yourself?!? I have to say that your theories are BULLSHIT![81]

This charge is never refuted. Instead the final chapter—positioning the panels in a two column, three stack grid against a gray background, as if to indicate its meta-narrative status— features the present-day Bashi's face. While she smokes, looking tired and occasionally disgruntled, she mulls over the narrative's ending. She frames the dilemma in terms of emotional import, of subject representations as multiple or singular. The narrating-I asks how she can conclude the work with wit, logic, and narrative drama, without appearing to be a split personality ("Persönlichkeit gespalten"), "paranoid," or "simply crazy" ("einfach Krank in Kopf"),[82] much as she thought she was on her first encounter with her six-year-old self. She is still continuing to speak when a very small figure—herself at six—appears again in the bottom left corner of the panel, smiling up at Bashi's dominating face.

In confronting and challenging the adult on the facing full page (Figure 5.8), the past selves "construct" the image of Bashi at her drawing table. She wears the same garb that she does in the opening panel. Now, however, the drawing shows that she has been composed of these selves throughout, at the same time that they are making her. Reckoning with each self has brought to representation their collaboration well as continuing distinctions among them. The avatars shrink but do not disappear in the final panels, which wittily juxtapose representational levels in metalepsis and mise-en-abime as the author's hand appears as the artist rendering the artist. The small figures, in an abstract psychic idiom, "ghost" the self,[83] Julia Watson argues. They also remain insistently concrete partial selves or complexes that resist incorporation and synthesis in favor of production and alliance.

A large hand holding a pencil appears in the foreground, sketching the inset panel, revealed to be a piece of paper propped up on an easel, with clips at the top to hold up the paper. Bashi cleverly presents the mise-en-abime as replicating the one that she as the artist sits in. The book on the shelves in the background, the photos and knickknacks in the room, imply that she sits in her own study drawing herself in the same location. She looks startled at the appearance of the miniature past selves on her desk. Rather than crossed, as they are in the inaugural image, her arms are open and raised away from the desk. Rather than looking out with a cool gaze at the reader, the large figure is preoccupied with her own avatars. She can't see the hijabed selves behind her, who pin up a party

The Mother Mark and Other Tongues **149**

FIGURE 5.8 *Nylon Road*, 2006, p. 127. Courtesy of Parsua Bashi and Kein & Aber AG.

banner that says "ENDE" (The End), not yet straightened out. The panel clearly displays a cooperative effort among the selves of the past and the "subject" of the present as she is drawn by her own wand. This scene is further enclosed within the larger page as a drawing that Bashi's hand is placing on the desk of the studio where the scene takes place. The complex operations of psychomachia and Muttermal in *Nylon Road* variously restate the mother-daughter relations that exist within the subject. Previous generations of feminists appear, as well as Bashi's own mother, who along with her father, encourages her to leave Iran after the revolution and is skeptical of her desire to marry so young. The absence of the mother tongue puts particular emphasis on the mark as a communicative device and a meeting zone of storyworlds, so often anchored by the face and the hand and restored to a female lineage of representation.

Notes

1 Parsua Bashi, *Nylon Road: Eine Graphische Novelle*, trans. Miriam Wiesel (Zürich: Kein & Aber, 2006), 34. Parsua Bashi, *Nylon Road: A Graphic Memoir of Coming in Age in Iran*, trans. Teresa Go and Miriam Wiesel (New York: St. Martin's-Griffin, 2009). A Spanish translation was also issued in 2009. Bashi's other works are *Briefe aus Teheran*, trans. Suzanne Baghestani (Zürich: Kein & Aber, 2010) and an essay with photographs by Martin Walker, *Persische Kontraste: Orientalisches Memo: Ausschnitte persischer Kacheln von Profan- und Sakralbauten zeigen die Vielfalt orientalischer verordnetes Grau in Iran von heute gegenüber* (Zürich: Walkwerke, 2008). For information about Bashi, see Frank and Karin Heer, "Pop Up: Parsua Bashi," *Annabelle* www.annabelle.ch/kultur/bucher/pop-up-parsua-bashi-12848. Accessed May 18, 2018. For information about her reception in journalistic reviews, see Julia Watson, "Parsua Bashi's *Nylon Road*: Visual Witnessing and the Critique of Neoliberalism in Iranian Women's Memoir" *Gender Forum* 65 (2017): 78–79.
2 The capture of movement is evocative of Massumi's "movement-vision" of the spectator. Here the movement is not a tactile sense related to proprioception but a disorientation and reorientation based on the physical movement of the spectator in relation to the field. A similar "felt sensation" in the viewer may be elicited based on the shifting interpretations between thing and body. Masssumi, *Parables*, 57. Stephens, *Skin Acts*, 82–83, discusses the similarities between Massumi's conception and the work of C. L. R. James.
3 Joseph Darda notes that the "instabilities of the multimodal text" afford various techniques for portraying "disjunctures." They lend the genre in this medium "political force, undermining hegemonic social structures, representing the unrepresentable, and positioning the reader as an intimate participant in its construction." "Graphic Ethics: Theorizing the Face in Marjane Satrapi's *Persepolis*," *College Literature* 40.2 (2013): 32.
4 Sidonie Smith, "Human Rights and Comics: Autobiographical Avatars, Crisis Witnessing, and Transnational Rescue Networks," in *Graphic Subjects: Critical Essays on Autobiography and Graphic Novels*, ed. Michael A. Chaney (Madison: University of Wisconsin Press, 2011), 61–66.
5 Iman Sohrabi, written communication to author, March 4, 2018.
6 Charles Hatfield, *Alternative Comics: An Emerging Literature* (Jackson: University Press of Mississippi, 2005), 115.
7 Deleuze and Guattari, *A Thousand Plateaus*, 167–68.
8 Kai Mikkonen, *The Narratology of Comic Art* (London and New York: Routledge, 2017), 35, calls this visual dimension of the graphic text "narrative salience."

9 Jan Baetens, "Dominique Goblet: The List Principle and the Meaning of Form," in *Graphic Subjects: Critical Essays on Autobiography and Graphic Novels*, ed. Michael A. Chaney (Madison: University of Wisconsin Press, 2011), 86.
10 Miriam Kent, "Unveiling Marvels: *Ms. Marvel* and the Reception of the New Muslim Superheroine," *Feminist Media Studies* 15.3 (2015): 522–23. Also see Arjana, *Veiled Superheroes*, 48–52.
11 For a full account of the genealogy of this figure, see J. Richard Stevens, "Mentoring Ms. Carol Danvers," in *Ms. Marvel's America: No Normal*, ed. Jessica Baldanzi and Hussein Rashid (Jackson: University Press of Mississippi, 2020), 3–20, 65–88.
12 Julie Davis and Robert Westerfelhaus, "Finding a Place for a Muslimah Heroine in the Post-9/11 Marvel Universe," *Feminist Media Studies* 13.5 (2013): 800–801. Arjana, *Veiled Superheroes*, 11–12, points out that Dust's problematic characteristic is her native tongue, Arabic, rather than one of the dominant languages of Afghanistan, Dari, Pashto, Uzbek, or Tajik.
13 Arjana, *Veiled Superheroes*, 37–38. These figures are only the most visible among a host of recent Muslimah superheroes, among them the animated Pakistani *Burka Avenger*. Egyptian Deena Muhamad's web comic *Qahera* (named after "Cairo"), which appeared during the Arab Spring (2012–13), focuses on feminist and other social justice issues. Vigilante figures appear in the English-language web comic *Raat*, by Wasiq Haris, and *Bloody Nasreen*, an English language graphic novel created by Shahan Zaidi. Both creators live in Karachi and set their works in Pakistan. *Qahera*, http://qaherathe-superhero.com/. Accessed March 14, 2019. There are English and Arabic versions. *Raat*, www.raatcomic.com/. Accessed March 14, 2019. *Bloody Nasreen*, Arjana, *Veiled Superheroes*, 71–114.
14 For a discussion of the different cover images used in the German and English editions, see Watson, "Parsua Bashi's *Nylon Road*," 79.
15 Jan Baetens and Hugo Frey, *The Graphic Novel: An Introduction* (New York: Cambridge University Press, 2015), 123.
16 Neil Cohn, *The Visual Language of Comics: Introduction to the Structure and Cognition of Sequential Images* (London: Bloomsbury, 2013), 93.
17 Cohn, *The Visual Language*, 93.
18 Mikkonen, *The Narratology of Comic Art*, 35. The distinction is a modification of Genette 1980, 35.
19 Bashi, *Nylon Road: Eine Graphische Novelle*, 103, 115, 76; Bashi, *Nylon Road: A Graphic Memoir of Coming in Age in Iran*, 103, 115, 76.
20 Cohn, *The Visual Language*, 93.
21 Bashi, *Nylon Road: Eine Graphische Novelle*, 6; Bashi, *Nylon Road: A Graphic Memoir of Coming in Age in Iran*, 6.
22 Bashi, *Nylon Road: Eine Graphische Novelle*, 6; Bashi, *Nylon Road: A Graphic Memoir of Coming in Age in Iran*, 6.
23 *Nylon Road: A Graphic Memoir of Coming in Age in Iran*, 6.
24 Bashi, *Nylon Road: Eine Graphische Novelle*, 12; Bashi, *Nylon Road: A Graphic Memoir of Coming in Age in Iran*, 12.
25 Bashi, *Nylon Road: Eine Graphische Novelle*, 13; Bashi, *Nylon Road: A Graphic Memoir of Coming in Age in Iran*, 13.
26 Bashi, *Nylon Road: Eine Graphische Novelle*, 10; Bashi, *Nylon Road: A Graphic Memoir of Coming in Age in Iran*, 10.
27 Bashi, *Nylon Road: Eine Graphische Novelle*, 14; Bashi, *Nylon Road: A Graphic Memoir of Coming in Age in Iran*, 14.
28 Bashi, *Nylon Road: Eine Graphische Novelle*, 15; Bashi, *Nylon Road: A Graphic Memoir of Coming in Age in Iran*, 15.
29 Thierry Groensteen, *System of Comics*, trans. Bart Beaty and Nick Nguyen (Jackson: University of Mississippi Press, 2007), 6, 144–48.
30 Bashi, *Nylon Road: Eine Graphische Novelle*, 47; Bashi, *Nylon Road: A Graphic Memoir of Coming in Age in Iran*, 47.

31 Bashi, *Nylon Road: Eine Graphische Novelle*, 70; Bashi, *Nylon Road: A Graphic Memoir of Coming in Age in Iran*, 70.
32 Bashi, *Nylon Road: Eine Graphische Novelle*, 64; Bashi, *Nylon Road: A Graphic Memoir of Coming in Age in Iran*, 64.
33 Bashi, *Nylon Road: Eine Graphische Novelle*, 65–66; *Nylon Road: A Graphic Memoir of Coming of Age in Iran*, 64-65.
34 Bashi, *Nylon Road: Ein Graphische Novelle*, 15; Bashi, *Nylon Road: A Graphic Memoir of Coming in Age in Iran*, 15.
35 Bashi, *Nylon Road: Eine Graphische Novelle*, 72–73; Bashi, *Nylon Road: A Graphic Memoir of Coming in Age in Iran*, 73.
36 Bashi, *Nylon Road: Eine Graphische Novelle*, 73; Bashi, *Nylon Road: A Graphic Memoir of Coming in Age in Iran*, 73.
37 Bashi, *Nylon Road: Eine Graphische Novelle*, 74; Bashi, *Nylon Road: A Graphic Memoir of Coming in Age in Iran*, 74.
38 Bashi, *Nylon Road: Eine Graphische Novelle*, 18; Bashi, *Nylon Road: A Graphic Memoir of Coming in Age in Iran*, 18.
39 Bashi, *Nylon Road: Eine Graphische Novelle*, 18; Bashi, *Nylon Road: A Graphic Memoir of Coming in Age in Iran*, 18.
40 Bashi, *Nylon Road: Eine Graphische Novelle*, 19; Bashi, *Nylon Road: A Graphic Memoir of Coming in Age in Iran*, 18.
41 Martha A. Malamud, *A Poetics of Transformation: Prudentius and Classical Mythology* (Ithaca: Cornell University Press, 1989), 56.
42 Malamud, *A Poetics of Transformation*, 73.
43 Kaja Silverman casts this agency exerted over the image as that which the male gaze desires in classic Hollywood cinema. *The Acoustic Mirror: The Female Voice in Psychoanalysis and Cinema* (Bloomington: Indiana University Press, 1988), 39.
44 Watson, "Parsua Bashi's *Nylon Road*," 75.
45 Bashi, *Nylon Road: Eine Graphische Novelle*, 35; Bashi, *Nylon Road: A Graphic Memoir of Coming in Age in Iran*, 35.
46 Bashi, *Nylon Road: Eine Graphische Novelle*, 32; Bashi, *Nylon Road: A Graphic Memoir of Coming in Age in Iran*, 32.
47 Bashi, *Nylon Road: Eine Graphische Novelle*, 106; *Nylon Road: A Graphic Memoir of Coming in Age in Iran*, 106.
48 Bashi, *Nylon Road: Eine Graphische Novelle*, 34; *Nylon Road: A Graphic Memoir of Coming in Age in Iran*, 34.
49 Bashi, *Nylon Road: Eine Graphische Novelle*, 34; Bashi, *Nylon Road: A Graphic Memoir of Coming in Age in Iran*, 34.
50 Watson, "Parsua Bashi's *Nylon Road*," 82.
51 Silke Horstkotte and Nancy Pedri, "Focalization in Graphic Narrative," *Narrative* 19.3 (2011): 331.
52 See for instance, C. Schneider, "The Cognitive Grammar of 'I': Viewing Arrangements in Graphic Autobiographies," *Studies in Comics* 4.2 (2013): 307–32; David Herman, "Beyond Voice and Vision: Cognitive Grammar and Focalization Theory," in *Point of View, Perspective and Focalization: Modeling Mediation in Narrative*, ed. Peter Hühn, Wolf Schmid, and Jörg Schönert (Berlin: Walter deGruyter, 2009), 119–42.
53 Kai Mikkonen, "Focalisation in Comics: From the Specificities of the Medium to Conceptual Reformulation, *Scandinavian Journal of Comic Art* 1.1 (2012): 83–84.
54 Bashi, *Nylon Road: Eine Graphische Novelle*, 124–25; Bashi, *Nylon Road: A Graphic Memoir of Coming in Age in Iran*, 124–25.
55 Bashi, *Nylon Road: Eine Graphische Novelle*, 51; Bashi, *Nylon Road: A Graphic Memoir of Coming in Age in Iran*, 51.
56 Bashi, *Nylon Road: Eine Graphische Novelle*, 50; Bashi, *Nylon Road: A Graphic Memoir of Coming in Age in Iran*, 50.

57 Bashi, *Nylon Road: Eine Graphische Novelle*, 52; Bashi, *Nylon Road: A Graphic Memoir of Coming in Age in Iran*, 52.
58 Bashi, *Nylon Road: Eine Graphische Novelle*, 53; Bashi, *Nylon Road: A Graphic Memoir of Coming in Age in Iran*, 53.
59 Bashi, *Nylon Road: Eine Graphische Novelle*, 54; Bashi, *Nylon Road: A Graphic Memoir of Coming in Age in Iran*, 54.
60 Bashi, *Nylon Road: Eine Graphische Novelle*, 54; Bashi, *Nylon Road: A Graphic Memoir of Coming in Age in Iran*, 54.
61 Bashi, *Nylon Road: Eine Graphische Novelle*, 55; Bashi, *Nylon Road: A Graphic Memoir of Coming in Age in Iran*, 55.
62 Bashi, *Nylon Road: Eine Graphische Novelle*, 56; Bashi, *Nylon Road: A Graphic Memoir of Coming in Age in Iran*, 56.
63 Bashi, *Nylon Road: Eine Graphische Novelle*, 56; Bashi, *Nylon Road: A Graphic Memoir of Coming in Age in Iran*, 56.
64 Bashi, *Nylon Road: Eine Graphische Novelle*, 58; Bashi, *Nylon Road: A Graphic Memoir of Coming in Age in Iran*, 58.
65 Bashi, *Nylon Road: Eine Graphische Novelle*, 59; Bashi, *Nylon Road: A Graphic Memoir of Coming in Age in Iran*, 59.
66 Bashi, *Nylon Road: Eine Graphische Novelle*, 60; Bashi, *Nylon Road: A Graphic Memoir of Coming in Age in Iran*, 60.
67 Bashi, *Nylon Road: Eine Graphische Novelle*, 61; Bashi, *Nylon Road: A Graphic Memoir of Coming in Age in Iran*, 61.
68 Bashi, *Nylon Road: Eine Graphische Novelle*, 75; Bashi, *Nylon Road: A Graphic Memoir of Coming in Age in Iran*, 75.
69 Bashi, *Nylon Road: Eine Graphische Novelle*, 77; Bashi, *Nylon Road: A Graphic Memoir of Coming in Age in Iran*, 77.
70 For information about Shirin Ebadi and other activists, see Catherine Z. Sameh, *Axis of Hope: Iranian Women's Rights Activism across Borders* (Seattle: University of Washington Press, 2019).
71 Bashi, *Nylon Road: Eine Graphische Novelle*, 78; Bashi, *Nylon Road: A Graphic Memoir of Coming in Age in Iran*, 78.
72 Bashi, *Nylon Road: Eine Graphische Novelle*, 79; Bashi, *Nylon Road: A Graphic Memoir of Coming in Age in Iran*, 79.
73 Bashi, *Nylon Road: Eine Graphische Novelle*, 106; Bashi, *Nylon Road: A Graphic Memoir of Coming in Age in Iran*, 106.
74 Bashi, *Nylon Road: Eine Graphische Novelle*, 107; Bashi, *Nylon Road: A Graphic Memoir of Coming in Age in Iran*, 107.
75 Bashi, *Nylon Road: Eine Graphische Novelle*, 110; Bashi, *Nylon Road: A Graphic Memoir of Coming in Age in Iran*, 110. The German actually translates as "follow them."
76 Bashi, *Nylon Road: Eine Graphische Novelle*, 111; Bashi, *Nylon Road: A Graphic Memoir of Coming in Age in Iran*, 111.
77 Bashi, *Nylon Road: Eine Graphische Novelle*, 112; Bashi, *Nylon Road: A Graphic Memoir of Coming in Age in Iran*, 112.
78 Bashi, *Nylon Road: Eine Graphische Novelle*, 123; Bashi, *Nylon Road: A Graphic Memoir of Coming in Age in Iran*, 123.
79 Bashi, *Nylon Road: Eine Graphische Novelle*, 119.
80 Bashi, *Nylon Road: Eine Graphische Novelle*, 123; Bashi, *Nylon Road: A Graphic Memoir of Coming in Age in Iran*, 123.
81 Bashi, *Nylon Road: Eine Graphische Novelle*, 124; Bashi, *Nylon Road: A Graphic Memoir of Coming in Age in Iran*, 124.
82 Bashi, *Nylon Road: Eine Graphische Novelle*, 126; Bashi, *Nylon Road: A Graphic Memoir of Coming in Age in Iran*, 126.
83 Watson, "Parsua Bashi's *Nylon Road*," 75.

CONCLUSION

Muslim Girl, the online magazine I cited in the opening chapter, ran a 2019 interview with four young Muslim-American journalists. Prominent as a topic in their discussion was the status of their "visibility," or marking, as Muslim. Emma Bare, a freelance journalist, observed, "I think what we are seeing right now is a focus on white-passing and white adjacent women on TV. Some Muslim women are only POC [persons of color] when they wear a hijab. And it's damaging to only focus on those stories."[1] The women continue to discuss the problems of marked and unmarked identities, particularly in relation to race and to hijab. Their own terms slide between voice and vision, racial and religious identity, belief and practices that can be "read" immediately and unambiguously. But Palestinian-American Noura Erakat makes little distinction between the Muslim Americans' problems and the problem of appearance for other young women. She parodied a typical reaction that she has encountered among older professionals: "'*She's just so cute and she doesn't understand reality yet.*' You can see that happening even with AOC [New York Representative Alexandria Ocasio-Cortez], that's just a challenge of being a woman."[2]

My focus here has not been on the contemporary explosion of Muslim women's self-representation on digital media and in public life as well as in traditional art forms. Rather, I treat the productions that emerged in the first decade or so of the twenty-first century, a period when more Muslim women were entering mainstream literature and art in Europe and America. As minority producers, particularly after 2001, they were made to negotiate with the frozen signifier of the veil and its attributes in order to gain mainstream representation. I argue that their work constitutes not merely reactive supplements to the sign or even counter-projections in response to the inert black blot, flat and

DOI: 10.4324/9781003189299-7

Conclusion   155

motionless, that obliterates agency and particularity. Rather I contend that this image acted as a spur to different representations of embodiment, agency, community, and alliance. These subtexts and even overt challenges to the emblem have been overread or misread through the ocular epistemology of the West, broadly speaking, and the fields of signification that operate in it. Even works that use the conventional idioms of choice or postfeminism may reformulate the masquerade and the luminous spectacle. (This is not to say, of course, that all recent mainstream representations of Muslim women by EuroAmerican Muslim women do so. Sika Dagbovie-Mullins and Eric Berlatsky note of the new Ms. Marvel, Kamala Khan, for instance, that problems such as Islamophobia "can easily be overcome without structural, political, or social resistance" since power is also an issue of "individual choice.[3]) In the works I discuss, in contrast, varieties of practice, belief, and culture contribute to structural commentary. Those who enjoy white or dominant luminosity seek relief in the shadows associated with Muslimah. Women's alliances and older legacies of feminism emerge, displaced, as a consolation or substitute for the obliteration of age. So do the limitations of visibility as the primary vehicle of representation and recognition for women, particularly in the visual fields of nonmajority locations created by postimperialism, epidermal racial codes, nationality, and Christian-derived "secular" frameworks.

Issues of class and race enter into these productions selectively, as in *Brick Lane* and *The Girl in the Tangerine Scarf*. Desire, romance, and sexuality are more consistent themes, and they remain in this period in default heterosexual and cis contexts.[4] Beauty resurfaces as a way of complicating social contexts, through widening the notion of domestic space, decoration, and vantage point. In multimodal and digital visual productions, conceptions, practices, and aesthetic repositories advance contemporary antipatriarchal theory as it is formulated in Western mainstream representations. The interlocking oscillations of surface and pattern preoccupy Iranian-German Parastou Forouhar's work. Multiplication of figures and focus on the face in relation to the rest of the form allow for enactment of coalition politics in Parsua Bashi's *Nylon Road*. Both artists draw attention to the cultural scaffolding that secures the representation of neoliberal individualism and draw attention to the aporias of antipatriarchal theories.

I conclude with a glimpse of a young Muslim-American artist who enthusiastically represents queer and antiracist female identity in her work, and to relate her imaginary to the representational strategies I discuss. Saba Taj, based in North Carolina, describes herself as "a queer Muslim femme mixed-media visual artist and activist whose work centers around identity and challenging Islamophobia and sexism." Taj discusses "struggle[s]" with her Muslim identity and "its seeming contradictions with the other parts" of herself. Yet she has come to "wholly embrace" it by "rejecting monolithic interpretations of what it means to be Muslim."[5] Elsewhere, under the name Saba Chaudry Barnard, she describes herself as a first-generation Pakistani-American who grew up as the "token of diversity" in her private school in North Carolina.[6]

In 2018, Taj showed the sculpture "Alpha, Delta, Burqa" in *The Third Muslim: Queer and Trans* Muslim Narratives of Resistance and Resilience*,[7] at the SOMArts Cultural Center, in San Francisco.[8] In it, three mannequins, standing on a platform in a line, wear burqas and niqab: one figure is dressed in a pink and floral patterns, with the panels running vertically and netting over the face; another is cloaked in navy blue; the other is in black with gold trim, a fringe that suggests curtains and flashy lamé. The figures in dark fabric show a bit of gold face or a gold, bare foot. Bumps protrude from the draped cloth, suggesting breasts, humps, arms or even hidden objects under the swaths of cloth. The title helps to unite the default male terrorist and the hijabi in a single form. It recalls Jasbir Puar's formulation of the queering of the Muslim terrorist by American homonationality as well as Fanon's female Algerian revolutionaries, who secreted weapons in their abayas. Shirin Neshat, too, has represented a Muslimah with a gun pointed at the viewer, in her "Rebellious Silence" (1994) images from the series the "Women of Allah." The pink and floral patterns and gold trim nonetheless suggest conventionally feminine decoration and light-heartedness. Taj's mixture portrays hijab itself as a source of confusion, terror and semiotic incoherence: the masquerade comes into new focus in this piece. The very form encodes fear of the unknown in its physical form, or celebration of it, as the bodies underneath are not easily fixed and readable. Unlike the robes worn by women in the cinematic Abu Dhabi, these burqas cannot be detached. Sexual ambiguity or "collapse" into trans- or nonbinary sex constitutes its danger, as well as a potential source of somatic liberation. Of Neshat's images, Rafia Zakaria notes: "A veil is revealed then to be not just a fabric but a partition and a boundary. Transgressing it represents intrusion and domination."[9] Taj treats veiling as less simple to define and therefore to transgress. What exactly do these forms project? How or what do they contain? What do they animate and occupy as sculptural forms?

Taj has produced at least two series of portraits that deal directly with the iconography of veiled women, both of them using attributes or citations to revise the frozen signifier of the black or brown hijabi. In both series, the artist highlights her interest in light and color as a feature of Muslimah portraiture, whether in the "inner light" of the sitter's qualities or the color and dynamism of their character. The seven portraits in "An Noor, or The Light,"[10] first exhibited in 2014 at the Carrack Modern Museum of Art in Durham, North Carolina, show figures in a variety of postures and attitudes using the iconography associated with Western art history as well as with pop and political emblems. Her allusions to Christian Renaissance painting are particularly striking: the robed woman with a flat, gold-leaf halo, recalls portraits of the Virgin Mary, sometimes in combination with children. But the series also alludes to "Norman Rockwell's 'Rosie the Riveter', Giotto's 'Madonna Enthroned,' the Queen of Swords from

Tarot, and even Superman and Napoleon," the artist says.[11] The most dramatic is "Maesta" or majesty (2014, mixed media, 96 in. x 72 in.).[12] It features a dark-skinned woman in hijab holding forth or presenting an infant, above an empty, indented pillow, covered in a long, turquoise cloth. Two other children, also male, flank her on either side. Their smaller size echoes patron figures, rendered in smaller scale in medieval Christian iconography; the arrangement dramatically evokes the presentation of the Christ child by the Madonna.[13] All figures bear plate-like halos in gold leaf, with edges stamped or otherwise raised. One of the boys on the ground looks up to the mother, his face yearning, in profile. The others look out at the viewer. The dramatic background against which the figures stand unites the American flag with a celestial heaven, a round circle with scattered gold stars that are also raised. Red and white stripes, which dominate the rest of the background, are overlain with light blue arabesques or tracery. The remarkable syncretism of the image evokes Latin American migrants or refugees at the same time that it unmoors the hijabed woman as Muslim, the seemingly marooned family as Christian, or the allusions as religious. Like "Alpha, Delta, Burqa," the work both dislocates and renders semiotically rich the conventional attributes of visual identity.

Taj, like Forouhar and Bashi, produces humorous and satirical pieces to make her political critique and to claim a range of affect and emotion. Her acrylic portrait series "Technicolor Muslimah," originally exhibited in 2012 at the Carrack Modern, consists of 15 close-up portraits of American Muslim women in bright colors using props. Novelty glasses, a Mouseketeer hat, a tiara, a cheese wedge, and a headphone device that holds a cola can and a tube to sip it through feature in the series.[14] The sitters assume various poses and attitudes in relation to the props. All of them wear head coverings. Only the final one is presented without an attribute: she looks out at the viewer with a more sober, composed face and is identified only as "Maryam."

Taj's large format portraits and self-portraits insist on the individual character of the sitter through a focus on the face. At the same time they refuse solemnity, suggesting "capture" in fixed categories is nothing but a joke, a joke that also signifies an American identity visually, according to the artist. "The hijab truly recedes into the background" in these portraits of "dynamic" women, according to the artist.[15] "Arsheen, Materials Scientist/Engineer" (2011, 18 in. × 18 in.) shows a woman in hijab with her hand up, twirling one curl of a large handlebar mustache, which is part of a gag disguise.[16] The twirling hand, highly modeled with green and blue highlights, dominates the foreground plane, as if to emphasize the bearer's manipulation of her image. Though at first glance, the sitter seems to be smiling, her lips are largely covered by the mustache. Only a small portion of her lower lip is visible. Her eyes, cheeks, and posture seem to telegraph a smile. The red scarf, blue tunic, and greenish background suggest a stagey palette that also seems highly mimetic. The portrait might be read as depicting a trans or queer identity. It also might serve a send-up of a stereotype of dark-haired women, who are seen as unfeminine because of their facial hair—ridicule that is directed at the bride Gamrah by her friends in *Girls of Riyadh*. Finally the mustache may be read simply as a playful costume because the hijabi is presented as normative, like the sitter's presumably "straight" face. "Nida, Renaissance Woman" similarly shows a woman in hijab holding a hand up next to her face. The sitter explicitly shares the joke. Nida holds a banana up to her ear like the receiver of a landline telephone.[17] Her face is presented in a slight profile, her head tilted as her eyes, behind black-framed glasses, move to look toward the banana-receiver or to someone outside the frame. Red tones dominate the figure in bright contrast to the yellow fruit and green background. Her mouth opens in a broad smile. The sitter seems caught in gesture as if in a snapshot.

"To humanize Muslims—to make Muslims appear to be more human—is a radical act," Taj proclaimed in a TED talk given in 2017.[18] Taj accomplishes this task through the kind of playful facialization and individual portraiture executed in the "Technicolor Muslimah" series but also through posthuman imagery in "Creatures from the Earth (2016),"[19] and "Of Beasts/Of Virgins (2019)."[20] Both series draw on ethnological and cultural stereotypes to invert species rhetoric in a "reclamation of the grotesque."[21] Critics have noted the works' affinity with "Afrofuturist" fiction, cinema, and visual art. Taj has also been grouped with artists with Muslim and "Muslim-adjacent" backgrounds "who envision future landscapes through a queer lens." Among them are the Iranian-American artist Hushidar Mortzaie, French-Palestinian performance artist Jassein Hindi, and Muslim-American musician Layla Qadr.[22] Taj has also been allied with American Afrofuturist painter Wagnechi Mutu, a Kenyan-American woman, and American digital artist and illustrator Manzel Bowman.[23]

Taj describes her technique in the collages of "Of Beast/Of Virgin" as a ripping up and cutting up of fetishized images, whether exotic or primitive in their cast. "Severing arms and gouging out eyes" of these representations and reassembling them into hybrid creatures is a "violent" and "transformative" experience for the artist.[24] She remains "within the limits" of these frozen signifiers but makes a new, posthuman, and often gender-queer narrative from them. The depictions envisage scenes extrapolated from a Muslim textual tradition, which includes "visions of the future and other dimensions, monsters, and life on other planets."[25] One such representation from Taj's "Creatures" series depicts the prophet Isa, called Jesus in the Christian tradition, defeating al-Masih ad-Dajjal, or the Antichrist, on the Day of Judgement. The Antichrist is modeled on Donald Trump.[26] The presence in these and other images in the series use the eye as an amulet or protective device from the "gaze that harms," and may be decked over the female nude as well as over other species. The "third eye" in the forehead signifies the curative outcome or healing of this incorporation.[27]

Though both draw from the vocabulary of the "speculative,"[28] these more lyrical painted images contrast strongly with the collages of "Of Beast/Of Virgin."

Critic Deborah Kreiger says Taj's work is not "just a shuffling and reorganization of human and animal features," but

> a total re-imagination of these different bodily components and what they might mean together. It's a total re-conception of evolutionary adaptations and organs. In this new world… humanity and all organic life must come up with entirely new ways of living, discarding the usual biological templates.[29]

"Suck My Dowry" (2016) features what appear to be illustrated or photographically enhanced human figures in saris with animal or object heads and arm extensions, human or insectlike. The figures appear on a red and yellow spray-painted background: the band of yellow running behind them separates the red background from the glittery black foreground. The figures, which overlap slightly as they appear frontally to the plane, stand in an ornamental gold bowl that might be read as sitting on a glittery black table or on water, as if they float. The figure to the left, which has a small body but large antlers or insect protuberances, extends up to cross the red plane of the background. The head rounds a triangular shaped, amber-colored jewel. The choli reveals a narrow strip of brown midriff. Human arms are arranged over her pelvis, one hand grasping the other wrist. Silver antlers might be read as metal protuberances that are crafted, or as insect legs with bulbous extensions, as they bend up. They dominate but do not topple or compress the decorous female-identified figure. The shorter figure adjacent to the left reaches only to the bottom of the left antler. This figure wears an insectlike head that appears to be a stylized mask or representation in black and white, with short, antennae-like extensions, the right one of which touches the adjacent figure. Its head, an inverted triangle shape, sits on a human neck. The figure is seated and wears voluminous, rich-red robes. The arm on the left, a human one, sits on the lap. The arm to the right is taken from another image that suggests a cowboy in grey scale, though the arm is fitted seamlessly to the torso of the figure. This arm is foreshortened, as it holds a gun aimed at the frontal plane.

Drawing on the lyric chimerical, the slick technofuturist, the symbolic animal, or on idealized images from the historical imagination of magazines and other mass-produced photographic media, Taj clearly extends the possibilities of EuroAmerican Muslim women's iconography. She associates this turn in her work to with becoming tired of trying to "humanize" Muslim figures after the September 11 attack. Her new approach imagines a narrative of destruction and rebirth, which is mythic as well as fantastic, posthuman as well as gender-queer. These series call up a disjointed collapsing of past, present, and future zones that depict a belief founded in resistance to a wealthy, indifferent elite.[30] Such visions suggest reorganization not just of representation, but of nonlife and nonhuman status or entities, drawn in part from the imagination of Islamic texts, to depict performative genres of embodiment and materiality.

Notes

1 Leila Ettachifini, "Four Muslim Women on How to Survive in Media," *Vice* 27 March 2019. www.vice.com/en_us/article/8xypxx/muslim-women-media-rewards-challenges-tokenization. Accessed May 29, 2019.
2 Ettachifini, "Four Muslim Women."
3 Sika Dagbovie-Mullins and Eric Berlatsky, "The Only Nerdy Pakistani-American-Slash-Inhuman in the Entire Universe: Postracialism and Politics in the New *Ms. Marvel*," in *Ms. Marvel's America: No Normal*, ed. Jessica Baldanzi and Hussein Rashid (Jackson: University Press of Mississippi, 2020), 80.
4 *Brick Lane* features a young gay man as well as a wife and mother whose mode of dress suggests an ambiguous alliance with a masculine identity, though without any comment on the movement of her desire. Siba al-Harez's *The Others* (Al Akharoun, 2006) features a lesbian protagonist. But while scholarship and popular literature about gay Muslim men have begun to appear, representations of same sex desire between women remains scarce, especially in mainstream works. Samar Yazbek's *Ra'ihat al-qirfah* (Cinnamon's Scent, 2008) portrays same-sex practice while eschewing queer or lesbian identification, as do other Arabic representations, according to Rima Sadek, "Same-Sex Relations in Modern Arabic Fiction between Empowerment and Impossibility: A Case Study of Samar Yazbek's *Cinnamon*, in *Memory, Voice and Identity: Muslim Women's Writing across the Middle East*, 106–17. The notable exception to this absence in pop productions is emerging in young adult novels in English, such as Sarah Farizan's *If You Could Be Mine* (2013) and *Tell Me Again How a Crush Should Feel* (2014). Seba al-Herz, *Al Akharoun* (Beirut: Dar al-Saqi, 2006); *The Others*, trans. Seven Story Press (New York: Seven Story Press, 2009); Samar Yazbek *Ra'ihat al-qirfah* [Cinnamon's Scent] (Beirut: Dar al-Adab, 2008); *Cinnamon*, trans. Emily Danby (London: Arabia Books, 2012).
5 Carol Kuruvilla, "Queer Muslim Artist Saba Taj Sees Her Art as an Act of Resistance," *Huffington Post Religion*, June 24, 2016. www.huffingtonpost.com/entry/saba-taj-muslim-artist_us_576c63c7e4b0f16832390d80. Accessed July 13, 2018.
6 Saba Chaudhury Barnard, "Technicolor Muslimah: A Lighter and Brighter Side," *Muslima: Women's Arts and Voices*. http://muslima.globalfundforwomen.org/content/technicolor-muslimah. Accessed July 13, 2018.
7 The artist has elsewhere referred to the piece as "F** the Veil" and "Fuck Veil Art," but the title I give was used in the exhibition.
8 "The Third Muslim, January 15–February 22, 2018." www.somarts.org/thirdmuslim/.
9 Rafia Zakaria, *Veil* (New York: Bloomsbury, 2017), 86.
10 Saba Chaudhury Barnard, "An-Noor: The Light." http://muslima.globalfundforwomen.org/content/noor. Accessed July 12, 2018.
11 Barnard, "An-Noor: The Light."
12 The work is acrylic paint, gold leaf, silver leaf, glitter, rhinestones, sequins, modeling paste, and paper on canvas. https://vtnews.vt.edu/articles/2018/04/mac-sabataj.html. Accessed July 14, 2018.
13 Katarina Pfannkuch "Portraits of Islam: Oh Veiled Mother of God!" *Zenith* June 8, 2017. https://magazine.zenith.me/en/culture/portraits-islam. Accessed July 14, 2018.
14 Saba Chaudhury Barnard, "Technicolor Muslimah: A Lighter and Brighter Side" *Muslima: Women's Arts and Voices*, http://muslima.globalfundforwomen.org/content/technicolor-muslimah. Accessed July 13, 2018.
15 Barnard, "Technicolor Muslimah."
16 Saba Taj [Saba Chaudhury Barnard], "Arsheen, Materials Scientist/Engineer" (18 in. x 18 in., 2011) acrylic on canvas www.itssabataj.com/painting?lightbox=dataItem-jgijuk1m1. Accessed July 13, 2018.

Conclusion 161

17 Saba Taj, "Nida, Renaissance Woman" (18 in. × 18 in., 2011), acrylic on canvas. www.itssabataj.com/painting?lightbox=dataItem-jgijuk1m4. Accessed July 13, 2018.
18 Saba Taj, "Art, Resistance, and the Dominant Narrative," TEDX Duke, April 10, 2017. www.youtube.com/watch?v=mnE0Qn2eJMw. Accessed November 9, 2019.
19 Allcott Gallery, *Creatures from the Earth Made of Earthly Materials* (University of North Carolina, Chapel Hill, 2016). "Of Beast/Of Virgin," Twelve Gates Arts, Philadelphia, PA.
20 Allcott Gallery, *Creatures from the Earth Made of Earthly Materials* (University of North Carolina, Chapel Hill, 2016). "Of Beast/Of Virgin," Twelve Gates Arts, Philadelphia, PA, December 7, 2018–January 26, 2019.
21 Taj, "Art, Resistance, and the Dominant Narrative."
22 Zulfikar Ali Bhutto, "Queer Muslim Futurism," *Archer Magazine* February 19, 2019 http://archermagazine.com.au/2019/02/queer-muslim-futurism/. The author is the grandson of the Pakistani leader of the same name. Hindi lives in Berlin.
23 Deborah Krieger, "Speculative Collages of Saba Taj at Twelve Gates Arts Reimagine the Future through a Queer, Brown Perspective," *Artblog* January 3, 2019. www.theartblog.org/2019/01/speculative-collages-of-saba-taj-at-twelve-gates-arts-re-imagine-the-future-through-a-queer-brown-perspective/. Accessed November 8, 2019.
24 Taj, "Art, Resistance, and the Dominant Narrative."
25 Ali Bhutto, "Queer Muslim Futurism."
26 Taj, "Art, Resistance, and the Dominant Narrative."
27 Taj, "Art, Resistance, and the Dominant Narrative."
28 Krieger, "Speculative Collages."
29 Krieger, "Speculative Collages."
30 Ali Bhutto, "Queer Muslim Futurism."

BIBLIOGRAPHY

Abdel-Fattah, Randa. *No Sex in the City*. London: Random House-Penguin, 2014.
Abdelrazek, Amal Talaat. *Contemporary Arab American Women Writers: Hyphenated Identities and Border Crossings*. Youngstown, New York: Cambria Press, 2007.
Abdullah, Mariam. "Rajaa al-Sanea: Beyond Girls of Riyadh." *Al-Akhbar English*. October 20, 2011. Accessed June 22, 2014. http://english.al-akhbar.com/node/1110.
Abdullah, Muhammad, and Safeer Awan. "Islamic Postfeminism and Muslim Chick-Lit: Coexistence of Conflicting Discourses." *Pakistan Journal of Women's Studies* 24, no. 2 (2017): 93–105.
Abdurraqib, Samaa. "Hijab Scenes: Muslim Women, Migration, and Hijab in Immigrant Muslim Literature." *MELUS* 31, no. 4 (2006): 55–70.
Aboulela, Leila. *Elsewhere Home*. London: Telegram, 2018.
Aboulela, Leila. *Lyrics Alley*. New York: Grove, 2010.
Aboulela, Leila. *Minaret*. New York: Black Cat, 2005.
Aboulela, Leila. *The Translator*. New York: Black Cat, 2006.
Abu-Jaber, Diana. *Arabian Jazz*. New York: Norton, 2003.
Abu-Jaber, Diana. *Birds of Paradise*. New York: Norton, 2011.
Abu-Lughod, Lila. *Do Muslim Women Really Need Saving?* Cambridge, MA: Harvard University Press, 2013.
Afshari, Reza. *Human Rights in Iran: The Abuse of Cultural Relativism*. Philadelphia: University of Pennsylvania Press, 2001.
Agamben, Giorgio. *Homo Sacer: Sovereign Power and Bare Life*, translated by Daniel Heller Roazen. Stanford: Stanford University Press, 1998.
Agamben, Giorgio. *Means without End: Notes on Politics*, translated by Vincenzo Binetti and Cesare Casarino. Minneapolis: University of Minnesota Press, 2000.
Agamben, Giorgio. *State of Exception*, translated by Kevin Attell. Chicago: University of Chicago Press, 2005.
Ahmad, Ali. "*Brick Lane*: A Note on the Politics of 'Good' Literary Production." *Third Text* 18, no. 2 (2004): 200–201.

Ahmad, Dohra. "Not Yet beyond the Veil: Muslim Women in American Popular Literature." *Social Text* 27, no. 2 (2009): 105–31.
Ahmed, Gutbi Mahdi. "Muslim Organizations in the United States." In *The Muslims of America*, edited by Yvonne Yazbeck Haddad, 11–36. Oxford: Oxford University Press, 1991.
Ahmed, Leila. *A Border Passage: From Cairo to America: A Woman's Journey*. New York: Penguin, 1999.
Ahmed, Rehana. "*Brick Lane*: A Materialist Reading of the Novel and Its Reception." *Race and Class* 52, no. 2 (2010): 25–42.
Ahmed, Samira. *Love, Hate, and Other Filters*. New York: Soho, 2018.
Ahmed, Sara. *The Cultural Politics of Emotion*. New York: Routledge, 2004.
Alamdari, Kazem. "The Power Structure of the Islamic Republic of Iran: Transition from Populism to Clientelism, and Militarization of the Government." *Third World Quarterly* 26, no. 8 (2005): 1285–301.
Alcoff, Linda Martin. *Rape and Resistance: Understanding the Complexities of Sexual Violation*. London: Polity, 2018.
Alcoff, Linda Martin. *Visible Identities: Race, Gender, and the Self*. Oxford: Oxford University Press, 2006.
Al-Ghadeer, Moneera. "*Girls of Riyadh*: A New Technology of Writing or Chick Lit Defiance." Review of *Banat al-Riyadh* [Girls of Riyadh], by Rajā' al-Sāniʿ. *Journal of Arabic Literature* 8, no. 2 (2004): 199–201.
Al-Herz, Seba. *Al Akharoun*. Beirut: Dar al-Saqi, 2006.
Al-Herz, Seba. *The Others*, translated by Seven Story Press. New York: Seven Story Press, 2009.
Al-Hibri, Aziza. "Divine Justice and the Human Order: An Islamic Perspective." In *Humanity before God: Contemporary Faces of Jewish, Christian, and Islamic Ethics*, edited by William Schweiker, Michael Johnson, and Kevin Jung, 238–55. Minneapolis: Fortress, 2006.
Ali, Ayaan Hirsi. *The Caged Virgin: An Emancipation Proclamation for Women and Islam*. New York: Free Press, 2006.
Ali, Kecia, and Oliver Leaman. *Islam: The Key Concepts*. New York: Routledge, 2008.
Ali, Kecia. *Sexual Ethics and Islam: Feminist Reflections on Qur'an, Hadith, and Jurisprudence*. London: Oneworld, 2006.
Ali, Monica. *Alentejo Blue*. New York: Scribner's, 2006.
Ali, Monica. *Brick Lane*. New York: Scribner's, 2003.
Ali, Monica. *In the Kitchen*. New York: Scribner's, 2009.
Ali, Monica. "No One Is Sacrosanct." *London Telegraph*, April 8, 2011. www.telegraph.co.uk/culture/books/bookreviews/8434547/No-one-is-sacrosant.html.
Ali, Monica. "The Outrage Economy." *Guardian*, July 24, 2006, 4.
Ali, Monica. *Untold Story*. New York: Scribner's, 2011.
Ali, Monica. "What If Diana Had Lived?" *London Telegraph*, January 15, 2011. www.telegraph.co.uk/culture/books/8261683/What-if-Diana-had-lived.html.
Allen, Kim. "Girls Imagining Careers in the Limelight: Social Class, Gender and Fantasies of 'Success.'" In *In the Limelight and Under the Microscope: Forms and Functions of Female Celebrity*, edited by Su Holmes and Diane Negra, 149–73. London: Continuum, 2011.
al-Herz, Seba. *Al Akharoun*. Beirut: Dar al-Saqi, 2006.
al-Herz, Seba. *The Others*, translated by Seven Story Press. New York: Seven Story Press, 2009.

Alloula, Malek. *The Colonial Harem*, translated by Myrna Godzich and Wlad Godzich. Minneapolis: University of Minnesota Press, 1986.
Al-Rasheed, Madawi. "Deconstructing Nation and Religion: Young Saudi Women Novelists." In *Novel and Nation in Muslim Women's Literary Contributions and National Identities*, edited by Daniella Kuzmanovic and Elisabeth Özdalga, 133–51. Oxon: Palgrave Macmillan, 2015.
Alsanea, Rajaa. *Girls of Riyadh*, translated by Rajaa Alsanea and Marilyn Booth. New York: Penguin, 2008.
al-Shaykh, Hanan. *A Thousand and One Nights: A Retelling*. New York: Anchor, 2014.
al-Shaykh, Hanan. *Women of Sand and Myrrh*, translated by Catherine Cobham. New York: Anchor, 1989.
Alsultany, Evelyn. *Arabs and Muslims in the Media: Race and Representation after 9/11*. New York: New York University Press, 2012.
Amini, Fariba, comp. "It Happened on Hedayat Street: The Forouhar's House, November 23, 1998." *The Iranian*, November 22, 2002. http://iranian.com/Arts/2002/November/Forouhar/index.html.
Anderson, Jon W. "Wiring Up: The Internet Difference for Muslim Networks." In *Muslim Networks from Hajj to Hip Hop*, edited by miriam cooke and Bruce Lawrence, 252–63. Chapel Hill: University of North Carolina Press, 2005.
Ang, Ien. *Watching Dallas: Soap Opera and the Melodramatic Imagination*. London: Routledge, 1985, 2013.
Ardjah, Melanie. "The Limited Time of the Butterflies." In *Parastou Forouhar: Im Zeichen des Ornaments*, edited by Meyer Werner and Melanie Ardjah, 79–83. Stadt Göppingen: Kunsthalle Göppingen, 2018.
Arjana, Sophia Rose. *Muslims in the Western Imagination*. Oxford: Oxford University Press, 2015.
Arjana, Sophia Rose. *Veiled Superheroes: Islam, Feminism, and Popular Culture*. Lanham, MD: Lexington Books, 2018.
Arora, Bharti. *Writing Gender, Writing Nation: Women's Fiction in Post-Independence India*. New York: Routledge, 2020.
Arzumanova, Inna. "Veiled Visibility: Racial Performances and Hegemonic Leaks in Pakistani Fashion Week." In *Racism Postrace*, edited by Roopali Mukherjee, Sarah Banet-Weiser, and Herman Gray, 264–82. Durham: Duke University Press, 2019.
Asad, Talal. *Genealogies of Religion: Discipline and Reasons of Power in Christianity and Islam*. Baltimore: Johns Hopkins University Press, 1993.
Asad, Talal. "Thinking about the Secular Body, Pain, and Liberal Politics." *Cultural Anthropology* 26, no. 4 (2011): 657–75.
Asaad, Lava. "'A Girl Is Like a Bottle of Coke': Emptied and Recycled Identities in *Always Coca-Cola*." In *Memory, Voice and Identity: Muslim Women's Writing across the Middle East*, edited by Feroza Jussawalla and Doaá Omran, 131–38. New York: Routledge, 2021.
Awad, Amal. *Courting Samira*. Sydney: Awal Ahmad, 2012.
Awad, Asmaa Gamal Salem. "Writing Veiled Bodies Anew: A Study of Maya al-Haj's Burkini: I'tirāfāt Muhajjaba." In *Memory, Voice and Identity: Muslim Women's Writing across the Middle East*, edited by Feroza Jussawalla and Doaá Omran, 118–28. New York: Routledge, 2021.
Babb, Lawrence A. "Glancing: Visual Interaction in Hinduism." *Journal of Anthropological Research* 37, no. 4 (1981): 387–401.

Badran, Margot. "Between Secular and Islamic Feminism/s: Reflections on the Middle East and Beyond." *Journal of Middle East Women's Studies* 1, no. 1 (2005): 6–28.
Badran, Margot. *Feminism in Islam: Secular and Religious Convergences.* Oxford: Oneworld, 2009.
Badran, Margot. "Islamic Feminism Revisited." *Countercurrents*, February 10, 2006. www.countercurrents.org/gen-badran100206.htm.
Baetens, Jan. "Dominique Goblet: The List Principle and the Meaning of Form." In *Graphic Subjects: Critical Essays on Autobiography and Graphic Novels*, edited by Michael A. Chaney, 76–92. Madison: University of Wisconsin Press, 2011.
Baetens, Jon, and Hugo Frey. *The Graphic Novel: An Introduction.* New York: Cambridge University Press, 2015.
Bailey, David, and Gilane Tawadros, eds. *Veil: Veiling, Representation, and Contemporary Art.* Cambridge, MA: MIT Press, 2003.
Baldanzi, Jessica, and Hussein Rashid, ed. *Ms. Marvel's America: No Normal.* Jackson: University Press of Mississipi, 2020.
Banet-Weiser, Sarah. "What's Your Flava? Race and Postfeminism in Media Culture." In *Interrogating Postfeminism*, edited by Yvonne Tasker and Diane Negra, 201–27. Durham: Duke University Press, 2007.
Barlas, Asma. *Believing Women in Islam: Unreading Patriarchal Interpretations of the Quran*, rev. ed. Austin: University of Texas Press, 2019.
Barlas, Asma, and David Raeburn Finn. *Believing Women in Islam: A Brief Introduction.* Austin: University of Texas Press, 2019.
Barnard, Saba Chaudhury [Taj, Saba]. "Technicolor Muslimah: A Lighter and Brighter Side." *Muslima: Women's Arts and Voices*. http://muslima.globalfundforwomen.org/content/technicolor-muslimah.
Bashi, Parsua. *Briefe aus Teheran*, translated by Suzanne Baghestani. Zürich: Kein & Aber, 2010.
Bashi, Parsua, and Martin Walker. *Persische Kontraste: Orientalisches Memo: Ausschnitte persischer Kacheln von Profan- und Sakralbauten zeigen die Vielfalt orientalischer verordnetes Grau in Iran von heute gegenüber.* Zürich: Walkwerke, 2008.
Bashi, Parsua. *Nylon Road: A Graphic Memoir of Coming of Age in Iran*, translated by Teresa Go and Miriam Wiesel. New York: Griffin, 2009.
Bashi, Parsua. *Nylon Road: Eine graphische Novelle*, translated by Miriam Wiesel. Zürich: Kein & Aber AG, 2006.
Bauman, Zygmunt, and Leonidas Donskis. *Moral Blindness: The Loss of Sensitivity in Liquid Modernity.* Malden, MA: Polity, 2013.
Baumgardner, Jennifer, and Amy Richards. "Feminism and Femininity: Or How We Learned to Stop Worrying and Love the Thong." In *All About the Girl*, edited by Anita Harris, 59–69. London: Routledge, 2004.
Baumgardner, Jennifer, and Amy Richard. *ManifestA: Young Women, Feminism, and the Future.* New York: Farrar, Straus and Giroux, 2000.
Beattie, Ann. *Mrs. Nixon: A Novelist Imagines a Life.* New York: Scribner, 2011.
Becker, Lutz. "Art, Death, and Language." In *Parastou Forourhar: Art, Life and Death in Iran*, edited by Rose Issa, 16–19. London: Saqi, 2010.
Belghazi, Taieb. "Afterword." In *Muslim Networks from Hajj to Hip Hop*, edited by miriam cooke and Bruce Lawrence, 277–99. Chapel Hill: University of North Carolina Press, 2005.

Bibliography

Benton, Sarah. "The Princess, the People, and Paranoia." In *After Diana: Irreverent Elegies*, edited by Mandy Merck, 87–101. London: Verso, 1998.

Bernstein, J. M. *Torture and Dignity: An Essay on Moral Injury*. Chicago: University of Chicago Press, 2015.

Bhabha, Homi K. "Designer Creations." In *After Diana: Irreverent Elegies*, edited by Mandy Merck, 103–10. London: Verso, 1998.

Bhutto, Zulfikar Ali. "Queer Muslim Futurism." *Archer Magazine*, February 19, 2019. http://archermagazine.com.au/2019/02/queer-muslim-futurism.

Booth, Marilyn. "'The Muslim Woman' as Celebrity Author and the Politics of Translating Arabic: *Girls of Riyadh* Go on the Road." *Journal of Middle East Women's Studies* 6, no. 3 (2010): 149–82.

Booth, Marilyn. "Three's a Crowd: The Translator-Author-Publisher and the Engineering of *Girls of Riyadh* for an Anglophone Readership." In *Translating Women: Different Voices and New Horizons*, edited by Luise von Flotow and Farzaneh Farahzad, 105–19. Oxon: Routledge, 2016.

Booth, Marilyn. "Translator v. Author (2007): *Girls of Riyadh* Go to New York." *Translation Studies* 1, no. 2 (2008): 197–211.

Bose, Purnima. Review of *The Girl in the Tangerine Scarf*, by Mohja Kahf. *Indiana Magazine of History* 105, no. 1 (2009): 90–91.

Braudy, Leo. *The Frenzy of Renown: Fame and Its History*. New York: Oxford University Press, 1986.

British Council Literature. "Monica Ali." http://literature.britishcouncil.org/monica-ali.

Brooks, Ann. *Postfeminisms: Feminism, Cultural Theory, and Cultural Forms*. London: Routledge, 1997, 2002.

Brooks, Geraldine. *Nine Parts of Desire: The Hidden World of Islamic Women*. New York: Anchor Books, 1995.

Brouillette, Sarah. "Literature and Gentrification on Brick Lane." *Criticism* 51, no. 3 (2009): 425–49.

Brown, Tina. *The Diana Chronicles*. New York: Anchor House, 2007.

Bucar, Elizabeth. *Pious Fashion: How Muslim Women Dress*. Cambridge, MA: Harvard University Press, 2017.

Bunt, Gary. "Defining Islamic Interconnectivity." In *Muslim Networks from Hajj to Hip Hop*, edited by miriam cooke and Bruce Lawrence, 235–51. Chapel Hill: University of North Carolina Press, 2005.

Bunt, Gary R. *iMuslims: Rewiring the House of Islam*. Chapel Hill: University of North Carolina Press, 2009.

Burge, Amy. *Representing Difference in the Medieval and Modern Orientalist Romance*. Houndmills, Basingstoke: Palgrave, 2016.

Butler, Jess. "For White Girls Only? Postfeminism and the Politics of Inclusion." *Feminist Formations* 25, no. 1 (2013): 35–58.

Butler, Judith. *Precarious Life: The Powers of Mourning and Violence*. London: Verso, 2004.

Butler, Pamela, and Jinga Desai. "Manolos, Marriage, and Mantras: Chick-Lit Criticism and Transnational Feminism." *Meridians: Feminism, Race, and Transnationalism* 8, no. 2 (2008): 1–31.

Cacciottolo, Mario. "*Brick Lane* Protestors Hurt over 'Lies'." *BBC News*, July 31, 2006. http://news.bbc.co.uk/2/hi/uk_news/5229872.stm.

Cahill, Ann J. *Rethinking Rape*. Ithaca: Cornell University Press, 2001.

Cavaler, C. "Undemocratic Layout: Eight Methods of Accenting Images." *The Comics Grid: Journal of Comics Scholarship* 8, no. 8 (2018): 1–24.
Chakravorty, Mrinalini. "*Brick Lane* Blockades: The Bioculturalism of Migrant Domesticity." *Modern Fiction Studies* 58, no. 3 (2012): 503–28.
Chakravorty, Mrinalini. *In Stereotype: South Asia in the Global Literary Imaginary*. New York: Columbia University Press, 2014.
Chambers, Claire. *Britain through Muslim Eyes: Literary Representations, 1780–1988*. Houndmills, Basingstoke: Palgrave-Macmillan, 2015.
Chambers, Claire. *Making Sense of Contemporary British Muslim Novels*. London: Palgrave-Macmillan, 2019.
Chan-Malik, Sylvia. *Being Muslim: A Cultural History of Women of Color in American Islam*. New York: New York University Press, 2018.
Chaney, Michael A., ed. *Graphic Subjects: Critical Essays on Autobiography and Graphic Novels*. Madison: University of Wisconsin Press, 2011.
Chapman, Sandra. *The Girl in the Yellow Scarf: One of Indiana's Cold Case Murders Solved as a Town Tries to Leave behind Its Past*. Indianapolis: Prince Media Group, 2012.
Cheng, Anne Anlin. *Second Skin: Josephine Baker and the Modern Surface*. New York: Oxford University Press, 2011.
Cheng, Anne Anlin. *Ornamentalism*. New York: Oxford University Press, 2019.
Chute, Hillary. *Graphic Women: Life Narrative and Contemporary Comics*. New York: Columbia University Press, 2010.
Cohn, Neil. *The Visual Language of Comics: Introduction to the Structure and Cognition of Sequential Images*. London: Bloomsbury, 2013.
Colebrook, Claire. *Deleuze: A Guide for the Perplexed*. London: Continuum 2006.
Collins, Lisa Gail. *The Art of History: African American Women Artists Engage the Past*. New Brunswick, NJ: Rutgers University Press, 2002.
cooke, miriam. "The Muslimwoman." *Contemporary Islam* 1, no. 2 (2007): 139–54.
cooke, miriam. *Women Claim Islam: Creating Islamic Feminism through Literature*. New York: Routledge, 2001.
Cooper, Arnold M. "The Narcissistic-Masochistic Character." In *Masochism: Current Psychoanalytic Perspectives*, edited by Robert A. Glick and Donald J. Meyers, 117–38. Hillsdale, NJ: Analytic Press, 1988.
Cormack, Alistair. "Migration and the Politics of Narrative Form: Realism and the Postcolonial Subject in *Brick Lane*." *Contemporary Literature* 47, no. 4 (2006): 695–721.
Cousins, Mark. "From Royal London to Celebrity Space." In *After Diana: Irreverent Elegies*, edited by Mandy Merck, 77–86. London: Verso, 1998.
Cyphers, Eric. *Sex and the City 2: The Stories. The Fashion. The Adventure*. Philadelphia: Running Press, 2010.
Dagbovie-Mullins, Sika, and Eric Berlatsky. "The Only Nerdy Pakastani-American-Slash-Inhuman in the Entire Universe: Postracialism and Politics in the New *Ms. Marvel*." In *Ms. Marvel's America: No Normal*, edited by Jessica Baldanzi and Hussein Rashid, 65–88. Jackson: University Press of Mississippi, 2020.
Darda, Joseph. "Graphic Ethics: Theorizing the Face in Marjane Satrapi's *Persepolis*." *College Literature* 40, no. 2 (2013): 31–51.
Davis, Hilary E., Jasmin Zine, and Lisa K. Taylor. "An Interview with Mohja Kahf." *Intercultural Education* 18, no. 4 (2007): 383–88.
Davis, Julie, and Robert Westerfelhaus. "Finding a Place for a Muslimah Heroine in the Post-9/11 Marvel Universe." *Feminist Media Studies* 13, no. 5 (2013): 800–809.

Bibliography

Deleuze, Gilles. *Foucault*, translated by Seán Hand. Minneapolis: University of Minnesota Press, 1988.

Deleuze, Gilles, and Felix Guattari. *A Thousand Plateaus: Capitalism and Schizophrenia*, translated by Brian Massumi. Minneapolis: University of Minnesota Press, 1987.

Deleuze, Gilles, and Leopold von Sacher-Masoch. *Masochism: Coldness and Cruelty and Venus in Furs*, translated by Jean McNeil and Aude Willm. New York: Zone, 1989.

DeLillo, Don. *Libra*. New York: Viking, 1988.

Denny, Frederick Mathewson. *An Introduction to Islam*, 2nd ed. New York: Macmillan, 1994.

di Mattia, Joanna. "'What's the Harm in Believing?' Mr Big, Mr Perfect, and the Romantic Quest for *Sex and the City*'s Mr Right." In *Reading Sex and the City*, edited by Kim Akass and Janet McCabe, 17–32. London: I.B. Tauris, 2004.

Doane, Mary Ann. *Femmes Fatales: Feminism, Film Theory, Psychoanalysis*. London: Routledge, 1991.

Donnelly, Alison. "Visibility, Violence and Voice? Attitudes to Veiling Post-11 September." In *Veil: Veiling, Representation and Contemporary Art*, edited by David A. Bailey and Gilane Tawadros, 121–35. Cambridge: MIT Press, 2003.

Dubbati, Bakuzar. "The Woman in Hijab as a Freak: Super(Muslim)woman in Deena Mohamed's Webcomic *Qahera*." *Journal of Graphic Novels and Comics* 8, no. 5 (2017): 433–49.

Duggan, Bob. "Black Swan: Uncovering Iranian Women Artists." *Big Think*, January 30, 2011. Accesssed January 20, 2015. http://bigthink.com/Picture-This/black-swan-uncovering-iranian-women-artists.

Duvall, Spring-Serenity. "Celebrity Travels: Media Spectacles and the Construction of a Transnational Politics of Care." In *Circuits of Visibility: Gender and Transnational Media Cultures*, edited by Radha S. Hegde, 140–56. New York: New York University Press, 2010.

Dyer, Richard. *Stars*, 2nd ed. London: British Film Institute, 1998.

Elias, Ana Sofia, Rosalind Gill, and Christina Scharff, eds. *Aesthetic Labour: Rethinking Beauty Politics in Neoliberalism*. New York: Palgrave-Macmillan, 2017.

El Guindi, Fadwa. *Veil: Modesty, Privacy, and Resistance*. Oxford: Berg, 2003.

El Omari, Diana, Juliane Hammer, and Mouhanad Khourchide, eds. *Muslim Women and Gender Justice: Concepts, Sources, and Histories*. New York: Routledge, 2019.

Elsadda, Hoda. "Arab Women Bloggers: The Emergence of Literary Counterpublics." *Middle East Journal of Culture and Communication* 3, no. 3 (2010): 312–32.

El-Sawy, Amany. "Revolutionizing Scheherazade: Deconstructing the Exotic and Oppressed Muslim Odalisque in Mohja Kahf's Poetry." In *Memory, Voice and Identity: Muslim Women's Writing across the Middle East*, edited by Feroza Jussawalla and Doaá Omran, 234–46. New York: Routledge, 2021.

Encyclopedia of World Biography. "Monica Ali." www.notablebiographies.com/newsmakers2/2007-A-Co/Ali-Monica.html

Etemad, Katayoon, Faramarz Samavati, and Przemyslaw Prusinkiewicz. "Animating Persian Floral Patterns." In *Proceedings of the Fourth Eurographics Conference on Computational Aesthetics in Graphics, Visualization, and Imaging*, edited by Paul Brown, D.W. Cunningham, V. Interrante, and J. McCormack, 25–32. Aire-la-Ville, Switzerland: Eurographics Association, 2008.

Ettachifini, Leila. "Four Muslim Women on How to Survive in Media." *Vice*, March 27, 2019. www.vice.com/en_us/article/8xypxx/muslim-women-media-rewards-challenges-tokenization.

Fanon, Frantz. *Black Skin: White Masks*, translated by Richard Philcox. New York: Grove, 1952.

Falcus, Sarah, and Katsura Sako. "Women, Travelling, and Later Life." In *Ageing, Popular Culture, and Contemporary Feminism: Harleys and Hormones*, edited by Imelda Whelehan and Joel Gwynne, 203–18. Houndsmills, Basingstoke: Palgrave-Macmillan, 2014.

Farizan, Sarah. *Tell Me Again How a Crush Should Feel*. New York: Workman, 2014.

Ferriss, Suzanne, and Mallory Young, eds. *Chick Lit: The New Woman's Fiction*. New York: Routledge 2006.

Firat, Begim Ozden. *Encounters with the Ottoman Miniature: Contemporary Readings of an Imperial Art*. London: Bloomsbury, 2015.

Fischer, Jordan. "The History of Hate in Indiana: How the Ku Klux Klan Took over Indiana's Halls of Power." December 8, 2016. www.theindychannel.com/longform/the-ku-klux-klan-ran-indiana-once-could-it-happen-again.

Flaskerud, Ingvild. *Visualizing Belief and Piety in Iranian Shiism*. London: Continuum, 2012.

Fleetwood, Nicole R. *Troubling Vision: Performance, Visuality, and Blackness*. Chicago: University of Chicago Press, 2011.

Forouhar, Parastou. *Das Land, in Dem Meine Eltern umgebracht wurden: Liebeserklärung an den Iran*. Freiburg: Verlag Herder, 2011.

Forouhar, Parastou. "Documents." www.parastou-forouhar.de/english/Documents-Parwaneh-and-Dariush-Forouhar.html.

Foster, Hal ed., *Vision and Visuality: Discussions in Contemporary Culture*. Seattle: Bay-DIA, 1988.

Fraiman, Susan. *Extreme Domesticity: A View from the Margins*. New York: Columbia University Press, 2017.

Freud, Sigmund. "A Child is Being Beaten." In *The Standard Edition of the Complete Psychological Works of Sigmund Freud*, edited and translated by James Strachey, vol. 17, 175–204. London: Hogarth Press, 1957–74.

Freud, Sigmund. "The Economic Problem of Moral Masochism." In *The Standard Edition of the Complete Psychological Works of Sigmund Freud*, edited and translated by James Strachey, vol. 19, 157–70. London: Hogarth Press, 1957–74.

Freud, Sigmund. "Three Essays on the Theory of Sexuality." In *The Standard Edition of the Complete Psychological Works of Sigmund Freud*, edited and translated by James Strachey, vol. 7, 123–46. London: Hogarth Press, 1953.

Friedman, Susan Stanford. "Conjunctures of the 'New' World Literature and Migration Studies: Cosmopolitanism, Religion, and Diasporic Sisters of Scheherazade." *Journal of World Literature* 3 (2018): 267–89.

Ganji, Ali Akbar. *L'eminence rouge*. Tehran: Tarhno, 2001.

Gaucho, Suzanne. *Liberating Shahradazad: Feminism, Postcolonialism, and Islam*. Minneapolis: University of Minnesota Press, 2006.

Gavey, Nicola. *Just Sex? The Cultural Scaffolding of Rape*. London: Routledge, 2005.

Genette, Gerard. *Narrative Discourse: An Essay in Method*, translated by Jane E. Lewin. Ithaca: Cornell University Press, 1980.

Gerhard, Jane. "*Sex and the City*: Carrie Bradshaw's Queer Postfeminism." *Feminist Media Studies* 5 no. 5 (2005): 37–48.

Germanà, Monica. "From Hijab to Sweatshops: Segregated Bodies and Contented Space on Monica Ali's *Brick Lane*." In *Postcolonial Spaces: The Politics of Space in Contemporary Culture*, edited by Andrew Teverson and Sara Upstone, 67–82. Houndsmills, Basingstoke: Palgrave Macmillan, 2001.

Ghabra, Haneen Shafeeq. *Muslim Women and White Femininity: Reenactment and Resistance.* New York: Peter Lang, 2018.
GhaneaBassiri, Kambiz. *A History of Islam in America: From the New World to the New World Order.* Cambridge: Cambridge University Press, 2010.
Ghumkhor, Sahar. *The Political Psychology of the Veil: The Impossible Body.* Cham, Switzerland: Springer and Palgrave-Macmillan, 2019.
Gill, Rosalind. "The Affective, Cultural, and Psychic Life of Postfeminism: A Postfeminist Sensibility Ten Years On." *European Journal of Cultural Studies* 20, no. 6 (2017): 606–26.
Gill, Rosalind. "Postfeminist Media Culture: Elements of a Sensibility." *European Journal of Media Studies* 10, no. 2 (2007): 147–66.
Gill, Rosalind. "Post-postfeminism? New Feminist Visibilities in Postfeminist Times." *Feminist Media Studies* 16, no. 4 (2016): 610–30.
Gökariksel, Banu, and Ellen McLarney. "Introduction: Muslim Women, Consumer Capitalism, and the Islamic Culture Industry." *Journal of Middle East Women's Studies* 6, no. 3 (2010): 1–18.
Goldman, Jonathan. *Modernism Is the Literature of Celebrity.* Austin: University of Texas Press, 2011.
Gorra, Michael. "East Enders." Review of *Brick Lane,* by Monica Ali. *New York Times,* September 7, 2003. www.nytimes.com/2003/09/07/books/east-enders.html.
Goska, Danusha. "'The Girl in the Tangerine Scarf' Book Review." Review of *The Girl in the Tangerine Scarf,* by Mohja Kahf. *Save, Send, Delete* (blog), July 13, 2013. http://save-send-delete.blogspot.com/2013/07/the-girl-in-tangerine-scarf-book-review.html.
Grabar, Oleg. *Mostly Miniatures: An Introduction to Persian Painting.* Princeton: Princeton University Press, 2000.
Grace, Daphne. *The Woman in the Muslim Mask: Veiling and Identity in Postcolonial Literature.* London: Pluto Press 2004.
Greer, Germaine. "Reality Bites." *Guardian,* July 24, 2006.
Grewal, Inderpal. *Transnational America: Feminisms, Diaspora, Neoliberalisms.* Durham: Duke University Press, 2005.
Grewal, Zareena. *Islam Is a Foreign Country: American Muslims and the Global Crisis of Authority.* New York: New York University Press, 2013.
Grochowski, Tom. "Neurotic in New York: the Woody Allen Touches in *Sex and the City.*" In *Reading Sex and the City,* edited by Kim Akass and Janet McCabe, 149–60. London: I.B. Tauris, 2004.
Groensteen, Thierry. *Comics and Narration,* translated by Ann Miller. Oxford: University Press of Mississippi, 2013.
Groensteen, Thierry. *The System of Comics,* translated by Bart Beaty and Nick Nguyen. Jackson: University of Mississippi Press, 2007.
Grossman, Ron. "Flashback: Fifty Years Ago: MLK's March in Marquette Park Turned Violent, Exposed Hate." *Chicago Tribune,* July 28, 2016. www.chicagotribune.com/news/opinion/commentary/ct-mlk-king-marquette-park-1966-flashback-perspec-0731-md-20160726-story.html.
Guerrero, Lisa. "Sistah's Are Doin' It for Themselves: Chick Lit in Black and White." In *Chick Lit: The New Woman's Fiction,* edited by Suzanne Ferriss and Mallory Young, 89–101. New York: Routledge 2006.
Gunning, Dave. *Race and Antiracism in Black British and British Asian Literature.* Liverpool: Liverpool University Press, 2012.

Gwynne, Joel. "'The Lighter that Fuels the Blaze of Change': Agency and (Cyber) Spatial (Dis)Embodiment in *The Girls of Riyadh*." *Women's Studies International Forum* 37 (2013): 46–52.

Hafez, Sherine. *An Islam of Her Own: Reconsidering Religion and Secularism in Women's Islamic Movements*. New York: New York University Press, 2011.

Halm, Heinz. *The Shi'ites: A Short History*, 2nd ed., translated by Allison Brown. Princeton: Markus Wiener, 2007.

Hammer, Juliane, "Introduction to Muslim Women and Gender Justice." In *Muslim Women and Gender Justice: Concepts, Sources, and Histories*, edited by Dina El Omari, Juliane Hammer, and Mouhanad Khorchide, 1–14. New York: Routledge, 2019.

Haque, Danielle. "The Postsecular Turn and Muslim American Literature." *American Literature* 86, no. 4 (2014): 799–828.

Haute Hijab Staff. "The 28 Most Influential Hijabi Bloggers You Should Be Following in 2017." January 10, 2017. www.hautehijab.com/blogs/hijab-fashion/28-most-influential-hijabi-bloggers.

Harper, Stephen. "Madly Famous: Narratives of Mental Illness in Celebrity Culture." In *Framing Celebrity: New Directions in Celebrity Culture*, edited by Su Holmes and Sean Redmond, 311–28. London: Routledge, 2006.

Hartman, Saidiya. *Scenes of Subjection: Terror, Slavery, and Self-Making in Nineteenth-Century America*. Oxford: Oxford University Press, 1997.

Hartman, Saidiya. *Wayward Lives, Beautiful Experiments: Intimate Histories of Social Upheaval*. New York: Norton, 2019.

Harzewski, Stephanie. *Chick Lit and Postfeminism*. Charlottesville: University of Virginia Press, 2011.

Hassan, Riffat. "Feminism in Islam." In *Feminism and World Religions*, edited by Arvind Sharma and Katherine K. Young, 248–78. New York: SUNY Press, 1998.

Hassan, Riffat. "Woman-Man Equality in Creation: Interpreting the Qur'an from a Nonpatriarchal Perspective." In *Muslim Women and Gender Justice: Concepts, Sources, and Histories*, edited by Dina El Omari, Juliane Hammer, and Mouhanad Khorchide, 89–105. New York: Routledge, 2019.

Hatfield, Charles. *Alternative Comics: An Emerging Literature*. Jackson: University Press of Mississippi, 2005.

Hegde, Radha, ed. *Circuits of Visibility: Gender and Transnational Media Cultures*. New York: New York University Press, 2010.

Hemmings, Clare, and Amal Treacher Kabesh. "The Feminist Subject of Agency: Recognition and Affect in Encounters with the 'Other'." In *Gender, Agency, and Coercion*, edited by Sumi Madhok, Anne Phillips, and Kalpana Wilson, 29–46. Houndsmills, Baskingstoke: Palgrave-Macmillan, 2013.

Henry, Astrid. "Sex and the City and Third Wave Feminism." In *Reading Sex and the City*, edited by Kim Akass and Janet McCabe, 65–82. London: I.B. Tauris, 2004.

Herding, Maruta. *Inventing the Muslim Cool: Islamic Youth Culture in Western Europe*. Bielefeld, Germany: Transcript Verlag, 2013.

Herman, David. "Beyond Voice and Vision: Cognitive Grammar and Focalization Theory." In *Point of View, Perspective and Focalization: Modeling Mediation in Narrative*, edited by Peter Hühn, Wolf Schmid, and Jörg Schönert, 119–42. Berlin: Walter deGruyer, 2009.

Hidayatullah, Aysha. *Feminist Edges of the Qur'an*. New York: Oxford University Press, 2014.

Hiddleston, Jane. "Shapes and Shadows: (Un)veiling the Immigrant in Monica Ali's *Brick Lane*." *Journal of Commonwealth Literature* 40, no. 1 (2005): 52–72.

Higgins, Will. "'We Need to Acknowledge It': Martinsville Tries to Remake Its Racist Image." *Indianapolis Star*, November 2, 2017 www.indystar.com/story/life/2017/11/02/martinsville-remakes-racist-image/775258001.

Hinchcliff, Sharron. "Sexing Up the Midlife Woman: Cultural Representations of Ageing, Femininity, and the Sexy Body." In *Ageing, Popular Culture. and Contemporary Feminism: Harleys and Hormones*, edited by Imelda Whelehan and Joel Gwynne, 66–73. Houndsmills-Basingstoke: Palgrave-Macmillan, 2014.

Hirschkind, Charles. "Is There a Secular Body?" *Cultural Anthropology* 26, no. 4 (2011): 633–47.

Holland, Sharon. *Raising the Dead: Readings of Death and (Black) Subjectivity*. Durham: Duke University Press, 2000.

Hollows, Joanne. *Feminism, Femininity and Popular Culture*. Manchester: Manchester University Press-St. Martins, 2000.

Holmes, Su, and Sean Redmond. *Framing Celebrity: New Directions in Celebrity Culture*. London: Routledge, 2006.

Hoodfar, Homa. "The Veil in Their Minds and on Our Heads: Veiling Practices and Muslim Women." In *The Politics of Culture in the Shadow of Capital*, edited by Lisa Lowe and David Lloyd, 248–79. Durham: Duke University Press, 1997.

hooks, bell. "The Oppositional Gaze: Black Female Spectators." In *The Feminism and Visual Culture Reader*, edited by Amelia Jones, 94–105. New York: Routledge, 2010.

Horstkotte, Silke, and Nancy Pedri. "Focalization in Graphic Narrative." *Narrative* 19, no. 3 (2011): 330–57.

Hosseini, Khaled. *The Kite Runner*. New York: Riverhead Books, 2003.

Hosseini, Mir M. "Assassination of Dariush Forouhar." *Fouman.com*. Accessed April 12, 2014. www.fouman.com/Y/Get_Iranian_History_Today.php?artid=22.

Hussain, Yasmin. *Writing Diaspora: South Asian Women, Culture, and Ethnicity*. Aldershot, Hampshire: Ashgate, 2005.

Irigaray, Luce. *This Sex Which Is Not One*, translated by Catherine Porter, and Carolyn Burke. Ithaca: Cornell University Press, 1985.

Issa, Rose, ed. *Parastou Forouhar: Art, Life and Death in Iran*. London: Saqi, 2010.

It Happened One Night. Directed by Frank Capra. Columbia Pictures, 1934.

Jackson, Sherman. *Islam and the Blackamerican: Looking toward the Third Resurrection*. New York: Oxford University Press, 2005.

Jalaluddin, Uzma. *Ayesha at Last*. London: Saqi, 2019.

Janmohamed, Shelina. *Generation M: Young Muslims Changing the World*. London: I.B. Tauris, 2016.

Jay, Martin. "Scopic Regimes of Modernity." In *Vision and Visuality: Discussions in Contemporary Culture*, edited by Hal Foster, 3–23. Seattle: Bay-DIA, 1988.

Jay, Martin. "That Visual Turn: The Advent of Visual Culture." *The Journal of Visual Culture* 1, no. 1 (2002): 87–92.

Johansson, Sofia. "Sometimes You Wanna Hate Celebrities': Tabloid Readers and Celebrity Coverage." In *Framing Celebrity: New Directions in Celebrity Culture*, edited by Su Holmes and Sean Redmond, 343–58. London: Routledge, 2006.

Jones, Amelia, ed. *The Feminism and Visual Culture Reader*, 2nd ed. New York: Routledge, 2010.

Jussawalla, Feroza, and Doaá Omran, eds. *Memory, Voice and Identity: Muslim Women's Writing across the Middle East*. New York: Routledge, 2021.

Jussawalla, Feroza. "Introduction." In *Memory, Voice and Identity: Muslim Women's Writing across the Middle East*, edited by Feroza Jussawalla and Doaá Omran, 1–8. New York: Routledge, 2021.

Kabeer, Naila. *The Power to Choose: Bangladeshi Women and Labour Market Decisions in London and Dhaka*. London: Verso, 2000.

Kahf, Mohja. "Braiding the Stories: Women's Eloquence in the Early Islamic Era." In *Windows of Faith: Muslim Women Scholar-Activists in North America*, edited by Gisela Webb, 147–71. Syracuse: Syracuse University Press, 2000.

Kahf, Mohja. *Hagar Poems*. Fayetteville: University of Arkansas Press, 2016.

Kahf, Mohja. *E-mails from Scheherazad*. Gainesville: University Press of Florida, 2003.

Kahf, Mohja. "From Her Royal Body the Robe Was Removed: The Blessings of the Veil and the Trauma of Forced Unveilings in the Middle East." In *The Veil: Women Writers on Its History, Lore, and Politics*, edited by Jennifer Heath, 27–43. Berkeley: University of California Press, 2008.

Kahf, Mohja. "More than One Way to Break a Fast." In *Post-Gibran: Anthology of New Arab American Writing*, edited by Munir Akash and Khaled Mattawa, 263. Syracuse: Syracuse University Press, 1999.

Kahf, Mohja. "Packaging 'Huda': Sha'rawi's Memoirs in the United States Reception Environment." In *Going Global: The Transnational Reception of Third World Women Writers*, edited by Amal Amireh and Lisa Suhair Majaj, 148–72. New York: Garland Publishing, 2000.

Kahf, Mohja. "Poetry Is My Home Address." In *Scheherazade's Legacy: Arab and Arab American Women on Writing*, edited by Susan Muaddi Darraj, 7–20. Westport, CT: Praeger, 2004.

Kahf, Mohja. "Politics and Erotics in Nizar Kabbani's Poetry: From the Sultan's Wife to the Lady Friend." *World Literature Today* 74, no. 1 (2000): 44–52.

Kahf, Mohja. *The Girl in the Tangerine Scarf*. New York: PublicAffairs, 2006.

Kahf, Mohja. "The Muslim in the Mirror." In *Living Islam Out Loud: American Muslim Women Speak*, edited by Saleemah Abdul-Ghafur, 130–38. Boston: Beacon Press, 2005.

Kahf, Mohja. *Western Representations of the Muslim Woman: From Termagant to Odalisque*. Austin: University of Texas Press, 1999.

Kane, Jean. *Conspicuous Bodies: Provincial Belief and the Making of Joyce and Rushdie*. Columbus: Ohio State University Press, 2014.

Karentzos, Alexandra. "Tausend Tode Sterben: Erwachen aus dem Märchentraum." In *Tausendundein Tag, Nationalgalerie Hamburger Bahnhof*, 37–38. Berlin: Walter König; Hamburg: Nationalgalerie Hamburger Bahnhof, 2003.

Karim, Jamillah. *American Muslim Women: Negotiating Race, Class, and Gender within the Ummah*. New York: New York University Press, 2009.

Khabeer, Su'ad Abdul. *Muslim Cool: Race, Religion and Hip Hop in the United States*. New York: New York University Press, 2016.

Khabeer, Suad Abdul. "Representation as a Black Muslim Woman Is Good—And It's a Trap." *Vice*, March 29, 2019 www.vice.com/en_us/article/nexp3d/representation-as-a-black-muslim-woman-is-goodand-its-a-trap.

Kent, Miriam. "Unveiling Marvels: *Ms. Marvel* and the Reception of the New Muslim Superheroine." *Feminist Media Studies* 15, no. 3 (2015): 522–38.

Keshavarz, Fatemeh. *Jasmine and Stars: Reading More than Lolita in Tehran*. Chapel Hill: University of North Carolina Press, 2007.

Kung, Shao-ming. "'Walking' Experiences and Self-Empowerment of South Asian Female Immigrants in Monica Ali's *Brick Lane*." *NTU Studies in Language and Literature* 27 (2012): 131–61.

Bibliography

Kuruvilla, Carol. "Queer Muslim Artist Saba Taj Sees Her Art as an Act of Resistance." *Huffington Post Religion*, June 24, 2016. www.huffingtonpost.com/entry/saba-taj-muslim-artist_us_576c63c7e4b0f16832390d80.

Ksander, Yaël. "Martinsville and Diversity." *Indiana Public Media*. January 15, 2007. http://indianapublicmedia.org/momentofindianahistory/martinsville-and-diversity/.

Labib, Michaela Canepari. "The Multiethnic City: Cultural Translation and Multilingualism in Monica Ali's *Brick Lane*." *La Torre di Babele: Rivista Letteratura e Linguistica* 3 (2005): 205–23.

Lea, Richard, and Paul Lewis. "Local Protests over Brick Lane Film." *The Guardian*, July 17, 2006. www.theguardian.com/books/2006/jul/17/film.uk.

Levin, Carole. "'Would I Could Give You Help and Succor': Elizabeth I and the Politics of Touch." *Albion* 21, no. 2 (1989): 191–205.

Levin, Gabriel. "'Who Keened over the Bones of Dead Encampments': On the Hanging Odes of Arabia." *Parnassus: Poetry in Review* 29, no. 1/2 (2006): 6–27.

Lewis, Paul. "Brick Lane Protests Force Film Company to Beat Retreat." *The Guardian*, July 27, 2006. www.theguardian.com/uk/2006/jul/27/film.books.

Lewis, Reina. "Introduction: Mediating Modesty." In *Modest Fashion: Styling Bodies, Mediating Faith*, 1–13. London: I.B. Tauris, 2013.

Lewis, Reina. "Preface." In *Veil: Veiling, Representation and Contemporary Art*, edited by David A. Bailey and Gilane Tawadros, 8–14. Cambridge: MIT Press, 2003.

Lewis, Reina. "Uncovering Modesty: Dejabis and Dewigies Expanding the Parameters of the Modest Fashion Blogosphere." *Fashion Theory* 19, no. 2 (2015): 243–69.

Livesey, Graham. "Assemblage." In *The Deleuze Dictionary*, rev. ed., edited by Adrian Parr. Edinburgh: Edinburgh University Press, 2010, 18–19.

Loos, Alfred. *Ornament and Crime: Selected Essays*, translated by Michael Mitchell. Riverside, CA: Ariadne Press, 1998.

Lyall, Sarah. "A Different, Happy Ending for Diana? Monica Ali Novel Imagines a Future." *New York Times Arts Beat*, January 7, 2011. http://artsbeat.blogs.nytimes.com/2011/01/07/a-different-happy-ending-for-diana-monica-ali-novel-imagines-a-future/.

Macdonald, Myra. "Muslim Women and the Veil: Problems of Image and Voice in Media Representations." *Feminist Media Studies* 6, no. 1 (2006): 7–23.

MacFarquhar, Neil. "She Carries Weapons; They Are Called Words." *New York Times*, May 12, 2007. www.nytimes.com/2007/05/12/books/12veil.html?pagewanted=all&_r=0.

McCloud, Aminah Beverly. *Transnational Muslims in American Society*. Gainesville: University Press of Florida, 2006.

McCloud, Scott. *Understanding Comics: The Invisible Art*. New York: HarperCollins-William Morrow, 1994.

McDonald, Megan. "Sur/Veil: The Veil as a Blank(et) Signifier." In *Muslim Women: Transnational Feminism and the Ethics of Pedagogy: Contested Imaginaries in Post-9/11 Cultural Practice*, edited by Lisa K. Taylor and Jasmin Zine, 225–58. New York: Routledge, 2014.

McKittrick, Katherine. *Demonic Grounds: Black Women and the Cartographies of Struggle*. Minneapolis: University of Minnesota Press, 2006.

McPhee, Ruth. *Female Masochism in Film: Sexuality, Ethics, and Aesthetics*. Oxon: Ashgate, 2014.

McRobbie, Angela. *The Aftermath of Feminism: Gender, Culture and Social Change*. London: Sage, 2009.

Mahmood, Saba. *Politics of Piety: The Islamic Revival and the Feminist Subject.* Princeton: Princeton University Press, 2005.

Majaj, Lisa Suhair. "'Supplies of Grace': The Poetry of Mohja Kahf." *ArteEast*, September 6, 2006. www.arteeast.org/artenews/artenews-articles2006/september06/artenews.mohj-kahf.html.

Majed, Hasan Saeed. *Islamic Postcolonialism: Islam and Muslim Identities in Four Contemporary British Novels.* Newcastle upon Tyne: Cambridge Scholars Publishing, 2015.

Malamud, Martha A. *A Poetics of Transformation: Prudentius and Classical Mythology.* Ithaca: Cornell University Press, 1989.

Malik, Ayiesha. *Sofia Khan Is Not Obliged.* London: twenty7 books, 2015.

Manav, Ratti. *The Postsecular Imagination: Postcolonialism, Religion, and Literature.* New York: Routledge, 2013.

Marranci, Gabriele. *Understanding Muslim Identity: Rethinking Fundamentalism.* Houndsmills, Basingstoke: Palgrave Macmillan, 2009.

Marriott, David. "The Racialized Body." In *The Cambridge Companion to the Body in Literature*, edited by David Hillman and Ulrika Maude, 163–76. New York: Cambridge University Press, 2015.

Marx, John. "The Feminization of Globalization." *Cultural Critique* 63 (2006): 1–32.

Massumi, Brian. *Parables for the Virtual: Movement, Affect, Sensation.* Durham: Duke University Press, 2002.

Mattawa, Khaled. "Writing Islam in Contemporary American Poetry: On Mohja Kahf, Daniel Moore and Agha Shahid Ali." *PMLA* 123, no. 5 (2008): 1590–95.

Mazza, Cris. "Who's Laughing Now? A Short History of Chick Lit and the Perversion of a Genre." In *Chick Lit: The New Woman's Fiction*, edited by Suzanne Ferriss and Mallory Young, 22–23. New York: Routledge, 2006.

Mbembe, Achille. *Necropolitics*, translated by Steve Corocoran. Durham: Duke University Press, 2019.

Merck, Mandy. "Sexuality in the City." In *Reading Sex and the City*, edited by Kim Akass and Janet McCabe, 48–62. London: I.B. Tauris, 2004.

Mernissi, Fatima. *Scheherazade Goes West: Different Cultures, Different Harems.* New York: Simon and Schuster, 2001.

Metz, Christian. *The Imaginary Signifier: Psychoanalysis and Cinema*, translated by Celia Britton, Annwyl Williams, Ben Brewster, and Alfred Guzzetti. Bloomington: Indiana University Press, 1982.

Meyer, Werner. "On the Role of Ornament in the Work of Parastou Forouhar." In *Parastou Forouhar: Im Zeichen des Ornaments*, edited by Meyer Werner and Melanie Ardjah, 84–87. Stadt Göppingen: Kunsthalle Göppingen, 2018.

Meyer, Werner, and Melanie Ardjah. *Parastou Forouhar: Im Zeichen des Ornaments.* Stadt Göppingen: Kunsthalle Göppingen, 2018.

Mikkonen, Kai. "Focalisation in Comics: From the Specificities of the Medium to Conceptual Reformulation." *Scandinavian Journal of Comic Art* 1 no. 1 (2012): 71–95.

Mikkonen, Kai. "Graphic Narratives as a Challenge to Narratology: The Question of Focalization." *Amerikastudien / American Studies* 56, no. 4 (2011): 637–52.

Mikkonen, Kai. *The Narratology of Comic Art.* London: Routledge, 2017.

Mitchell, W. T. J. "Showing Seeing: A Critique of Visual Culture." *Journal of Visual Culture* 11, no. 2 (2002): 165–81.

Mirza, Fatima Farheen. *A Place for Us.* New York: SJP for Hogarth, 2018.

Mirzoeff, Nicholas. "On Visuality." *Journal of Visual Culture* 5, no. 1 (2006): 53–79.

Mirzoeff, Nicholas. *The Right to Look: A Counterhistory of Visuality*. Durham: Duke University Press, 2011.

Missler, Heike. *The Cultural Politics of Chick Lit: Popular Fiction, Postfeminism and Representation*. Oxon: Routledge, 2017.

Moallem, Minoo. *Between Warrior Brother and Veiled Sister: Islamic Fundamentalism and the Politics of Patriarchy in Iran*. Berkeley: University of California Press, 2005.

Moallem, Minoo. *Persian Carpets: The Nation as a Transnational Commodity*. New York: Routledge, 2018.

Monbiot, George. "Neoliberalism—The Ideology at the Root of All Our Problems." *Guardian*, April 15, 2016. www.theguardian.com/books/2016/apr/15/neoliberalism-ideology-problem-george-monbiot.

Montoro, Rocío. *Chick Lit: The Stylistics of Cappuccino Fiction*. London: Continuum, 2012.

Moors, Annelies. "'Discover the Beauty of Modesty': Islamic Fashion Online." In *Modest Fashion: Styling Bodies, Mediating Faith*, edited by Reina Lewis, 17–40. London: I.B. Tauris, 2013.

Moran, Joe. *Star Authors: Literary Celebrity in America*. London: Pluto Press, 2000.

Morey, Peter, and Amina Yaqin. *Framing Muslims: Stereotyping and Representation after 9/11*. Cambridge, MA: Harvard University Press, 2011.

Morey, Peter. *Islamophobia and the Novel*. New York: Columbia University Press, 2018.

Mukherjee, Roopali, Sarah Banet-Weiser, and Herman Grey, eds. *Racism Postrace*. Durham: Duke University Press, 2019.

Musser, Amber Jamilla. *Sensational Flesh: Race, Power, and Masochism*. New York: New York University Press, 2014.

Nafisi, Azar. *Reading Lolita in Tehran: A Memoir in Books*. New York: Random House, 2003.

Narayan, Uma. *Dislocating Cultures: Identities, Traditions, and Third World Cultures*. New York: Routledge, 1998.

Nash, Geoffrey. *Writing Muslim Identity*. London: Continuum, 2012.

Nasr, Vali. *The Shia Revival: How Conflicts within Islam Will Shape the Future*. New York: Norton, 2006.

Negra, Diane. *What a Girl Wants? Fantasizing the Reclamation of the Self in Postfeminism*. London: Routledge, 2009.

Negrin, Llewellyn. "Ornament and the Feminine." *Feminist Theory* 7, no. 2 (2006): 219–35.

Neroni, Hilary. *The Subject of Torture: Psychoanalysis and Biopolitics in Television and Film*. New York: Columbia University Press, 2015.

Newns, Lucinda. "Renegotiating Romantic Genres: Textual Resistance and Muslim Chick-Lit." *Journal of Commonwealth Literature* 53, no. 2 (2017): 1–17.

Nissim-Sabat, Marilyn. "Fanonian Musings: Decolonizing/Philosophy/Psychology." In *Fanon and the Decolonization of Philosophy*, edited by Elizabeth A. Hoppe and Tracey Nicholls, 39–54. Lanham, MD: Lexington Books, 2010.

Norberg, Jenny. *The Underground Girls of Kabul: In Search of Hidden Resistance*. Broadway Books, 2015.

Nguyen, Mimi Thi. "The Biopower of Beauty: Humanitarian Imperialism and Global Feminism in the Age of Terror." *Signs* 36, no. 2 (2011): 359–83.

Niblock, Sarah. "'My Manolos, My Self': Manolo Blahnik, Shoes and Desire." In *Reading Sex and the City*, edited by Kim Akass and Janet McCabe, 144–46. London: I.B. Tauris, 2004.

Oates, Joyce Carol. *Blonde*. New York: Ecco, 2000.

"Old Murder Case Moves Forward." *Indianapolis Star*, May 10, 2002.

Ommundsen, Wenche. "Sex and the Global City: Chick Lit with a Difference." *Contemporary Women's Writing* 5, no. 2 (2011): 107–24.

Ossman, Susan. "Seeing Princess Salma: Transparency and Transnational Intimacies." In *Circuits of Visibility: Gender and Transnational Media Cultures*, edited by Radha S. Hegde, 21–34. New York: New York University Press, 2010.

Pearls on the Ocean Floor. Directed by Robert Adanato. Adanto, Heidenberg, and Levin Produktion, 2010.

Penner, Diana. "Suspect Faces Murder Charges for the Third Time." *Indianapolis Star*, May 9, 2002, 1, 11.

Pereira-Ares, Noemí. "The Politics of Hijab in Monica Ali's *Brick Lane*." *Journal of Commonwealth Literature* 48, no. 2 (2013): 201–20.

Perfect, Michael. "The Multicultural Bildungsroman: Stereotypes in Monica Ali's *Brick Lane*." *Journal of Commonwealth Literature* 43, no. 3 (2008): 109–20.

Pfannkuch, Katarina. "Portraits of Islam: Oh Veiled Mother of God!" *Zenith* 8 June 2017. https://magazine.zenith.me/en/culture/portraits-islam.

Phelan, Peggy. *Mourning Sex: Performing Public Memories*. London: Routledge, 1997.

Phelan, Peggy. *Unmarked: The Politics of Performance*. London: Routledge, 1993.

Phillipa. "*Girls of Riyadh* and *Desperate in Dubai*: Reading and Writing Romance in the Middle East." Review of Amy Burge presentation. *Synaesthezia: An Arts Blog*, August 4, 2018. www.synaesthezia.com/girls-of-riyadh-and-desperate-in-dubai-reading-and-writing-romance-in-the-middle-east/.

Piela, Anna. *Muslim Women Online: Faith and Identity in Virtual Space*. New York: Routledge, 2012.

Poon, Angela. "To Know What's What: Forms of Migrant Knowing in Monica Ali's *Brick Lane*." *Journal of Postcolonial Writing* 45, no. 4 (2009): 426–37.

Poston, Larry A. "Da'wa in the West." In *The Muslims of America*, edited by Yvonne Yazbeck Haddad, 125–35. Oxford: Oxford University Press, 1991.

Puar, Jasbir. *Terrorist Assemblages: Homonationalism in Queer Times*. Durham: Duke University Press, 2007.

Rana, Junaid. *Terrifying Muslims: Race and Labour in the South Asian Diaspora*. Durham: Duke University Press, 2011.

Rana, Junaid. "The Story of Islamophobia." *Souls* 9, no. 2 (2007): 148–61.

Reid, R. T., and Bob Warden. "3,000 Protest against Nazis in Chicago's Loop." *Washington Post* June 25, 1978 www.washingtonpost.com/archive/politics/1978/06/25/3000-protest-against-nazis-in-chicagos-loop/b21c5ab5-2775-4d97-963b-acddc0a440f2/?utm_term=.cadb5ab5c379.

Reilly, Maura, and Linda Nochlin. *Global Feminisms: New Directions in Contemporary Art*. New York: Merrell and Brooklyn Museum, 2007.

Riedel, David. "Princess Diana Fascination Reaching Creepy Heights?" *CBS News*, June 29, 2011. www.cbsnews.com/news/princess-diana-fascination-reaching-creepy-heights/. Accessed June 8, 2013.

Rimer, Sara. "After Arrest, Town Shamed by '68 Killing Seeks Renewal." *New York Times*, May 17, 2002: A18.

Riviere, Joan. "Womanliness as a Masquerade." (1929). In *Formations of Fantasy*, edited by Victor Burgin, James Donald, and Cora Kaplan, 35–44. London: Methuen, 1986.

Roald, Anne Sofie. *Women in Islam: The Western Experience*. London: Routledge, 2001.

Rojek, Chris. *Celebrity*. London: Reaktion, 2011.

Rommespacher, Birgit. "Emanzipation als Konversion: Das Bild von Muslima in christliche-säkularen Diskurs." *Ethik und Gesellschaft: Ökumenische Zeitschrift für Sozialethik* 4, no. 2 (2010): 1–30.
Roth, Philip. *The Plot Against America*. New York: Houghton Mifflin, 2004.
Roupakia, Lydia Efthymia. "Cosmopolitanism, Religion, and Ethics: Rereading Monica Ali's *Brick Lane*." *Journal of Postcolonial Writing* 52, no. 6 (2016): 645–58.
Rouse, Carolyn Moxley. *Engaged Surrender: African American Women and Islam*. Berkeley: University of California Press, 2004.
Roy, Olivier. *Globalised Islam: The Search for a New Ummah*. London: Hurst, 2004.
Rubin, Michael, and Patrick Clawson. "Patterns of Discontent: Will History Repeat Itself in Iran?" *Middle East Review of International Affairs* 10, no. 1 (2006): 105–21.
Sadek, Rima. "Same-Sex Relations in Modern Arabic Fiction between Empowerment and Impossibility: A Case Study of Samar Yazbek's *Cinnamon*." In *Memory, Voice and Identity: Muslim Women's Writing across the Middle East*, edited by Feroza Jussawalla and Doaá Omran, 106–17. New York: Routledge, 2021.
Sahar, Naila. "Feminist Ethnography, Revisionary Historiography, and the Subaltern in Assia Djebar's *Fantasia: An Algerian Cavalcade*." In *Memory, Voice and Identity: Muslim Women's Writing across the Middle East*, edited by Feroza Jussawalla and Doaá Omran, 69–80. New York: Routledge, 2021.
Said, Edward. *Covering Islam: How the Media and Experts Determine How We See the Rest of the World*, rev. ed. New York: Vintage, 1997.
Sandoval, Chela. *Methodology of the Oppressed*. Minneapolis: University of Minnesota Press, 2000.
Salah, Trish. "Of Activist Fandoms, Auteur Pedagogy, and Imperial Feminism: From *Buffy the Vampire Slayer* to *I am Du'a Khalil*." In *Muslim Women: Transnational Feminism and the Ethics of Pedagogy: Contested Imaginaries in Post-9/11 Cultural Practice*, edited by Lisa K. Taylor and Jasmin Zine, 152–71, New York: Routledge, 2014.
Sameh, Catherine Z. *Axis of Hope: Iranian Women's Rights Activism across Borders*. Seattle: University of Washington Press, 2019.
Santesso, Esra Mirze. *Disorientation: Muslim Identity in Contemporary Anglophone Literature*. Houndmills, Basingstoke: Palgrave, 2013.
Scarry, Elaine. *The Body in Pain: The Making and Unmaking of the World*. New York: Oxford University Press, 1987.
Schmitz, Britta. "Tausendundeine Macht." In *Tausendundein Tag*, 15–16. Berlin: Walter König Hamburg: Nationalgalerie Hamburger Bahnhof, 2003.
Schneider, C. "The Cognitive Grammar of 'I': Viewing Arrangements in Graphic Autobiographies." *Studies in Comics* 4, no. 2 (2013): 307–32.
Sedgwick, Eve Kosofsky. *Touching Feeling: Affect, Pedagogy, Performativity*. Durham: Duke University Press, 2003.
Seedat, Fatima. "Beyond the Text: Between Islam and Feminism." *Journal of Feminist Studies in Religion* 32, no. 2 (2016): 138–42.
Seedat, Fatima. "Islam, Feminism, and Islamic Feminism: Between Inadequacy and Inevitability." *Journal of Feminist Studies in Religion* 29, no. 2 (2013): 25–45.
Seedat, Fatima. "On Spiritual Subjects: Negotiations in Muslim Female Spirituality." *Journal of Gender and Religion in Africa* 22, no. 1 (2016): 21–37.
Seedat, Fatima. "Sitting in Difference: Queering the Study of Islam." *Journal of Feminist Studies in Religion* 34, no. 1 (2018): 149–54.
Seierstad, Åsne. *The Bookseller of Kabul*, translated by Ingrid Christophersen. Boston: Back Bay Books, 2004.

Sengupta, Mitu. "Sex, the City and American Patriotism." *Counterpunch*, June 18, 2010. www.counterpunch.org/2010/06/18/sex-the-city-and-american-patriotism/.

Sex and the City. Created by Darren Star. Produced by HBO, 1998–2004.

Sex and the City 2. Directed by Michael Patrick King. Burbank, CA: Warner Home Video, 2010. DVD.

Shaik, Sa'diyya. "A *Tafsir* of Praxis: Gender, Marital Violence, and Resistance in a South African Muslim Community." In *Violence against Women in Contemporary World Religion: Roots and Cures*, edited by Daniel C. Maguire and Sa'diyya Shaik, 66–89. Cleveland: Pilgrim Press, 2007.

Shome, Raka. *Diana and Beyond: White Femininity, National Identity, and Contemporary Media Culture*. Champaign: University of Illinois Press, 2014.

Silverman, Kaja. *The Acoustic Mirror: Feminism, Psychoanalysis and Cinema*. Bloomington: Indiana Press, 1988.

Singer, Mark. "Who Killed Carol Jenkins: What a Thirty-three year old Murder Has Done to a Town." *New Yorker* 77, no. 42, January 7, 2002, 24–28.

Sittenfeld, Curtis. *American Wife*. New York: Random House, 2008.

Smith, Sidonie. "Human Rights and Comics: Autobiographical Avatars, Crisis Witnessing, and Transnational Rescue Networks." In *Graphic Subjects: Critical Essays on Autobiography and Graphic Novels*, edited by Michael A. Chaney, 61–72. Madison: University of Wisconsin Press, 2011.

Snorton, C. Riley. *Black on Both Sides: A Racial History of Trans Identity*. Minneapolis: University of Minnesota Press, 2017.

Soltani, Amir, and Khalil. *Zahra's Paradise*. New York: Macmillan, 2011.

Spielhaus, Riem. "Islam and Feminism: German and European Variations on a Global Theme." In *Muslim Women and Gender Justice: Concepts, Sources, and Histories*, edited by Dina El Omari, Julianne Hammer, and Mouhandad Khorchide, 46–61. New York: Routledge, 2020.

Spillers, Hortense. *Black, White, and in Color: Essays on American Literature and Culture*. Chicago: Chicago University Press, 2003.

Springer, Kimberly. "Divas, Evil Black Bitches, and Bitter Black Women: African American Women in Postfeminist and Post-Civil-Rights Popular Culture." In *Interrogating Postfeminism: Gender and the Politics of Popular Culture*, edited by Yvonne Tasker and Diane Negra, 249–76. Durham: Duke University Press, 2007.

Stepanov, Brigitte. "Djebar and Scherherazade: On Muslim Women, Past and Present." In *Memory, Voice and Identity: Muslim Women's Writing across the Middle East*, edited by Feroza Jussawalla and Doaá Omran, 211–22. New York: Routledge, 2021.

Stephens, Michelle Ann. *Skin Acts: Race, Psychoanalysis, and the Black Male Performer*. Durham: Duke University Press, 2014.

Stevens, J. Richard. "Mentoring Ms. Marvel: Marvel's Kamala Khan and the Reconstitution of Carol Danvers." In *Ms. Marvel's America: No Normal*, edited by Jessica Baldanzi and Hussein Rashid, 3–20. Jackson: University Press of Mississippi, 2020.

Strum, Phillipa. *When the Nazis Came to Skokie: Freedom for Speech We Hate*. Lawrence: University of Kansas Press, 1999.

Summers, Brandi Thompson. "Haute [Ghetto] Mess: Postracial Aesthetics and the Seduction of Blackness in High Fashion." In *Racism Postrace*, edited by Roopali Mukherjee, Sarah Banet-Weiser, and Herman Gray, 244–63. Durham: Duke University Press, 2019.

Syeda, Maha. "Make Up: Muslim Beauty Bloggers You Need to Follow." *Teen Vogue*, www.teenvogue.com/gallery/muslim-beauty-bloggers-to-follow.

Taj, Saba. "Art, Resistance, and the Dominant Narrative," TEDX Duke, 10 April 2017 www.youtube.com/watch?v=mnE0Qn2eJMw.
Taylor, Diana. *The Archive and the Repertoire: Performing Cultural Memory in the Americas*. Durham: Duke University Press, 2003.
Taylor, Lisa K., and Jasmin Zine. *Muslim Women, Transnational Feminism and the Ethics of Pedagogy. Contested Imaginaries in Post-9/11 Cultural Practice*. New York: Routledge, 2014.
Tehranian, John. *Whitewashed: America's Invisible Middle Eastern Minority*. New York: New York University Press, 2009.
Terry, Don. "34 Years Later, Sad Secret Surfaces: Childhood Memory May Solve Slaying." *Chicago Tribune* May 12, 2002: 1.
Teverson, Andrew, and Sarah Upstone, eds. *Postcolonial Spaces: The Politics of Place in Contemporary Culture*. Basingstoke: Palgrave Macmillan, 2011.
Thompson, Craig. *Habibi*. New York: Pantheon, 2011.
Tietenberg, Annette. "Vom Verschleiern und Enthüllen oder Warum Parastou Forouhars Arbeiten ein Kontextuelles Gewand-tragen." In *Tausendundein Tag*, Nationalgalerie Hamburger Bahnhof, 54–61. Berlin: Walter König; Hamburg: Nationalgalerie Hamburger Bahnhof.
Toossi, Katayoun Zarei. "The Conundrum of the Veil and Mohja Kahf's Literary Representation of Hijab." *Interventions* 17, no. 5 (2015): 640–56.
Turner, Graeme. *Understanding Celebrity*. London: Sage, 2004.
Upstone, Sara. *British Asian Fiction: Twenty-First Century Voices*. Manchester: Manchester University Press, 2010.
Upstone, Sara. "Representation and Realism: Monica Ali's *Brick Lane*." In *Culture, Diaspora, and Modernity in Muslim Writing*, edited by Rehana Ahmed, Peter Morey, and Amina Yaqin, 164–79. London: Routledge, 2012.
Upstone, Sara. "'Same Old, Same Old': Zadie Smith's *White Teeth* and Monica Ali's *Brick Lane*." *Journal of Postcolonial Writing* 43, no. 3 (2007): 336–49.
Wadud, Amina. "American Muslim Identity: Race and Ethnicity in Progressive Islam." In *Progressive Muslims: On Justice, Gender, and Pluralism*, edited by Omid Safi, 270–85. Oxford: Oneworld, 2003.
Wadud, Amina. *Inside the Gender Jihad: Women's Reform in Islam*. Oxford: Oneworld, 2006.
Wadud, Amina. "Islamic Feminism by Any Other Name." In *Muslim Women and Gender Justice: Concepts, Sources, and Histories*, edited by Dina El Omari, Juliane Hammer, and Mouhanad Khorchide, 33–45. New York: Routledge, 2019.
Wadud, Amina. "Foreword: Engaging Tawhid in Islam and Feminisms." *International Feminist Journal of Politics* 10, no. 4 (2008): 435–38.
Ware, Vron. "The New Literary Front: Public Diplomacy and the Cultural Politics of Reading Arabic Fiction in Translation." *New Formations* 73, no. 85 (2010): 56–77.
Watson, Julie. "Parsua Bashi's *Nylon Road*: Visual Witnessing and the Critique of Neoliberalism in Iranian Women's Graphic Memoir." *Gender Forum* 65 (2017): 73–101.
Wearing, Sadie. "Representing Agency and Coercion: Feminist Readings and Postfeminist Media Fictions." In *Gender, Agency, and Coercion*, edited by Sumi Madhok, Anne Phillips, and Kalpana Wilson, 219–39. Houndsills, Baskingstoke: Palgrave-Macmillan, 2013.
Werneburg, Brigitte. "'You Have to Have Faith in People': An Interview with the Iranian Artist Parastou Forouhar." *Deutsche Bank ArtMag* 55, June 2009. http://db-artmag.com/en/55/feature/an-interview-with-parastou-forouhar/.

Weheliye, Alexander G. *Habeas Viscus: Racializing Assemblages, Biopolitics, and Black Feminist Theories of the Human*. Durham: Duke University Press, 2014.

Whelehan, Imelda, and Joel Gwynne. *Ageing, Popular Culture, and Contemporary Feminism: Harleys and Hormones*. Houndsmills, Basingstoke: Palgrave-Macmillan, 2014.

Whitlock, Gillian. *Soft Weapons: Autobiography in Transit*. Chicago: University of Chicago Press, 2007.

Wilson, G. Willow. *Alif the Unseen*. New York: Grove, 2012.

Wilson, G. Willow and M. K. Perker. *Cairo*. New York: DC Vertigo, 2008.

Wilde, Oscar. *The Picture of Dorian Gray*, 2nd ed, edited by Michael Patrick Gillespie. New York: W. W. Norton, 1988.

Wolcott, James. "Hear Me Purr: Maureen Dowd and the Rise of Postfeminist Chick Lit." *New Yorker*, May 20, 1996, 54–57.

Women Without Men [Zanan-e Bedun-e Mardan]. Directed by Shirin Neshat and Shoja Azari. Essential Filmproduktion, 2009.

Wynter, Sylvia. "Beyond Miranda's Meanings: Un/silencing the 'Demonic Ground' of Caliban's Women." In *Out of the Kumbla: Caribbean Women and Literature*, edited by Carole Boyce Davies, and Elaine Savory Fido, 355–66. Trenton: Africa World Press, 1990.

Wynter, Sylvia. *On Being Human as Praxis*, edited by Katherine McKittrick. Durham: Duke University Press, 2014.

Wynter, Sylvia. "Toward the Sociogenic Principle: Fanon, Identity, the Puzzle of Conscious Experience, and What It Is Like to be 'Black." In *National Identities and Sociopolitical Changes in Latin America*, edited by Antonio Gómez-Moriana and Mercedes Durhán-Cogan, 30–66. London: Routledge, 2001.

Yazbek, Samar. *Cinnamon*, translated by Emily Danby. London: Arabia Books, 2012.

Yousuf-Sadiq, Nousheen. "Half and Half." In *I Speak for Myself: American Women on Being Muslim*, edited by Maria M. Ebrahimji and Zahra T. Suratwala, 18–22. Ashland, OR: White Cloud Press, 2011.

Zakaria, Rafia, *Veil*. New York: Bloomsbury, 2017.

Zakaria, Rafia. *The Upstairs Wife: An Intimate History of Pakistan*. Boston: Beacon, 2015.

Ziadé, Lamia. *Bye Bye Babylon: Beirut 1975–1979*, translated by Olivia Snaije. Northhampton, MA: Interlink Graphic, 2011.

Ziegler, Garrett. "East of the City: *Brick Lane*, Capitalism, and the Global Metropolis." *Race/Ethnicity: Multidisiplinary Global Contexts* 1, no. 1 (2007): 145–67.

INDEX

Pages in *italics* refers figure and pages followed by n refers note

abortion 82–3
Aboulela, Leila 72
affect: Ahmed on 37n13; in Ali's *Brick Lane* 44, 48–50, 52, 55–6, 64, 68n52; Ali's *Untold Story*, Princess Diana, and 48–9, 58–61; in Bashi's *Nylon Road* 135, 143–44; Forouhar and 96, 101, 108, 118; in Kahf's *Girl in the Tangerine Scarf* 73, 85; postfeminism and 6; *Sex and the City 2* and 16; stickiness of 49, 85; as synesthetic 48; Taj and 157
African-American Muslims *see* Girl in the Tangerine Scarf, The (Kahf)
Agamben, Giorgio 45–6, 61, 119n18
agency: in Ali's *Brick Lane* 43, 45, 50, 54–7; Ali's *Untold Story*, Princess Diana, and 50, 62; in Alsanea's *Girls of Riyadh* 29–31; in Bashi's *Nylon Road* 126; Forouhar and 95, 108–10, 113, 116–17, 125; in Kahf's *Girl in the Tangerine Scarf* 70, 73, 84, 86; male gaze and 152n43; Muslim women and 6; Robbie on postfeminist masquerade and 15; Scheherazade and 109; in *Sex and the City 2* 28, 33, 35–6; veiling and 14, 113; visibility and 1
Ahmed, Leila 75
Ahmed, Sara 49, 60, 90n7
Alentejo Blue (Ali) 47
al-Ghadeer, Moneera 24
al-Harez, Siba 160n4

al-Hibri, Azizah Y. 7
Ali, Kecia 7, 31
Ali, Monica: *Alentejo Blue* 47; immigrant status vs. Britishness of 46–8; *In the Kitchen* 47; overview 4; on reception of *Brick Lane* and *Untold Story* 44; *see also Brick Lane*; *Untold Story*
Ali, Noble Drew 76
Allen, Kim 35
al-Muttawa, Naif 126
Alsanea, Rajaa: authorial image and head covering 36; individual celebrity woman and 20; *tafsir, da'wa*, and 32; vernacular language, use of 19; *see also Girls of Riyadh, The*
Alsultany, Evelyn 46
Arzumanova, Inna 1, 34
Asad, Talal 55
'Ashura 97–9, 111, 117–18, 133
assemblage: in Ali's *Brick Lane* 49–57; concept of 44–5; Diana as feminine assemblage in Ali's *Untold Story* 57–63

Badran, Margot 7
Banat al-Riyadh (Alsanea) *see Girls of Riyadh, The*
Barlas, Asma 7, 31
Barnard, Saba Chauduy *see* Taj, Saba
Bashi, Parsua: Forouhar compared to 125, 127; *Persepolis* 134; *see also Nylon Road*

Bastard Out of Carolina (Allison) 73
Bauman, Zygmut 120n21
beauty: in Ali's *Brick Lane* 58; in Ali's *Untold Story* 48, 61; in Alsanea's *Girls of Riyadh* 32; in Bashi's *Nylon Road* 125–27; fashion and beauty blogs 25–6; Forouhar and 108; hijab as projection from standards of 85; in Kahf's *Girl in the Tangerine Scarf* 77–8, 83–5
Benton, Sarah 58
Berlatsky, Eric 155
Bernstein, J. M. 94
Bhabha, Homi 58
biopolitics: in Ali's *Brick Lane* 49; in Ali's *Untold Story* 46, 61–2, 73; in Kahf's *Girl in the Tangerine Scarf* 50, 73
Bloody Nasreen (Zaidi) 151n13
bodies and embodiment *see* beauty fashion habitus, bodily looking, seeing, and gaze veiling and the veil
Booth, Marilyn 8, 19–20, 24, 36
Bose, Purnima 87
Bowman, Manzel 158
braiding 132
Brick Lane (Ali): assemblage in 49–57; as domestic realism third-person narrative 48; figure skating fantasy 52–4; gay character in 160n4; location (London and Bangladesh) 50–2, 56–7; overview 4, 9, 43–6; pop currency and 46; reception 44; Rushdie's *Satanic Verses* compared to 46, 54; spiritual practice in 51
Bunt, Gary 25
Burge, Amy 17, 25, 27
Burka Avenger 151n13
Bushnell, Candace 18–9, 20

Cahill, Ann J. 110
Chakravorty, Mrinalini 46, 57
Chambers, Claire 1–2
Chan-Malik, Sylvia 89
Chanson de Roland 77
chick-lit genre 17–9
Christianity: belief, in 55; culture, Christian-derived 2; Forouhar's "Roman Martyrs" and 117; Hagar (Hajar) in 88; Islamic, hostility to 17; sin in Shi'a conception vs. 98; Taj and iconography of 156–57; terror, Christian 80
Cohen, Nina 26
Cohn, Neil 127–28

consumption and consumer capitalism: Ali's *Brick Lane* and 64; Ali's *Untold Story* and 60; in Alsanea's *Girls of Riyadh* 19; in Bashi's *Nylon Road* 128, 143–44, *145*; celebrity and 59; dismissal of, by young Muslims 89; gay men, postfordism, and 22; neoliberalism and 13n41; *Sex and the City 2* and 32–4
Cousins, Mark 59
culture industry, "Islamic" 64

Dagbovie-Mullins, Sika 155
Darda, Joseph 150n3
da'wa 3, 25, 32
Death of Ivan Ilyich, The (Tolstoy) 63
Deleuze, Gilles 15–6, 33, 44–5, 65n12, 107, 109–10
demonic ground 71–2, 79
Denny, Frederick 55
DeShell, Jeffry 18–9
Detwa, Winnie 26
Diana, Princess of Wales 44–7, 57–63; *see also Untold Story* (Ali)
Doane, Mary Ann 15–6, 93, 134
domestic realism 48, 53
Donnelly, Allison 118
Dowd, Maureen 18
Duggan, Bob 116
Dyer, Richard 35

Ebadi, Shirin 143
Elias, Ana Sofia 61
Elsadda, Hoda 38n40
E-Mails from Scheherazad (Kahf) 87
Erakat, Noura 154
Etemad, Katayoon 101

faciality and facialization: Bashi's *Nylon Road* and 124–25, *126*; Deleuze and Guattari's concept of 15–6; Forouhar and 109, 118; *Sex and the City 2* and 33–4
Fanon, Franz 72, 75, 156
fashion: in Ali's *Brick Lane* 64; Alsanea and 36; in Alsanea's *Girls of Riyadh* 17, 25; in Bashi's *Nylon Road* 128, 137, 144–50, *145*, *146*, *148*; blogs and 25–6; in Kahf's *Girl in the Tangerine Scarf* 81–2; Princess Diana and 58; in *Sex and the City 2* 16, 28–9, 33–4, 43; veil as fashion 1; *see also* veiling and the veil
fate 48, 56–7

184 Index

feminism: Ali's *Brick Lane* and 45, 49–50; Alsanea's *Girls of Riyadh* and 17, 30–1; Bashi's *Nylon Road* and 126, 143–44, 150; chick-lit and 18; commodity and choice feminism 5, 44–5; disguise, theories of 16; Forouhar and 94–5, 109, 113; "Islamic feminist" contested 7; Kahf's *Girl in the Tangerine Scarf* and 4, 70, 72, 86, 89; look, voice, and 1, 5; Muslim theologians, relation to 6–7; neoliberal 8; *Sex and the City 2* and 16, 29, 33, 35–6, 43; third-wave 12n23; visual representation and 2; *see also* postfeminism
Ferriss, Suzanne 18
Firat, Begum Ozden 101
"First Thing, The" (Kahf) 88
focalization 136–37
Forouhar, Dariush 94–5, 111
Forouhar, Parastou: about 4, 10, 93–5; Bashi compared to 125, 127; figure and book in two-dimensional works 100–06; figure and furnishings in "Commemorations" works 94–100; figure as architecture in two-dimensional works 106–12; figuring women and veiling in photography 113–18; gaze and 124; *mashrabiyaa* and adaptation of *tawhid* 96, 107–08, 113; ornamentation and 93–4, 102; Shi'a aesthetics and practices and 96–100, 113; state violence and torture discourse and 94–6, 106–10
Forouhar, Parwaneh Eskandari 94–5
Freud, Sigmund 45, 65n12

Garvey, Marcus 76
Gavey, Nicola 110
gay male sexuality 21–2, 160n4
gaze *see* looking, seeing, and gaze
Genette, Gerard 136
Ghabia, Haneen Shafeeq 15
GhaneaBassiri, Kambiz 74, 76
Ghumkhor, Sahar 2, 15, 124
Gill, Rosalind 5–6, 61
Girl in the Tangerine Scarf, The (Kahf): henna party 77–8; intertexts 73; location 73, 79, 86; marriage, pregnancy, and abortion 82–3; national vs. migrant/transnational Muslims and 71, 74–6; overview 4, 9, 70–2; prayer in 86–7; racial sociogeny in 72–6, 79–80, 85–6; sexual violence in 78–81; "standing before" and 71, 86; travels and returns 83–4; veiling and unveiling in 70, 72, 75, 81–2, 84–6
Girls of Riyadh, The (Alsanea): chick-lit romance genre and 18–20; email postings and Internet in 24–6; location 29–30; narrator's voice 17, 23, 35; overview 3, 8–9, 16–7; postfeminist global girl figure in 30–2, 35; surveillance and 25–6; translation into English 19–20, 24; weddings and marriage in 23–7, 30–2
Gökariksel, Banu 64
Grabar, Oleg 100, 102, 110
Grace, Daphne 84
Grewal, Zareena 71
Grochowski, Tom 20
Groensteen, Thierry 132
Guattari, Félix 15–6, 33, 44, 109–10
Gunning, Dave 57

habitus, bodily: in Ali's *Brick Lane* 52, 54; Forouhar and 108, 124; in Kahf's *Girl in a Tangerine Scarf* 84–5, 87
hadith 12n29, 30–1, 73–4
Hagar Poems (Kahf) 9–10, 87–9
Halm, Heinz 98
Hammer, Juliane 7
hamsa (hand of Fatima) 113, 133
Haque, Danielle 89n3
Hardy, Thomas 73
Hartman, Saidiya 85, 120n21
Harzewski, Stephanie 18–9
Hassan, Riffat 7
Hesford, Wendy 4–5, 11n11
Hidayatullah, Aysha A. 12n28, 31
hijab *see* veiling and the veil
Hindi, Jassein 158
homo sacer 46
Hoodfar, Homa 14
Horstkotte, Silke 136
Hussain (grandson of Muhammad) 97–8, 133

ijtihad 6–7
image: in Ali's *Untold Story* 43–4, 48–9, 58, 61–3; Alsanea's authorial image 36; in Alsanea's *The Girls of Riyadh* 20, 29; in Bashi's *Nylon Road* 127, 136; the disrobed Black woman's body and scopic fixity 85; Forouhar and 93, 101–02, 124; in Kahf's *Girl in the Tangerine Scarf* 78, 86–7; in *Sex and the City 2* 16, 35, 43; veil as 2–3

Internet 24–6
In the Kitchen (Ali) 47
Irigaray, Luce 37n10
Islam: African-American 76–7, 85; in Ali's *Brick Lane* 45, 48, 53–4, 57, 64; 'Ashura 97–9, 111, 117–18, 133; in Bashi's *Nylon Road* 141; Belief Practice 54–5; Christian images or stereotypes of 2, 109; culture industry, "Islamic" 64; *da'wa* 3, 25, 32; feminism and Muslim theologians 6–7; Forouhar and 94, 96–102; the hajj 83, 88; Islamophobia 73, 79–80, 155; Ka'ba, female metaphors for the 79; in Kahf's *Girl in the Tangerine Scarf* 70–7, 79, 81–3, 87; in Kahf's *Hagar Poems* 88; Khabeer on "Muslim Cool" 89; Muslim Student Association and Islamic Society of North America 74–5, 80; national vs. migrant/transnational Muslims 71, 74–6; postwar Muslim migration to U.S. 74; romance and Christian hostility to 17; Shari'ah 31–2, 109; Shi'a aesthetics and practices 96–100, 113; *tafsir* 3, 6–7, 32, 45, 48, 55; *tawhid* 3, 93, 107, 113; veil as frozen signifier of 15, 113; *see also* Qur'an; spiritual practice
Islamic Society of North America (ISNA) 74, 80
isnan 31

Jackson, Sherman 71
Janmohamed, Shelina 25
Jay, Martin 4
Jenkins, Carol 80–1, 84
Jussawalla, Feroza 109

Kabber, Naila 50
Kahf, Mohja: on audience 88; on difference 77; *E-Mails from Scheherazad* 87; *Hagar Poems* 9–10, 87–9; on the *mudjadila* 87; Muslim "angle of vision" and 71, 89; received as Muslim writer in America 88–9; on the sensual and the political 24; "standing before" and 71; *see also Girl in the Tangerine Scarf, The*
Kant, Immanuel 110
Karim, Jamillah 71
Kazemi, Zahra (Ziba) 143
Kaz, Mehrangiz 143
Khabeer, Su'ad Abdul 89
King, Michael Patrick 27, 29, 32–3
Krafft-Ebing, Richard 65n12

Lahiji, Shahla 143
Lewis, Reina 25–6, 75, 96
looking, seeing, and gaze: Ali's *Brick Lane* and 64; in Ali's *Untold Story* 59; Bashi's *Nylon Road* and 125–26, 128, 132; circuit of gazes 110, 125–26; female gaze 93; Forouhar and 93, 96, 107, 110, 113, 120n21, 124–25; Kahf's *Girl in the Tangerine Scarf* and 78–9, 87; male gaze 152n43; *mashrabiyaa* and mutuality of gaze 96; as preferred metaphor of recognition 2; in *Sex and the City* 29; Taj's "Creatures" and the gaze that harms 158; visual culture, feminist theory, and 4–5; *see also* image; spectacle; veiling and the veil; visibility
Loos, Alfred 101
luminosity: in Ali's *Brick Lane* 43; Ali's *Untold Story*, Princess Diana, and 43–4, 48, 58, 60, 64; in Alsanea's *The Girls of Riyadh* 17; Forouhar and 93; ineligibility for 3; postfeminism and 5, 17, 155; in *Sex and the City 2* 22–3, 36

Mahmood, Saba 54–5
marriage and weddings: in Ali's *Untold Story* 58; in Alsanea's *The Girls of Riyadh* 23–7, 30–2; in Kahf's *Girl in the Tangerine Scarf* 77–8, 82; in *Sex and the City 2* 21–3
Marx, John 50
mashrabiyaa 96, 108, 113
masochism: about 65n12; in Ali's *Brick Lane* 4, 44–5, 51; in Ali's *Untold Story* 4, 45, 48, 60–2, 64; feminist view of 45
masquerade: Ali's *Untold Story* and 62; Bashi's *Nylon Road* and 134; faciality and 15–6; femininity as 37n10; Kahf's *Girl in the Tangerine Scarf* and 72; *Sex and the City 2* and 16, 28; Taj and 156
Massumi, Brian 150n2
Mazza, Cris 18–9
McDonald, Megan 15
McKittrick, Katherine 73
McLarney, Ellen 64
McQueen, Shirley Richmond 80–1
McRobbie, Angela 5–6, 15, 17, 20, 58, 62
Merck, Mandy 21–2
Metz, Christian 4
Mikkonen, Kai 136
Mir-Hosseini, Ziba 32
Mirzoeff, Nicholas 5
Missler, Heike 18

Index

Mitchell, W. T. J. 4
Moallem, Minoo 33
Monbiot, George 13n41
Moorish Temple of Science 76
Moors, Annelies 81
Morey, Peter 55, 68n60
Mortzaie, Hushidar 158
Ms. Marvel 126, 155
mudjadila 87
Muhammad 31
Muhammad, Elijah 76–7
Muhammad, Fard 76
Muhammad, Warith Deen (W. D.) 76
Muslim Girl magazine 1, 5, 154
Muslim Student Association (MSA) 74, 80
Musser, Jamilla 45, 61, 65n12, 66n13
Mutu, Wagnechi 158

Narayan, Uma 14
Nash, Geoffrey 68n49
Nasr, Vali 97
National Socialists of America 80
Nation of Islam 76
neoliberalism 1, 8, 13n41
Neroni, Hilary 106–07, 119n18
Neshat, Shirin 113, 156
99, The (al-Muttawa) 126
Nylon Road (Bashi): English translation 128–30; fashion and figuration 144–50, *145*, *146*, 148; figure and design 126–34, *129*, *131*; mother tongue (Farsi), German, and metafocalization of language 134–43, *138*, *140*, *142*; "Muttermal" (mothermark) 125–26, 130–33, *131*, 135, 144; overview 4, 10, 124–26; paratextual figures 127; psychomachia in 133–34, 136–37

Others, The (al-Harez) 160n4

Passage to India, A (Forster) 73
Pedri, Nancy 136
Pereira-Ares, Noemi 49
Persepolis (Bashi) 134
Phelan, Peggy 1, 37n10
Picture of Dorian Gray, The (Wilde) 62
postfeminism: about 5–6; in Ali's *Untold Story* 43, 48, 58, 61–2, 64; in Alsanea's *The Girls of Riyadh* 17, 20, 30, 43; Forouhar and 93, 118; global-American girl figure in Alsanea's *The Girls of Riyadh* and *Sex and the City 2* 30–6; majority woman vs. other woman in 29; masquerade and 15–6, 62, 155; neoliberalism and 1
prayer *see* spiritual practice
pregnancy 82–3
Prudentius 133
Prusinkiewicz, Przemyslaw 101
psychomachia 133–34, 136–37
Puar, Jasbir 56, 156

Qabbani, Nizar 24
Qadr, Layla 158
Qahera (Muhamad) 151n13
queerness: Ali on 44; Diana and 58; portrayal of Muslims and 160n4; *Sex and the City 2* and 21–2; Taj and 155–59
Qur'an: in Ali's *Brick Lane* 51; decorative marginalia 102; Forouhar and 98, 102; gender equity and 31–2; in Kahf's *Girl in the Tangerine Scarf* 73, 78; *tafsir, ijtihad,* and *siyaq* 6–7

Raat (Haris) 151n13
racial sociogeny and xenophobia 72–6, 79–80, 85–6
Rana, Junaid 89n6
realism, domestic 48, 53
"Rebellious Silence" (Neshat) 156
Richmond, Kenneth 80–1
Riviere, Joan 15, 37n10
Roupakia, Lydia Efthymia 68n49
Roy, Olivier 25
Rushdie, Salman 46

Sacher-Masoch, Leopold von 45, 65n12
Sade, Marquis de 45, 65n12, 107
Saeed, Fatima 7
Salah, Trish 12n22
Samavati, Faramarz 101
same sex desire 22, 160n4
Santesso, Ezra Mirze 68n52
Satanic Verses, The (Rushdie) 46, 54
Satrapi, Marjane 113
Scarry, Elaine 95
Scharff, Christina 61
scopic regimes 4
seeing *see* looking, seeing, and gaze
Sengupta, Mitu 32–3
Sex and the City (Bushnell) 18–9
Sex and the City (HBO) 16–7, 19, 32
Sex and the City 2 (King): ageing, specter of 16, 28; chick-lit romance genre and 18; ethnographic trope 20–1; location

27–9; overview 8, 16; postfeminist global girl figure in 32–6; "real housewife of Abu Dhabi" 16, 33–6; the stock Muslim woman in 28–9; virginity, return to 22–3; weddings and marriage in 21–3
sexual violence: Bashi's *Nylon Road* and 143; Carol Jenkins case 80–1; Forouhar and 94; in Kahf's *Girl in the Tangerine Scarf* 78–81, 85–6; race and 85
Shah, Suzanne 88
Shaikh, Sa'diyya 7
Shome, Rakia 45–6, 60
Silverman, Kaja 152n43
siyaq 6–7
social media 24–6
sociogeny *see* racial sociogeny and xenophobia
Souief, Adhaf 72
spectacle: in Ali's *Brick Lane* and *Untold Story* 44, 53, 63–4; in Alsanea's *The Girls of Riyadh* 26; Forouhar and 118; Kahf's *Girl in the Tangerine Scarf* and 17, 86; luminous 155; in *Sex and the City 2* 22, 26, 33
Spillers, Hortense 45, 85
spiritual practice: in Ali's *Brick Lane* 51; Forouhar and 96–100; prayer in Kahf's *Girl in the Tangerine Scarf* 86–7
"standing before" 71, 86, 90n8
Stephens, Michelle Ann 35
Summers, Brandi Thompson 28
sunnah 31
surveillance 5, 26–7, 62, 82

tafsir 3, 6–7, 32, 45, 48, 55
Taj, Saba (aka Saba Chaudry Barnard) 155–59; "Alpha, Delta, Burqa" 156; "An Noor, or The Light" 156–57; "Arsheen, Materials Scientist/Engineer" 157–58; "Creatures from the Earth (2016)" 158–59; "Maesta" 157; "Nida, Renaissance Woman" 158; "Of Beasts/Of Virgins (2019)" 158–59; "Suck My Dowry" 159; "Technicolor Muslimah" series 157–58
tawhid 3, 93, 107, 113
Taylor, Diana 49, 134
Tehranian, John 75
Tempest, The (Shakespeare) 72, 77
Tess of the d'Urbervilles (Hardy) 73
Tolstoy, Leo 63
Toossi, Katayoun Zarei 84

Universal Negro Improvement Association 76
Untold Story (Ali): Britishness vs. immigrant status and 47–8; Diana as feminine assemblage in 57–63; as domestic realism third-person narrative 48; location 62; masochism in 48–9; overview 4, 9, 43–6; pop currency and 46; reception 44; Wilde's *Picture of Dorian Gray* compared to 62
Upstone, Sara 64, 67n21

veiling and the veil: Ali's *Brick Lane* and 44, 49; Alsanea and 36; in Alsanea's *The Girls of Riyadh* 26, 29–30; as blot 3, 15, 115, 126, 134, 154–55; consumer capitalism and 33–4; faciality and 15–6, 33–4; Forouhar and 113–18, 124; as frozen signifier of Islam 15, 113; history of 14–5; Kahf's *Girl in the Tangerine Scarf*, veiling and unveiling in 70, 72, 75, 81–2, 84–6; as master signifier 2–3; as paradoxical visual code in U.S. 75; as partition and boundary 156; as protection from beauty standards 85; racialization of, in U.S. 81; *Sex and the City 2* and 29, 33–4; in Taj's work 156–58; "visibility" and 1; white-passing and 154; *see also* masquerade
virginity 22–3, 44, 57–8
visibility and invisibility: agency and 6; Ali's *Brick Lane* and 4, 53, 64; Ali's *Untold Story* and 4, 58–9; Alsanea's *The Girls of Riyadh* and 23, 25, 35–6; Chan-Malik's reversal of 89; critique of concept 1; discussed in *Muslim Girl* magazine 154; feminist visual studies and 5; Forouhar and 96, 99; hijab and hypervisibility 2; Kahf's *Girl in the Tangerine Scarf* and 72, 79, 86, 88–9; limitations of 155; in *Sex and the City 2* 22, 33–4; *see also* veiling and the veil
visual culture 4–5, 24–5

Wadud, Amina 7, 31
Watson, Julia 134, 136
Wearing, Sadie 12n24
Weheliye, Alexander 85
Wolcott, James 18
"Women of Allah" (Neshat) 156
Women's March, Washington, DC (2018) 1

works: "Ashura Day" 111; "Blind Spot" 114–15, 117; "Bodyletter" series 117; "Countdown" 96–100; "Eslimi" series 101–06, 112; "Ewin Prison (2010)" 111; "Freitag" ("Friday") 113–14, *114*; "Genitals" 103–04, *104*; "Guns" 103, *103*, 104–06, *106*; "Mahrem" pattern book 101–03; "Ornament and Verbrechen" ("Ornament and Crime") 101; "Panorama" 107, 110; "Papillion Collection" 111; "Ping Pong Caesar" 117; "Red Is My Name, Green is My Name" 112, *112*; "Roman Martyrs" 117–18; "Rorschach Behnam" 114–16; "Swanrider" series *116*, 116–17; "Tausendundein Tag" ("A Thousand and One Days") *107*, 107–10, *111*, 112; "Trauerfeier" ("The Funeral") 96–100, *97*; "Villa Massimo" 117–18; "Written Room" 117

Wynter, Sylvia 71–3, 77, 79

xenophobia *see* racial sociogeny and xenophobia

Young, Mallory 18
Yousuf-Sadiq, Nousheen 85

Zakaria, Rafia 16, 156
Ziegler, Garret 49–50